THE WORLD'S RELIGIONS

The Study of Religion, Traditional and New Religions

THE WORLD'S RELIGIONS

Islam
edited by Peter Clarke

The Religions of Asia
edited by Friedhelm Hardy

Judaism and Christianity
edited by Leslie Houlden

*The Study of Religion, Traditional
and New Religions*
edited by Peter Clarke and Stewart Sutherland

THE WORLD'S RELIGIONS

The Study of Religion, Traditional and New Religions

EDITED BY

Peter Clarke and Stewart Sutherland

LONDON

First published in 1988
as part of The World's Religions
Reprinted in 1991 and 2001
by Routledge
11 New Fetter Lane, London EC4P 4EE

Routledge is an imprint of the Taylor & Francis Group

Printed in Great Britain by
Selwood Printing Ltd, Burgess Hill, West Sussex

ISBN 0-415-06432-5

WITHDRAWN

Contents

Contents

Religion and the Study of Religions

1 | Religion and the Religions

Peter Byrne

Introduction

The aim of this book is to offer a survey of the world's religions. We must ask ourselves at the outset what is the general character of the thing the more specialised chapters describe. There are three important questions which must be considered prior to any detailed description of the religious life of mankind in history: What is religion? What kind of unity does it possess? How far is it available for disinterested study? Each of the questions will be considered in separate subsections below.

Before they are tackled it is worth while to note some important features of the context in which they are considered—features which also help to reveal some of the assumptions underlying the approach behind this entire work. So it is vital to understand that what is offered in these pages is a work in the study of religions and not in theology. Theology is an attempt to express or articulate a given religious faith (see Smart, 1973: 6). Theology thus begins, and is shaped by, the fundamental beliefs of, say, Christianity. The theologian in his development of these beliefs may offer historical accounts of the scriptures or church of his religion, but such accounts will be part of an attempt to state and defend the fundamentals of his faith for his fellow believers and the age in which they live. The student of religion attempts to offer a reflective account of the various facets of one religion or of many. He aims at detachment and disinterestedness in observation so far as these are possible. In describing the beliefs, practices and institutions of a particular religion he seeks neither to defend nor attack them, but only to understand. So it should be possible to offer a study of religion (or of religions) without committing oneself or one's reader to the truth or falsity of that religion (or religions). Whereas to present a theology is to claim endorsement of some religious beliefs. It is in the spirit of detachment and disinterestedness that the present volume is offered.

3

The degree to which a detached study of religions can be successful in reaching a full understanding of religious traditions will be discussed when our third question about the general character of religion is considered below ('How far is religion available for disinterested study?'). We may note now how the aims behind the study of religions, as opposed to theology, give a distinctive sense to these questions about the general character of religion. For the student of religion and the theologian will be inclined, because of their divergent interests, to give quite different answers to the question 'What is religion?'. A typical theological account of the nature of religion is to be found in the writings of the great systematiser of medieval Catholic thought, St Thomas Aquinas (?1225–73). 'Religion' here figures as the name of a moral virtue, the virtue of offering due worship and service to God (see Aquinas, 1974: 2a2aeQ81). It is opposed to the vices of idolatry and superstition (see Aquinas: 2a2aeQ92 and 94). Thus one cannot recognise the presence of religion in someone's life without judging the truth and adequacy of his beliefs about God and the theological appropriateness of the forms of worship he engages in. But the student of religion tries to use the concept of religion as a neutral, descriptive category. He neither desires nor needs to judge of the truth of someone's beliefs in deciding that person is engaged in religion. Concerned to give an impartial treatment of religions as important historical and social phenomena, he does not contrast religion with idolatry or superstition, but with those other aspects of individual and social life, e.g. politics, art, science and economics, which are worthy of separate treatment from the student of human nature.

The use of 'religion' to signify a descriptive category is relatively new in European thought, as is the concern for an impartial historical and sociological survey of religions. Three important movements of thought seem to be essential to this use of 'religion' and the study that underlies it. First there is the detachment already remarked upon, which involves a readiness to stand back from the religious traditions of one's own culture. This leads to the second thing: comparison. In standing back from the faith of one's own people, one will be ready to look at the faiths of other cultures and to see one's own as but one instance of a general phenomenon to be found throughout culture. The third underpinning of this approach is an historical perspective upon religion. Detachment and comparison will inevitably bring with it a readiness to see the ways one's own and other nations' religions have changed in the course of time and have been enmeshed in the general progress and decay of human societies.

We are now able to turn to our first question about the general character of religion: 'What is religion?'. We must consider whether the detachment, comparison and historical reflection behind the study of religions presupposes or leads to some definition of religion that will fix its essential nature, or sum up in a sentence or two what we are looking to study in various societies or epochs.

4

What is Religion?

At first glance it seems as if a clear definition of 'religion' is both desirable and necessary for the study of religion. A clear understanding of what religion is is needed if, in advance of historical and sociological enquiry, one is to know what is to be rightly included within the scope of study. Only with the kind of understanding a definition of 'religion' (and hence of 'a religion') provides will one know what is to count as a religion for the purposes of study. And after a survey of world's religions has been completed it would seem desirable to sum up the general conclusions reached about the nature of religion in the course of the survey by improving, filling out and making more precise the original 'operational definition' on the basis of which enquiry was launched (for this argument see Wiebe, 1981: 11–13). The way in which an operational definition of religion might be constructed appears straightforward. One would examine the definition of 'religion' implicit in ordinary usage, adapting it and making it more precise in the light of the scholarly purpose one has in using the word (in this case picking out in a neutral fashion a particular historical and social reality in human life).

The search for definition is common enough in branches of the human sciences, but it faces enormous difficulties in the case of 'religion'. For the rest of this subsection we shall treat of the problems that arise in giving an initial, operational definition of 'religion'. These difficulties begin with disputes arising from the ordinary usage of 'religion' and from the conflicting purposes scholars may bring to the business of defining and studying religion.

The clues to defining 'religion' that come from the ordinary use of the word are best considered by separating the denotation and connotation of 'religion'. The denotation of 'religion' is given by listing all those systems of belief, or whatever, we would normally agree on calling religions or examples of religion. Its connotation includes the properties or features of these systems we take to be constitutive of their being religions. The problem with ordinary usage as a guide to an operational definition of 'religion' is that the denotation and connotation of 'religion' are both confused and contradictory therein (see Ferre, 1967: 31–4). There is no question that we could *begin* to set out the denotation of 'religion'. We would start our list of religions with: Christianity, Judaism, Islam, Hinduism, Buddhism. But we would get no clear guidance from ordinary usage as to whether Confucianism was to be included here or under the denotation or 'ethical systems', or as to whether Voodoo was a religion or a mere system of magic. Further we might, without solecism in either case, say that Maoism in the 1960s and 1970s was the new religion of China *and* that China then had no religion because its dominant ideology was so fiercely atheistical. Reflection upon the connotation of 'religion' will produce similar results. Thinking of items on our list of religions like Christianity, Judaism and Islam we might conclude that the chief feature that made something a religion was the presence of a given doctrine: belief in God. Reminding ourselves now of obvious instances of polytheistic religions (e.g. Homeric religion) we may broaden the connotation to 'belief in gods or spiritual beings'. But so seemingly obvious a definition will run into trouble very quickly. It will rule out from the denotation of 'religion' things ordinary usage would at the very least have us pause over (i.e. forms of Buddhism which are apparently atheistic, Jainism, Confucianism and Taoism) and definitely include things like magical practices usage would bid us be hesitant about. If we modify the statement of the belief said to be crucial in making something a religion so that it refers now to something broader (say, 'belief in sacred things or things of ultimate value') we will still be in difficulty. For ordinary usage will be happy to list in the denotation of 'religion' tribal or folk-religions ('the religion of the Eskimos', 'the religion of the Nuer' etc.) in which the element of doctrine/belief may be undeveloped and unimportant. The nineteenth-century anthropologist William Robertson Smith argued that the ancient, tribal religions of mankind were largely systems of rites. They were 'series of acts and observances' in which doctrine and myth were secondary (W.R. Smith, 1927: 20–1). And if this is even half true, to define 'religion' simply in terms of a kind of belief may be quite misleading.

Ordinary usage not being clear about the denotation of religion, and giving no sure guide even to the genus into which 'religion' fits, there is plenty of scope for scholars with different interests in the study of religions to resort to different operational definitions. The possibility of bringing different purposes to the definition of 'religion' reflects the fact of their being different kinds of reflection upon religion and different aims and purposes behind these modes of reflection. Thus a definition of 'religion' may be influenced by avowedly theological purposes even though it wishes to treat 'religion' as a descriptive category. When Max Mueller defines religion as 'A disposition which enables man to apprehend the Infinite under different names and varying guises' (Mueller, 1893: 13) he is modifying an element present in the ordinary connotation of 'religion' (i.e. 'religion is belief in God') to suit a theological purpose behind his study, a purpose which becomes evident when he concludes that all religions place the human soul in the presence of God, despite their surface differences (see Mueller, 1893: 192). Equally a definition could be advanced by a sociological theorist of religion to suit the purpose of showing that religion was a wholly social and human construct, as the following definition appears to do:

> a religion is (1) a system of symbols which acts to (2) establish powerful, pervasive and long-lasting moods and motivations in men by (3) formulating concepts of a general order of existence (4) and clothing these conceptions with such an aura of factuality that (5) the moods and motivations seem uniquely realistic. (Geertz, 1966: 4)

Given that different scholarly interests provide divergent ways of resolving the vagaries of ordinary usage, we must be clear as to the purpose of the study now in hand. Since this purpose is to provide a neutral survey of the broad sweep of mankind's religious life, it seems to call for a definition of 'religion' which does not immediately imply any controversial claims about religion's truth or origin and which preserves as broad a denotation for 'religion' as possible. The definition should allow us to make the necessary discrimination between the religious aspect of human life in history and, say, its economic or political aspects, whilst begging as few questions as possible over which particular forms of belief and practice illustrate this aspect. Boundary questions, such as those concerning the relation between religion and magic, can thus be commented on in the course of surveying tribal religions, rather than being settled arbitrarily in advance.

In producing a definition to meet the above purpose, the first requirement is to establish as broad a genus for 'religion' as possible. So we shall define 'religion' as a type of human institution. It is a complex to be found in human history having the following four important dimensions: the theoretical (e.g. beliefs, myths and doctrines), the practical (e.g. rites, prayers and moral codes), the sociological (e.g. churches, leaders and functionaries) and the experiential (e.g. emotions, visions and sentiments of all kinds). A religion is an institution in human life showing a significant mixture of this complex of theoretical, practical, sociological and experiential dimensions (see Wach's definition in Kitagama, 1967: 41 and Smart, 1971: 15ff.). It is an institution which may be further distinguished by three types of differentiae which qualify the dimensions making up its genus. These may be specified as the *object* of this complex, its *goal* and its *function*. The object of the complex of dimensions that make up the institution that is religion is given in describing the content of its theoretical dimension and the focus of its practical and experiential ones. Its beliefs will concern God, or the gods or more generally sacred things. Its practices and characteristic experiences will be devoted to and focus on supernatural beings or sacred aspects of reality. The goal of this complex will be shown in its practical and sociological dimensions (and in part defined by its theoretical). This goal will be salvation or the achievement of some ultimate good or well-being. The function of the entire system of dimensions will typically be to provide an overall meaning to an individual's life, or in the case of the religion of a group, to integrate and unify the society which they form. To sum up: a religion is an institution with a complex of theoretical, practical, sociological and experiential dimensions, which is distinguished by characteristic objects (gods or sacred things), goals (salvation or ultimate good) and functions (giving an overall meaning to life or providing the identity or cohesion of a social group).

A number of points now need to be made about this definition. We may see first that its very broadness provides a way of understanding the great variety of more specific definitions which have competed with one another in scholarly literature upon religion. For each of these rivals will usually be found to select only some of the dimensions of religion to provide its genus and to fasten upon some limited differentiae to fix the species to which religion belongs. Thus E.B. Tylor's famous definition of 'religion' as 'belief in spiritual beings' (Tylor, 1903: 424) selects the theoretical element as the most important aspect of religion's genus and differentiates it by a particular kind of belief. Religion becomes a kind of philosophy, which Tylor distinguishes from other types by the label 'Animism' (a general view that the world is moved and controlled by superhuman and spiritual beings) and its other dimensions are then but secondary. By contrast the following definition from a recent author initially selects two of our dimensions to provide the genus and picks out the particular function of these dimensions to fix the species:

> Religion, then, can be defined as a system of beliefs and practices by means of which a group of people struggles with these ultimate problems of human life. It expresses their refusal to capitulate to death, to give up in the face of frustration, to allow hostility to tear apart their human aspirations. (Yinger, 1970: 7)

Such a difference in selection by Tylor and Yinger leads to a difference in fixing religion's denotation: Tylor's definition will make us hesitate about including the 'atheistic' religions in the denotation, whilst Yinger's will see the downgrading of belief in personal gods as unimportant in the light of the common function the beliefs and practices of theistic and atheistic religions share. These different definitions with their attendant consequences can now be seen to be selections from the dimensions which give religion its genus and from the various differentiae of these dimensions. Such selection can be motivated by a variety of reasons: the impressiveness of a certain aspect of the ordinary use of religion (or of a chosen example of religion) or the bringing of a specific purpose to the business of definition. No such reasons lie behind our definition so it eschews such selection and remains as inclusive as possible.

      The inclusiveness of our definition shows that it is in good measure vague. We allow in the first instance that a religion need not clearly show all four dimensions in developed form. We can thus accept that at the penumbra of religion there may be primitive, ancient religions which, as Robertson Smith suggested, display the theoretical dimension in but a weak fashion. We can equally accept the Society of Friends as practising a religion in which the sociological dimension has atrophied to a large extent and in which the ritual aspects of the practical dimension have all but disappeared. We look only for a 'significant mix' of these four dimensions. We have also allowed for a number of diverse differentiae so that we produce yet further species of our genus. Moreover many of these differentiae are themselves vague. Thus one of the most important differentia of religion relates to its object and is given by the great French sociologist Durkheim thus: 'A religion is a unified system of beliefs and practices relative to sacred things ...' (Durkheim, 1976: 47). The advantage of this way of fixing the object of religion is that the object becomes broad enough to include religious realities (such as nirvana) which are none the less not divine. But how is the sacred to be defined itself? We may contrast sacred objects and realities with profane on the grounds the former are thought of as transcendent, extraordinary and beyond anything in normal experience, but a full understanding of the nature and range of the sacred can only come with an actual study of the complexity of beliefs about the sacred that can be found in religious history. It is impossible to give an adequate idea of this complexity in some simple formula (cf. Eliade, 1958: xii).

Vague though our definition is, it will still serve to pick out the religious aspect of human life in history from other aspects of that life. It is useful, for example, to be able to distinguish religions in history from systems of belief we say are 'merely philosophies' even though they may have an object, goal and at least personal function which parallel those of religion proper. The demand that the theoretical dimension to religion be significantly linked with at least some of the other three enables us to do this. We might, on the other hand, come across institutions in human life which display the four dimensions of theoretical, practical, sociological and experiential but from which are absent any of the differentiae which mark out religion in the genus. In such institutions there would be no concern with the divine or the sacred, no attempt to rise beyond utilitarian goals and aims and no desire to function as the ultimate source of meaning or identity in life. Political institutions may thus show the dimensions of religion but lack any significant combination of the differentiae of central examples of religion. Some indeed regard the combination of science and technology in the modern world as a significant instance of the displacement of religion by something parallel but different to it. But though our definition has some obvious discriminating power, it will not, because it is vague, sort out the nicer boundary disputes which occur, say, in distinguishing religion from magic. For in some magical systems we may have elements of the four dimensions and at least one of the important differentiae of religion in the presence of belief in spiritual, superhuman beings. Yet other differentiae will be lacking. The goal and function of a system of magic may be entirely mundane and utilitarian, being concerned solely with the attainment of worldly and limited ends. Whether such a system is likened in the end to a crude kind of religion or a crude kind of science/technology (as Sir James Frazer famously does in the opening and closing chapters of *The Golden Bough*) will be left to a detailed study of its relation to central examples of religion.

We may summarise the above points by saying that our definition of religion serves to pick out religion as a recognisable aspect of human life in history but does so in an open-ended way. It serves the purposes of a broad enquiry into religion by giving it a general direction whilst not settling in advance important questions which can only be properly decided upon after detailed study has finished. This kind of operational definition of 'religion' works by listing the more important features which contribute to something's being an instance of religion, but refuses to say exactly what combination of such features is essential for something's being a religion and refuses to define in advance what each feature precisely means (cf. Alston, 1967: 142–3). To some this will seem like the abdication of the attempt to define 'religion' at all, since the operational definition given does not state in unambiguous terms the necessary and sufficient conditions for something's being a religion. A statement of religion's necessary and sufficient conditions would be a list of precise features such that, if an institution lacked them, it could not be classed as a religion, and if it did possess them, it could not fail to be a religion. All that our list of dimensions and differentiae of religion does is allow a number of different statements of sufficient conditions for something's being a religion to be produced, since we know that the possession of a significant number of these features in varying combinations will be enough to enable something to be a religion. But we neither close the list of possible combinations of religion-making features, nor do we attempt to define each feature precisely. But how may we suppose that 'religion' has a meaning we can understand, if we cannot thus state necessary and sufficient conditions for the use of the term?

One answer to the above question would be this: 'religion' is a family-resemblance term and religions form a family. Ludwig Wittgenstein explained the family-resemblance idea of meaning in the following way (he is discussing the words 'language' and 'game'):

> Instead of producing something common to all that we call language, I am saying that these phenomena have no one thing in common which makes us use the same word for all—but that they are all *related* to one another in many different ways. And it is because of this relationship, or these relationships, that we call them all 'language' . . . Consider for example the proceedings that we call 'games' . . . What is common to them all?—Don't say 'There *must* be something common, or they would not be called 'games' '—but *look and see* whether there is anything common to them all.—For if you look at them you will not see something that is common to *all*, but similarities, relationships, and a whole series of them at that . . . we see a complicated network of similarities overlapping and criss-crossing: sometimes overall similarities, sometimes similarities of detail. I can think of no better expression to characterise these similarities than 'family resemblances'; for the various resemblances between members of a family: build, features, colour of eyes, gait, temperament, etc. etc. overlap and criss-cross in the same way.—And I shall say: 'games' form a family. (Wittgenstein, 1958: 31–2)

If the family-resemblance idea of meaning applies to 'religion' then we should expect to find the following facts in our understanding of the word. 1. There will be a characteristic set of features found in examples of religion (such as those described above). 2. There will be no single set of such features to be found in each and every example of religion. 3. There will be no limits to set in advance to the kind of combinations of the characteristic features newly discovered or developing religions could be found to exemplify, nor will there be absolute limits to the additional features such new examples could add to the set. 4. The various examples of religion will be related to one another not therefore by them all sharing a single set of features but through a series of significant overlaps in the features they possess; there will be a network of relationships but no one set of things they all share. 5. The meaning of the word 'religion' will none the less be projectible, that is, having rehearsed the characteristic features of religion in an inclusive definition like that given above or having gained a knowledge of some central examples one will be able to say of newly-found examples whether they are religions or not.

The merit of accepting, at least initially, a family-resemblance meaning for 'religion' is that it agrees with our intuition that religion is an open-ended and ever-developing aspect of life. To think there social existence to be drawn in advance is to falsify our perception that religion will enmesh and intermingle with what surrounds it. Since, too, religion is part of human history it will be ever-changing and therefore it would be wrong not to be open to the possibility that new forms of religion await to be discovered, forms which indeed could extend our apprehension of what religion can be and amount to. The analogy with a family, an ever-developing unity of diverse yet organically-related elements, is more than apt to bring out these facts about religion. We should also be ready to extend the family-resemblance model to the prior picture we have of the particular religions.

This last point is worth stressing. Many believe that to be able to identify different religions and baptise them with names such as 'Hinduism' and 'Christianity' presupposes that there is some easily definable common element that distinguishes them from one another. But if we can legitimately distinguish a host of Indian forms of belief and worship by the term 'Hinduism', this is not because there is some essential unity among them that can be seen on the surface. We have, in fact, coined an umbrella term which refers to a mass of phenomena which does not aspire to be a unity and which is not united by any single item of belief, mode of worship etc. (see Smith, 1978: 65–6). The use of the single term to cover all these phenomena rests only on there being a significant family likeness between them of the sort Wittgenstein has described for us. Nor is this lack of unity simply a feature of the religious traditions of India. In Christianity there is evidently a greater desire to present the religion as a unity and its various sects will accordingly tend to present themselves as representatives of '*the* Church of Christ'. But even in this instance, the actual forms of religion to which we give the label 'Christianity' have shown, and continue to show, the most astonishing variety. Consider in this light the difference between the Christian Unitarianism to be found in parts of Victorian England and the Catholic

Christianity of the peoples of Latin America. Even an alleged common feature in all, such as 'the preaching of Christ' (or '. . . the Gospel' or '. . . the New Testament') will be found to take different shapes in different examples of the religion and to bring with it no essential likeness. Again we will have to fall back upon a family-resemblance picture.

The reason for the variability within specific religions is the same as that for the variability of the general phenomenon, 'religion'. To speak of 'Hinduism' or 'Christianity' is to refer to aspects of the belief, practice, organisation and experience of human beings. These aspects of human life show the variability that human beings show. We might wish as students of human life that human beings believed and behaved more uniformly but they do not. There is limitless scope for novelty and for receptivity to the differing influences of time and place amongst human beings. It is the humanity of religion and the religions which commands that we begin our study with an open-ended definition of 'religion'.

What Kind of Unity does Religion Possess?

The difficulties in giving a clear operational definition for 'religion' do not reflect an inability to pick out the general area of human life that the study of religion is concerned with. The problems surround the precise description of its distinguishing features and the search for uniformity in those features. We have in this latter source of difficulty a reflection of a general problem in all attempts to classify phenomena, for all classification is an attempt to seek unity in diversity. Many students of religion have thought that the attempt to seek unity in the diversity of religious phenomena cannot stop merely with the acknowledgement of the problems confronted in giving a precise operational definition. These problems, they will argue, show only the great divergence in the outward characteristics of the various things we call 'religions'. Further study will reveal an inner unity amongst them, an identity, or sharing, of fundamental characteristics that only comes to light once one has penetrated the varying outer forms of religion. All religions, they argue, share an inner core of some sort, which underlies their outward characteristics.

The relation between the alleged common core to religions and their outward characteristics can be understood on the model of 'essence and manifestation'. The common core to all religions is then said to be the essence of religion. There are different religions because this essence is manifested in different historical and cultural contexts. The unique features of a particular religion can be explained by showing how the core features of religion would produce the outward characteristics of the religion in question, given the particular setting that this religion is placed in. The core features of religion are thus believed to be its true essence in that they are the unvarying, underlying features fundamental in explaining all else.

Such a definition of 'religion' that arose from a search for religion's inner essence or core would have two distinct advantages over an operational definition. It could, in the first place, be said to be a true account of the nature of religion. An operational definition on the other hand would at best be a true summary of ordinary usage, but its adequacy would largely be a matter of its suitability to the purposes behind it. But if we discovered an inward core to religion we would be able to describe the true source of religion's unity and the true explanation of its manifold characteristics. Such a definition would produce a second valuable consequence in so far as it would be the means of settling the boundary disputes over the demarcation of religion in a sure and non-arbitrary fashion. The religions shown to possess the core would have been linked together in fundamental respects. Those things our operational definition had previously allowed to be marginal examples of religious phenomena but which did not possess the core of religion would have been shown to be essentially unlike the central cases.

The power of an account of religion's essence to produce a strong, clear demarcation of religion points to the way one could test any such account. If the account excludes from the denotation of 'religion' central examples of religious phenomena according to a reasonable operational definition, then it is false and inadequate. If we cannot come up with any precise specification of a common core to all religions which does not exclude some such examples, then all religions do not have a common core and religion does not have an essence.

There seem to be two main sources of the belief in an essence to religion, in the belief that all religions share a common core. One we may call 'theological', the other 'scientific'.

The theological source of the belief arises from a concern with the truth of religion. Those who wish to contend that religion in general is correct in its claim that there is a sacred realm beyond the profane or that there is a God will naturally be embarrassed by the apparent diversity and conflict amongst the contrasting beliefs of the world's religions. Divergence and disagreement will also cast a similar shadow over the belief that there is in human religion a valid concern with a transcendent goal or meaning to life. One way of avoiding the worst consequences of these conflicts is to claim that the differences conceal an underlying unity. In essence, by reference to some inner core of belief, experience or ethic, the major religions at least will be found to be in harmony. Underneath their outward differences they offer the same truth and way. This concern with religious truth and an inner core to religion is frequently felt by those who wish to construct a theology of world religions as part of articulating and expressing their own faith. The problem posed by many parts of the human race following religions different from one's own is overcome if a harmony at the level of inner essence is discovered. Many Christian theologies of world religions proceed along these lines and the apologetic value of postulating this

13

deeper harmony is increased if the inner core is shown to commit other faiths to the perceptions of the Christian religion. Furthermore, a theory of religion's inner core may be of apologetic value if it could be shown that, by reference to the core, one's own religion is the highest, most fully developed example of religion: the specific form of faith in which religion's inner essence is given fullest, most perfect expression. Many Christian accounts of 'other religions' have been inspired by just such theological aims (cf. Smart, 1973: 60-1).

Given the terms of this study, we cannot endorse so evidently theological a motive in searching for religion's essence. But we can take cognisance of another source of the search. One might well believe that a truly scientific treatment of religion must be committed to the belief in a common core to all religions, for only if this belief is true will the world's religions be explicable in a truly scientific way. The student of religion will be able to see his investigation into religion by analogy with the way a scientist investigates the nature and properties of a natural substance. If a chemist is investigating the properties of, say, water or gold he knows that, since he is dealing with a natural substance, it is no mere matter of linguistic custom that things are or are not examples of water or gold. We may feel inclined to call substances which look and behave like water and gold by these terms, but it is a question of *truth* whether they are properly so called, for all true examples of these substances will share the common essences of them. A sample of liquid, a piece of metal will either have the molecular structure of these substances or it will not. It is by this criterion that we say no matter how much 'fool's gold' looks and feels like gold it is not as a matter of truth and fact real gold. The real, as opposed to merely conventional, unity of the objects he investigates enables the scientist to delimit the scope of his enquiries in a precise way and to seek genuinely true laws to explain how that which he investigates behaves. There are laws descriptive of the behaviour and properties of water, because all examples of the substance share a common inward constitution which determines their behaviour and properties in a strict fashion. To sum up: we can have a true science of natural substances only because they have common essences as well as common outward properties, for this in turn means that we can classify them in a precise and non-arbitrary manner and explain their myriad properties and reactions in terms of genuine laws.

The attractiveness of the belief in an essence to all religions to those who wish the study of religions to be a true science lies in the thought that a precise delimiting of the object of study and the true laws to explain its characteristics are thereby possible. With a common core there is a real non-conventional and non-arbitrary way of picking out 'true' examples of religion and there is hope of being able to explain the many facets of religion by generalisations from its essence. In considering examples of suggested cores for religion we thus need to bear two questions in mind. We must ask whether any suggested essence really does show a real, inner unity in the central examples of religion. If no account of the core does this, but all force us to dismiss from the category of religion some central cases (on our preliminary classification) then the scientific analogy behind the belief in religion's essence is weak. We must further ask if the suggested accounts of religion's essence really seem to explain the many characteristics of the various central examples of religion our operational definition of 'religion' gives us. If no account of an essence to religion seems to have this explanatory power then, again, the scientific analogy is weak.

The entire question of whether a true science of religion is possible is an important one and we shall touch upon it later in considering how far a disinterested study of religion is possible. In now turning to sample accounts of religion's essence or common core, we shall discuss examples of theories which locate the essence/core in religion's beliefs, in its origins and in its experiences.

An early example of an attempt by a Western scholar to find an essence to all religion comes from the work of the seventeenth-century humanist Edward Herbert. Exhibiting very clearly the theological motives that can lie behind the search for a common core to all religions, Herbert argues that, if God exercises a universal providence over the whole of mankind, we should expect to find in all religions a reliable account of how God is to be served. There must therefore be some 'common notions' in religion or 'catholic articles' which all true religions agree in. Herbert thinks he has found these common notions in the following five simple beliefs: 1. 'That there is one supreme God'; 2. 'That he ought to be worshipped'; 3. 'That virtue and piety are the chief parts of divine worship'; 4. 'That we ought to be sorry for our sins and repent of them'; 5. 'That divine goodness doth dispense rewards and punishments both in this life and after it' (Herbert, 1705: 3–4). The brevity of the list of common notions in religion, and the generality of individual items in it, points to one of the major problems in attempting to unite all religions around a set of common beliefs. (It is a problem which carries over into other attempts to seek a common core as well.) The set of beliefs has to be both vague enough to stand a chance of being seen to be behind the theologies of many outwardly different religions and yet it must be precise enough to point to a factor which really unites those many different religions. What Herbert has done is to locate this vague but genuinely unifying factor in monotheism and an awareness of right and wrong. To this day this has remained a popular way of seeking a unity in the world religions.

The problem that we have pointed to facing Herbert's attempt at unity shows initially in how he links both Christianity and Classical paganism together by reference to his common notions in religion. The Classical world apparently believed in many gods who were often regarded as being identical with parts of the natural world (e.g. sun, heavens, moon) rather than as supreme and transcendent. Ancient heathenism and

Christianity are still linked, however, for, according to Herbert, the heath-ens' worship of the sun etc. 'was symbolical' (Herbert, 1705: 31). Thus he is forced to seek a 'true', 'inner' meaning behind the outward form of pagan beliefs. Such an inner meaning *ought* to be there if his belief about God's presence in all religions is correct, but can we follow him in this 'symbolical' interpretation of Classical polytheism if we do not accept his theological starting-point? The question here raised about the attempt to see a common theology in all faiths gains force upon noting that Herbert acknowledges *popular* polytheism could not be interpreted symbolically. Polytheistic and pagan beliefs were taken seriously by many with the result that in place of religion, defined by the common notions, we had superstition and idolatry (see Herbert, 1705: 381–2). But now all religion is being unified by Herbert's common core of belief only at the cost of setting aside many forms of theology and worship as superstitious and idolatrous. We have: not an attempt to seek a common core to all religions, but a theological judgement that all correct, worthwhile religions will share certain beliefs. Herbert's theology is more unifying than some, because it is less specific, but he is none the less trying to establish what is correct in religion rather than what is essential to all its manifestations.

When we reflect, as Herbert could not, on the greater variety of doctrine and myth apparent with the recognition of non-theistic religions, the normative, theological character of attempts to see a single set of beliefs as unifying all religions is even more evident. Only if we are prepared to wield the distinction between 'true' and 'false' religion with vigour can we hope to unite all religions around a common set of beliefs. But that this is so, shows in turn that this form of the search for a common core to religion has no place in a disinterested, neutral survey of mankind's religious life throughout the world and its history.

The second form of the belief in an essence to all religions we wish to consider focuses upon the idea that all religions are identical in origin. There is a common essence to all religions because they all spring from the same original root (see Alston, 1967: 141). This approach to the search for religion's essence is popular wherever a strongly evolutionary perspective upon human life is influential. For if one thinks that human life and culture is the product of an evolutionary process, one may be led to conclude that the key to understanding it will lie in its origins. Since it is reasonable to suppose that human culture had similar origins in different parts of the world, one can assume a uniform starting-point for mankind's religions. Accepting the crucial role of origins in an evolutionary account of any aspect of cultural life, one will conclude there is common essence (i.e. explanatory key) to all religions.

There are numerous examples of this version of the essence theory, for it was particularly in vogue amongst late nineteenth-century scholars in Europe impressed by the success of evolutionism in biology and other fields. Thus E.B. Tylor argues in his famous work *Primitive Culture* that all religions share in a common root, which is also their essence, through 'animism'. Animism is the first philosophy of life and nature primitive man can be supposed to have thought out. It shaped the first human societies, the first religions from which all the rest flowed and is still at the heart of the religious faiths found today. It consists of the simple belief in souls (i.e. spiritual, non-material personalities) which animate man and his environment and control nature. Because of the centrality of the evolutionary origins of religion, animism in Tylor's account is the key to understanding the manifold beliefs and practices now extant and is the hidden unity beneath that manifold. Despite the popularity of searching for the essence of religions through origins, there are a number of grave difficulties in this approach. They can be instructively set out by reference to Tylor's theory. How, we may first ask, could we know that animism was or was not the first philosophy of life and nature from which all religions sprung? We have no direct access to the period of human history when culture and religion first arose, for by definition it occurred long before written records were possible. We can investigate the archaeology of the first human communities, but the traces they have left behind are meagre, rarely found and leave only the slimmest basis for inference as to the shape of the earliest human religions. Tylor overcomes this problem by largely basing his account upon the evidence of the beliefs of contemporary primitive peoples. These are tribal peoples who employ a low standard of technology and food production by European standards and can thus be taken to be living examples of the very first human communities. Leaving aside the much debated point of whether their religious life is really united by the philosophy of animism, it may be doubted whether they truly fill the evidential gap that threatens the anthropologist's speculations about the origins of all religions. For how do we know that their material culture has not developed slower than their spiritual? How do we know that either one or both are not degenerations from a state more sophisticated than that enjoyed at present? Even if their religious life were uniform, no sure clue is provided to the earliest origins of all religious life.

In fact the search for origins can be seen as a misleading detour in the search for religion's essence. For granted that all religions originate from, say, the same philosophy of nature, this will not unite them now unless they are all still true to that origin. It is an obvious fallacy (the 'genetic fallacy') to assume that because something originated in X it must still be essentially X and no more. Thus Tylor still has to show that all religions are *still* united in essence by the animistic philosophy (a point recognised in Chapter 11 of *Primitive Culture*). But then the origins theory of religion's essence collapses into one of the other types of theory. In Tylor's case it becomes another version of the view that all religions are united around a common belief or beliefs, but in his case a vague philosophy of nature has replaced the minimal theology Herbert lays down.

17

There is good reason to doubt whether any single philosophy of nature is or has been shared by all the central examples of religion. Animism, as defined by Tylor, will not do. For we read that in early Buddhism (to take but one example), though a variety of beings, including *devas* (gods), populate the universe, they occupy a secondary place, being impermanent and subject to a higher, impersonal cosmic law (see von Glasenapp, 1970: 30). The 'gods', therefore, did not occupy a fundamental role in the theoretical, practical, sociological or experiential dimensions of this central example of a religion.

The two sample accounts of religion's essence so far considered flounder upon the doctrinal and theological complexities exhibited by the world's religions. Given these complexities it is hard to find a common set of beliefs shared by all, or a common philosophical outlook in which they all agree. One way of continuing the search for religion's essence which bypasses the doctrinal and philosophical differences among religions is provided by the notion that we must look for the shared possession of a certain type of experience. A shared mode of experience underlying doctrinal differences is the common core to all religions and the essence of religion, the key to understanding its other dimensions.

Numerous writers have prosecuted the search for religion's essence in this fashion. One of the most famous is Rudolf Otto, who in his influential work *The Idea of the Holy* describes the numinous experience and of it concludes 'There is no religion in which it does not live as the real innermost core, and without it no religion would be worthy of the name' (Otto, 1950: 6). This experiential essence to religion is described by Otto as having three essential features: mystery, power and love. The religious experience is firstly an experience of something 'wholly other', that is, of something felt to be totally different from mundane objects of awareness. It is of something alien, foreign and transcendent. It does in addition strike those who have it with a sense of immense power. Before it awe, dread and fear are appropriate. The human subject of the experience feels himself and the objects around him as nothing in comparison with what is revealed in the numinous experience. The third important feature of the experience is shown in the way that, despite the mystery and power given in it, it draws and fascinates those who have it. They are not repelled, but rather their interest and concern is demanded by what is shown to them in the experience.

There are reasons for believing that something like Otto's numinous experience is present in many religions otherwise different in points of doctrine or explicit philosophical outlook (why this is so will become apparent below). Despite this there are a number of grounds for doubting whether we have stumbled upon the essence or common core to all religions. Some of these grounds relate to the specifics of Otto's account, others apply generally to accounts placing religion's essence in experience.

18

A specific point of criticism comes from the difficulty of seeing that Otto's analysis fits the character of many types of mystical experience. In mysticism the object of religion is sought through contemplation and inner quest. The characteristic result is a unitive experience in which the object is not felt as 'wholly other' but as identical with, or somehow within, the self. A concentration upon numinous experiences has been held to come from over-attention to the strand of worship in the religions, worship being a religious attitude or discipline which encourages the idea of a gulf between the believer and the object of his devotions (see Smart, 1964: 129–31).

A further question mark over the status of the numinous as the essence to all religion casts doubts about the validity of any search for religion's unifying essence in a mode of experience. The reason why the numinous experience looks like an important unifying feature, binding together at least all those religions in which worship is an important strand, is because its description captures many of the general features of man's experience of the sacred. But 'the sacred' is not the name of a *specific* object common to all religions; no more is it the name of a *specific* experience. Otto's description is unifying because it picks out some of the *generic* features (transcendence, power and attraction) that specific experiences of the sacred exemplify. We must be clear, however, that specific experiences of the sacred exemplify these generic features in different ways. This is not an accident. It arises through the mutual interaction of experience and doctrine in the religions. Those religions which all may be said to have as their generic object 'the sacred' differ enormously in the beliefs they hold about what specifically for them is sacred, and these idiosyncratic beliefs naturally colour in part how the sacred is experienced in religion. Otto's appearance in *The Idea of the Holy* of presenting a precise, specific, non-generic experience is created by the concentration upon Jewish and Christian sample experiences used to illustrate the numinous, for here we have experiences coloured and shaped by similar and overlapping beliefs about the object of experience. Otto himself affirms that the true essence of religion is not the numinous in isolation but the category of 'the Holy' (see Chapters 14 and 17 of *The Idea of the Holy*), this being the numinous experience mediated, interpreted by some definite conceptions and beliefs. They turn out to be elements of conception and belief associated with the concept of God as we find it in the philosophical theology of the Christian tradition. No wonder then that, if organisation around the category of the Holy is the mark of the full development of something as an example of religion, 'we find that Christianity ... in this as in other respects, stands out in complete superiority over all its sister religions' (Otto, 1950: 142). Here, then, we have a general point of principle against any attempt to seek a specific religious experience that will unite all religions despite their doctrinal and philosophical differences. There is no such specific experience because doctrines shape experiences, so the specifics of doctrine will affect the specifics of experience. Only if experience and doctrine in religion were sharply separable (with perhaps differing doctrinal structures floating free above a unifying, specific experience to be found in all religions) could this be otherwise.

There are other ways of seeking an essence to religion than by the three modes we have illustrated (belief, origin and experience). Another important approach, for example, undertakes to discover a common, unifying feature in the function religion might have in personal and social life (see, e.g. Durkheim, 1936). In the course of discussing our examples of the quest for religion's essence we have noted one crucial problem that faces all such attempts. They have to locate religion's essence in something sufficiently precise enough to have a real unifying and explanatory force, but sufficiently general not to be tied to the specifics of some central examples of religion rather than others. Our discussion also throws up another general difficulty for all forms of the quest. We see that it is hard to find a core with the right combination of precision and generality in any of the beliefs of the religions or in anything that is fundamentally affected by their differing beliefs (such as their different philosophical outlooks or modes of experience). The measure of the difficulty in finding a core to religion which bypasses doctrine and belief may now be shown. For we can hope to find a common essence to religion only if we can hope to demonstrate that the theoretical dimension to religion is strictly secondary in making institutions examples of religion and in explaining their fundamental characteristics.

One may feel that this goal of relegating to the secondary and consequential the theoretical dimension in religion is too far-fetched to make the task of seeking an essence and common core to all religions seem at all attractive. Abandoning the task, one may still hope that the study of religions will produce interesting facts from one religion which illuminate our general conception of religion, and through that, other religions as well. One will have given up, however, any attempt to discover an absolute, definitive unity amongst religions or to explain the characteristics of religion by universal laws modelled on those in science.

Is Religion Available for Disinterested Study?

If our brief discussion of the search for religion's essence raises a question mark over a fully scientific explanation of religion, it remains to be considered how far a more modest scientific approach to religion is possible. In offering this volume as a work of detached, disinterested scholarship we have in fact been claiming that an acceptably modest scientific description of religion in history is possible. This is a description free of doctrinal commitment and bias, based upon objective, scholarly research. Such an approach, being distinct from that of theology, presupposes that one may seek to understand the world's religions without being a committed participant in them. It assumes, in short, that understanding a religion is possible without believing it.

Whether belief and understanding can thus be separated is something we must now pursue, as well as the related issue of how the historian's or sociologist's description of a religion is related to the beliefs of those who actually practise it. Many have thought that a neutral understanding of religion is impossible in some degree or other. This may reflect either a worry about a neutral approach to any human institution or doubts arising from the specific institution religion is. To tackle these doubts we must remind ourselves that we have defined 'religion' in terms of genus and differentiae. Its genus is a human institution—a complex of theoretical, practical, sociological and experiential dimensions. Its differentiae are provided by the characteristic object, goal and function of this complex. Our question about whether it is possible to have a neutral, outsider's understanding of religion now divides into two: Is it possible to have a neutral understanding of *any* complex of human belief, behaviour etc.? Can we have such an understanding for the *specific* types of belief, behaviour etc. that we find in religion?

The general question about the relation between understanding and belief raised here is important because of the common recognition that human behaviour has an 'inside' as well as an 'outside'. This distinction is evident if we reflect on the difference between the behaviour of an inanimate object and even a moderately complex piece of human behaviour, such as a gesture of greeting. The difference between say, describing a kettle boiling and describing something like the latter is shown in the way an account in terms of mere externals will do in the first case but not in the second. A kettle's boiling is a sequence of physical changes and to describe it is to do no more than plot these changes. But a description of the externally observable events that constitute one person's act of greeting to another would leave out some vital features of the act altogether. It would ignore those features which gave it its meaning as this act rather than another. It is an act of greeting because it has a certain kind of point. Its having this point is a matter of its being informed by beliefs and desires of a given kind and of it conforming to accepted conventions and rules for giving expression to those beliefs and desires. Unlike a sequence of mere physical changes, we may say that a piece of human behaviour has an 'inside' as well as an 'outside'. It is informed by beliefs and desires, and is related to conventions and rules of a human community. This 'inside' to human behaviour is even more apparent if we consider the experience and feelings that accompany behaviour and which also inform and shape it. Attention to both the externals and the inside of human behaviour is necessary if its meaning is to be discovered and hence if it is to be understood.

We might seem able to conclude quickly that an understanding of any human institution cannot be separated from the beliefs of those who participate in it. For any such institution will have an inside as well as an outside. Discovery of its inside will be necessary to determine the meaning of its component parts but will include precisely the beliefs of its participants. The beliefs of the participants will shape the meaning of the institution. But we must note the very limited nature of this conclusion. If to uncover the meaning of a human institution is in part to uncover the beliefs of those who participate in it, this is not to say that we must *share* those beliefs. It is only to say that we must describe them in describing the 'inward' side to the institution on pain of missing its meaning. As non-participating observers we should look to the beliefs and conventions present in the institution in helping us complete our description of it. We need sympathy, imagination and insight to uncover these beliefs, but this does not entail that we share them. We need to describe the beliefs of the participants to describe the institution in its fullness, but we do not need in addition to hold them.

If we equate a scientific approach to the description of religion with one that is neutral, scholarly and disinterested, we have not ruled it out in noting the importance of the 'inside' to any human institution. A scientific approach would only have been defeated if we assumed that neutrality, scholarship and disinterest meant being confined to the externals of an institution only. But there is no reason to suppose that the elements of objective study exclude the sympathetic and imaginative insight needed to penetrate beyond the externals of an institution. In the case of human belief and behaviour sympathy and imagination turn out to be the preconditions for the discovery of the whole range of data needed by objective scholarship.

This conclusion about the relation between belief and understanding drawn from the general character of a human institution can be applied to the specific case of a religion in the following way. Consider a scholar describing the meaning of the ritual of the Eucharist in a particular Christian denomination. No adequate description of this rite could confine itself to the externals of what goes on. It would have to mention and delineate its point—let it be an act of remembrance of the Saviour. In characterising the point of the rite many beliefs about the object of Christianity (i.e. God-in-Christ) would have to be mentioned and explained. The worshippers' beliefs about the object of their religion would thus need to be called upon to make up the description of the rite. But this does not entail that the scholar himself shares these beliefs, only that he be ready to uncover and use them in his account. All the beliefs about Christ and the Eucharist mentioned in his account would be in reported speech, and thus neither endorsed nor denied. Though the object of the religion would figure very considerably in the observer's account, it would, to use the technical expression, be 'bracketed' (see Smart, 1973: 57). All the statements about God and Christ in the description of the Eucharist would, on this score, be preceded by an explicit or implicit 'The participants believe that . . .' The nature of the object of religion would figure in the description only in and through the participants' beliefs about that object. So the 'inside' of the ritual could be grasped in the scholarly account without committing either the scholar or his readers to the actual existence of a religious object having that nature.

Our brief discussion of the general difficulties in describing human institutions has revealed a complexity in the relationship between an outsider's understanding of them and a participant's beliefs and experiences. The latter are crucial in yielding an understanding of the institution but not because endorsing them is a precondition of understanding them. Rather, uncovering and describing them will reveal to the outsider the full meaning of what goes on in the institution. The object of the outsider's reflection and, he hopes, understanding is in large measure the participant's beliefs. If we wish to restrict the possibility of an objective, neutral study of religion we must seek something more specific in religion to block this kind of approach to it.

One common way of arguing from the specifics of religion to the impossibility of a neutral understanding of it has been found in its experiential dimension. Thus it has been argued that religion's essence lies in its experiential dimension and that in the case of religion the experiential dimension is beyond definition or description (see Wiebe, 1981: 9–10). If this were the case, the only means of understanding the 'inside' to the institution is actually to have the experiences which determine it. Since they are beyond description nothing believers say or write can help the non-participant understand religion. Only by becoming a participant can one understand the unique, inexpressible experience that lies at the heart of religion. This line of thought is suggested by Otto's comments on the numinous experience:

> This mental state is perfectly *sui generis* and irreducible to any other, and therefore, like every absolutely primary and elementary datum, while it admits of being discussed, it cannot be strictly defined. There is only one way to help another to an understanding of it. He must be guided and led on by consideration and discussion of the matter through the ways of his own mind, until he reaches the point at which 'the numinous' in him perforce begins to stir, to start into life and into consciousness. (Otto, 1950: 7)

No doubt part of the reasoning behind Otto's conclusion that we can understand religious experience, and thus the core of religion, only if it is awakened in us lies in his stress upon it as the experience of something 'wholly other'. The observer of religion doesn't merely confront beliefs about and experiences of objects he happens not to have met himself, but could still understand. For he cannot be apprised of the character of these alleged objects by the use of general categories of which he has had experience in other cases. The objects of religious belief and experience, being transcendent, are not well described by general categories of description into which objects of common acquaintance also fit. Thus the believer himself feels the presence of a gap between the descriptions he offers and the object of his religion, just because those descriptions are drawn from ordinary things. Here we have a point which reflects the general character of the sacred as a class of objects of belief, ritual and experience. The sacred is other than the ordinary, the mundane, and thus not easily defined by ordinary descriptions and classifications.

There can be no question that the content of religious beliefs and experiences is out of the ordinary in a quite special sense and that this creates peculiar difficulties in understanding. The resources of imagination, sympathy and insight that the neutral scholar must employ will have to be greater than in the description of many other aspects of human life. Further reflection, however, will show that he is not without important aids in understanding even the content of beliefs and experiences focusing on the sacred.

One source of interpretation comes from the fact that beliefs and experiences concerning the sacred do not exist in isolation. It is, for example, clear from Otto's discussion of the numinous experience that it is in concrete cases always found connected with a web of notions and doctrines in particular religions. It is shaped by these connections and in turn contributes to the concepts and beliefs that surround it. In its developed forms it is not a bare experience but an encounter with the object of a specific religion. Thus its character can in part be ascertained by noting the connections established between it and other things in the various dimensions of a religion. The fact that particular beliefs and experiences concerning the sacred are connected with other beliefs and experiences, and with practices and sociological structures, brings with it a further source of understanding for the non-participant. These connections entail that such beliefs and experiences are parts of a publicly shareable and shared human institution. Experiences of the sacred may in a manner be private and unique but they are bound up with dimensions of belief, behaviour, experience and social organisation that define a human, cultural phenomenon (see Wiebe, 1981: 9–10). Being a cultural phenomenon religion exists as a public entity. The experiential dimension to religion does not militate against this fact. For what makes an individual's experiences of the sacred *religiously* significant (as opposed to being merely private experiences of one knows not what) is that they do connect with and contribute to the public phenomenon that is a religion. To be counted as experiences of the sacred they must be characterised as experiences of something, where the relevant concept used to delineate the object is recognisably drawn from some system of religious thought or other, even if it is a system initiated by the experience itself. This entails that all experiences of the sacred have the public connections described if they are to be counted as experiences of the sacred. If someone had an experience that was literally indescribable or literally of nothing, there would be no more reason to classify it as a religious experience than there would to classify it as belonging to some totally different area of life.

One cannot deny that there are esoteric experiences in the religions. There are experiences (sometimes associated with forms of mysticism) described as being of the Ineffable or of Nothingness. Such experiences do of course create a problem for the interpreter. But it should be noted that words like 'Ineffable' and 'Nothingness' do function here as descriptions: they are means of positively characterising the experiences in question, which in turn connect the experiences with doctrines, rituals etc. in comprehensible ways. Thus 'Ineffable' gets its force from associations with doctrines to the effect that the sacred object surpasses and is distinct from all mundane things. 'Nothingness' as a characterisation may be connected with doctrines and practices associated with the religious importance of the extinction of the self or of the emptying of mind of all discrete, finite objects of consciousness. Such characterisations do not, then, blunt the force of what has been urged concerning the publicity and connectedness of individual religious experiences and beliefs. In the last analysis the force of these characterisations is derived from what comes before and what comes after them in the life of religion.

A further source of help to the observer trying to understand the character of beliefs and experiences comes from the undoubted fact that the sacred connects with the mundane in countless ways. Thus, to cite Otto's particular account of the sacred again, it is evident that both the numinous experience itself and the concepts used to rationalise it are connected with experiences and descriptions of the ordinary and everyday. Otto notes how the numinous experience has 'numerous analogies' with other experiences, despite being qualitatively *sui generis* in some sense. He mentions the experience of the sublime in nature as a closely analogous feeling (Otto, 1950: 44). If the experience is rationalised in the manner of Christian theology (in terms of an all-powerful, all-good creator God), then it is being shaped by concepts derived from public conceptions of mundane things (power, goodness, making). For all the unique and 'wholly other' character of the numinous, one who has not had experience of it is not without bearings in understanding it. A general truth about the character of the sacred here emerges. The characteristic objects of religion may be regarded as distinct from ordinary, mundane things in various and varying respects. But they are all regarded as connected with and related to ordinary things in important ways.

There are two strong reasons from within the dynamics of religion why the sacred should thus be connected with the ordinary. In the first case: if it were not it would be of no interest and importance. Religion does not merely focus on realities felt to be extraordinary but on ones which are vital to human life. They must be realities which suggest a goal for human striving, the following of which will have an important role in human individual or social life. They must therefore be thought of as interacting in important ways with ordinary life and its concerns. In addition, if the sacred were not related to ordinary things and realities there would be no route into religion for even those who aspire to be participants. Religion would be a completely closed book quite incapable of being comprehended by anyone. Nothing else in human culture would provide a means for being able to understand or participate in it. Not only the phenomenon of conversion, but also the obvious interpenetration of religion and the other aspects of human culture shows the connectedness of religious belief and experience with other things. If religion were completely esoteric, it would be of no interest to anyone; and it would not exist. We do not, again, deny that religion may speak of the 'ineffable' or the 'utterly mysterious'. One way of relating a felt reality to ordinary things may be the way of differencing and distinguishing it from them. The importance for us of the religious object might lie in its unlikeness to anything ordinary. We can describe and relate one thing to another by stressing unlikeness and difference.

If we consider the differentiae of religion as a human institution, we must conclude that it has many aspects which will stretch the sympathetic and imaginative resources of the neutral scholar to the uttermost. We have not, however, found anything to suggest that, unlike other phenomena in human culture, it is not available for disinterested study. 'Disinterest' and 'neutrality' are not labels for 'lack of sympathy' or 'external observation'. The scholar must get to grips with the living 'inside' of religion, but he need not share the beliefs, experiences etc. which make up that 'inside'. Nor need he govern his research and observation by the desire to make them prove preconceived theological commitments.

Conclusion

Much has been said in the last section of the difference between a theological approach to religion and an approach of disinterested scholarship. The point of view of the believer has likewise been distinguished from that of the non-participating observer of religion. It would be wrong to leave the impression that such distinctions were hard and fast.

It may, for example, be very important for one who is a committed participant in a particular religion to adopt on occasion the stance of a disinterested observer of the religious scene. The fruits of others' neutral scholarship may equally be of great importance to the participant. No one is any the better for being ignorant of the actual historical or sociological details of his own religion. To stand back from one's own faith, to examine it and other faiths with disinterested scrutiny, may be of great importance in fully understanding what one believes and why one believes it. Scholarly enquiry into one's own faith may be the means of uncovering beliefs and assumptions about one's religion that are best dismissed as prejudiced and harmful. Looking at the faiths of others may give one a new insight into one's own, in revealing how people of different cultures have coped with common problems, such as suffering and death. It may be a powerful check to the parochialism which assumes that one's own culture represents the experience of humanity as a whole.

For the kind of reason mentioned above much theology has in fact been engaged in scholarly historical and critical research. Much of the pioneering work in the West in the global study of religions was undertaken by theologians interested in discovering the facts of the relationship between Christianity and the larger religious life of mankind. The best theologians have understood that one cannot articulate one's faith without understanding it. Acts of disinterested reflection which take in what others have thought and believed may be an aid to such understanding. An understanding of one's own religion, and of religion in general, is not given just in being a participant in it.

As we reflect upon religion in the contemporary world it is with a heightened sense of the facts of the historical antiquity, and geographical variety and extent of human culture. More and more we will come to realise accordingly the truth of Max Mueller's dictum of 100 years ago: he who knows one religion, knows none (Mueller, 1893: 13).

Bibliography

Alston, W. P. 'Religion', in P. Edwards (ed.), *The Encyclopedia of Philosophy* (Macmillan, New York, 1967), pp. 140–5.

Aquinas, Thomas *Summa Theologiae*, tr. Dominican Fathers (Eyre & Spottiswoode, London, 1974)

Durkheim, E. *The Elementary Forms of the Religious Life* (Allen & Unwin, London, 1976)

Eliade, M. *Patterns in Comparative Religion* (Sheed and Ward, London, 1958)

Ferre, F. *Basic Modern Philosophy of Religion* (Scribners, New York, 1967)

Frazer, J. *The Golden Bough*, abridged edn (Macmillan, London, 1922)

Geertz, C. 'Religion as a Cultural System' in M. Banton (ed.), *Anthropological Approaches to the Study of Religion* (Tavistock, London, 1966), pp. 1–46

Glasenapp, H. von *Buddhism—a Non-Theistic Religion*, tr. Irmgard Schlögel (Allen and Unwin, London, 1970)

Herbert, Edward *De Religione Gentilium*, tr. as *The Antient Religion of the Gentiles* by William Lewis (London, 1705)

Kitagawa, J. 'Primitive, Classical and Modern Religions' in Kitagawa (ed.), *The History of Religions* (University of Chicago Press, Chicago, 1967), pp. 39–65

Mueller, F.M. *An Introduction to the Science of Religion* (Longman, London, 1893)

Otto, R. *The Idea of the Holy*, tr. J. Harvey (Oxford University Press, Oxford, 1950)

Smart, R.N. *Philosophers and Religious Truth* (SCM, London, 1964)

—— *The Religious Experience of Mankind* (Collins, Glasgow, 1971)

—— *The Science of Religion and the Sociology of Knowledge* (Princeton University Press, Princeton, 1973)

Smith, W.C. *The Meaning and End of Religion* (SPCK, London, 1978)

Smith, W.R. *Lectures on the Religion of the Semites*, 3rd edn (Black, London, 1927)

Tylor, E.B. *Primitive Culture*, vol. 1, 4th edn (Murray, London, 1903)

Wiebe, D. *Religion and Truth* (Mouton, The Hague, 1981)
Wittgenstein, L. *Philosophical Investigations* (Blackwell, Oxford, 1958)
Yinger, J. M. *The Scientific Study of Religion* (Macmillan, New York, 1970)

Some of the material for this chapter is taken from an article by the author in *The Scottish Journal of Religious Studies*, Vol. 1, No. 1 (1980), and is reproduced by kind permission of the editor.

2 | The Study of Religion and Religions

Stewart Sutherland

There are many reasons or motives which may lead someone to study religion or particular religions. One may simply be *interested* in the subject, or in some aspect of it. Alternatively one may be engaged 'existentially' with some of the questions to which religion and religions offer answers: that is to say one may be looking for a belief or set of beliefs. More mundanely one may be sitting examinations which will test one's knowledge of these matters.

To focus upon the reasons or motives however is at this stage not very helpful. What is more important is to try to grasp what the successful outcome of the study of religion or religions should be. In one sense this is a straightforward matter, for the successful outcome of anything worth studying ought to be an extension of knowledge and understanding. This obvious answer, however, raises as many questions as it settles. There are three main types of question which arise, and they are all central to the nature and rationale of this book:

1. What will one know if one knows more about religion(s) and what is it that one will understand if one has a greater understanding of religion(s)?

2. If one seeks such knowledge or understanding where should one focus one's attention?

3. What methods should one use to increase knowledge or understanding?

Let us answer these questions in turn, recognising at the outset what will become even more apparent as we proceed: the answer to any one of these questions is ultimately dependent upon the answers given to the other two.

Knowledge and Understanding

What will one know, if one knows more about religion(s) and what is it that one will understand if one has a greater understanding of religion(s)?

In his discussion of the idea that all religions may have a common core (see pp. 3–28), Peter Byrne considers the comparison some had drawn between looking for knowledge or understanding of religion, and looking for knowledge or understanding of a substance in the natural world. This someone who 'knows' what gold is, knows how to distinguish it from what looks like it, 'fool's gold', and ultimately such knowledge is based upon knowledge of the properties which the substance gold has. Now it would be very nice if knowing about religion or religions could be characterised in an equivalently straightforward way. However, for all the reasons spelt out in Peter Byrne's chapter, such a comparison is too simple and simplified.

A fundamental difficulty in such a comparison is that gold is gold, with its various physical properties whatever human beings may believe about it, or whatever value they attach to it. It is part of the natural world which is there and is what is, without reference to what we may or may not think of it. Religion, however, is not part of the natural world in that way, for if there were no human beings there would be no religion: whereas there was gold before there were any human beings, and there may well still be gold after the human race is extinct. This is an element of what we mean when we say that religion is in part at least a social phenomenon. It has to do with what human beings do and think and say. Thus in studying religion(s) one is studying, amongst other things, human beings and human societies. To grasp this is to have avoided many of the pitfalls of the study of religion. It is also, as we shall see, to have given ourselves some hints about where we must focus our attention, and also of the methods which we must use.

It will be useful to pause briefly to underline this point. Some regard the study of religion(s) as at best distracting, and at worst impossible. They do this because they believe that the study of religion(s) is and can only be the study of 'God' or of what is 'transcendent'. They then recall or point out that if God is God, or if we do really mean 'what transcends human thought', then study in any acceptable sense will be impossible, for God is above all knowing and beyond all of our limited conceptions and is not a suitable candidate for study: for worship, or love, or even hatred, yes, but not for the cool reflective gaze of the student. Now there are many questions which could be raised here, which are not the concern of this book, but which are properly the focus of theological enquiry (for example St Thomas Aquinas's *Summa Theologiae*, or Karl Barth's *Church Dogmatics*, both of which consider with great subtlety the question of the knowledge which we may have of God). These questions are not our concern because the study of religion(s) is not, for example, the study of what God is, but is the study of what men and women *believe* or *say* that God is. Equally the study of religion(s) is not the study of what we must do to have eternal life, but is the study of what human beings *do* in pursuit of eternal life, and of what they *say* we must do to find it. Thus the study of religion(s) must at least begin with the study of human beings and their doings and sayings.

Of course for many it will go well beyond this. On the one hand there are those who would also press the question of whether what such human beings say and believe is true, and on the other, there are those who might, in assuming that it is not true, look for an explanation of why human societies should, without exception, include people who do engage in religious practices and/or hold religious beliefs.

If it is clear that the study of religion(s) is founded in the study of human beings and human society, are we any nearer answering our first question of what it is that we hope to know or understand through the study of religion(s)? We are a little nearer, but we still have some considerable way to go. For some the idea of study is the amassing of facts or information so that they may achieve a reputation for erudition, whether in playing *Trivial Pursuit* with their relatives, or entering television quiz-games, or with more *gravitas*, in the arena of scholarship.

Thus they might be seeking, in magpie fashion, knowledge of a number of facts about religion, e.g. that in Brazil the number of Protestants in 1890 was 143,743, in 1940 was 1,074,857 and in 1961 was 4,071,643, or that an Islamic writer named al-Ghazali wrote a book called *The Incoherence of Philosophers* in which he attacked the growing influence of philosophy on Islamic theology. Or we may be interested in such facts as that in 1976 211 of the 236 adults resident in Hardenburgh, New York State, became ministers of the Universal Life Church. (The explanation of this apparently massive response to a veritable trumpet-blast of religious vocation is that evidently, in the USA, citizens who are ministers or clergy may be exempt from some taxes. An enterprising though almost illiterate former hobo called Kirby J. Hensley founded the Universal Life Church to provide a mail-order ordination service, thus allowing the recipients of his airmail dog-collars to reclassify their homes as churches and thereby to save on taxes payable!)

Now knowledge of such facts which are in each case, in some sense, knowledge of facts about or of religion, may well be important in non-trivial ways and in some cases essential for further study or deeper understanding. Indeed of such facts there is virtually no end and drawing upon and analysing them is a precondition of the discussions of all the contributions to this book. In putting the point in that way I am implying that the search for knowledge and understanding may rest upon, but it must go far beyond, the acquisition of such snippets of information.

This suggests a second answer to our question of what sort of knowledge or understanding we hope to attain. On this view we may be seeking knowledge in the sense of the specific sort of understanding which an expertise or particular discipline can give us. Thus, for example, an historian can tell us much about the historical fortunes of a particular religious tradition, or a sociologist can inform us about the statistical correlations between particular social groupings and classes on the one hand, and membership of particular religious groups or branches of the Christian Church on the other. Or an expertise in ancient Greek and Hebrew can contribute an understanding of the Scriptures of the Christian religion which is not possible for those who study these Scriptures only in translation. These are all examples of the application of a skill or a discipline to the analysis of facts, and the extension of the understanding of religion(s).

What each example makes plain is that understanding or knowledge may take many forms and draw upon many disciplines, and the consequent fragmentation of knowledge and understanding is a fundamental feature of the world in which we live, whether we think of understanding religion(s) or understanding agriculture. To that extent it is a feature also of this book, for the multi-faceted nature of religion(s) requires a variety of skills and techniques in its analysis. Equally the interests of any particular reader may best be served through the use of one particular discipline rather than another (see below).

What is true, however, is that it is unlikely that any *one* discipline will provide a universal key to unlock all the secrets of religion(s) to those in search of understanding and knowledge. In addition to the answers to specific questions (e.g. Is there a correlation between industrialisation and the decline of religion?, or, Is Islamic Fundamentalism best understood as a political movement?, or, Do any of the Gospels present an accurate picture of the historical Jesus?) there are questions of a much wider nature, where it is not clear that an historian *qua* historian or a sociologist *qua* sociologist can provide adequate answers.

This shows itself in two ways. In the first instance there are many questions about religion(s) which require the skills of more than one discipline to answer them. Thus for example even within the limited range of the exegesis of religious texts practitioners will use historical, linguistic, textual, and increasingly also, anthropological and sociological skills. In the second place we do seem to return to the further group of questions of a much wider nature already mentioned which are perhaps more easily formulated than answered.

These questions are for many the driving force behind the study of religion(s) and are questions which signal the desire for a third and much less easily definable knowledge or understanding. We might for example be puzzled about what religion is, or about how to understand a particular religious practice. Someone who is not a Muslim might be puzzled about why some of his colleagues or neighbours kneel and bow low five times each day, facing always in the same direction. He may begin to understand if he is told that they are praying, but his puzzlement may go deeper than that. It may show itself in the further question of '*Why* do they pray five times daily in that way?', but it may in fact be a question about what prayer is.

One answer to the question, 'Why do they pray five times daily?' may be found in the teachings of the Qur'an and in the traditions of Islam and an answer which spells out the details here will be an increase in knowledge and understanding. What it will not do, however, is give the sort of understanding which the questioner seeks. The puzzlement may be about what prayer is, or about why men and women should pray at all. Two centuries ago the philosopher Kant wrote of Christian prayer that a man might be embarrassed to be found alone in a room on his knees. Now Kant knew perfectly well what the practices and conventions of Christianity are regarding prayer, and someone who wanted to contest his view, or to imply that he did not 'really' understand what prayer is, would have to do rather more than reiterate biblical injunctions about the manner of and the importance of prayer. He would have to give Kant an account of the nature of prayer which justifies other descriptions than 'a man alone in a room on his knees'. On the one hand he would have to persuade Kant that the practice of prayer has a point or meaning which Kant has missed, and on the other, in the course of that, he would have to give content and meaning to expressions such as 'watch and pray that ye may not enter into temptation', or 'worship the Lord in the beauty of holiness'. Whether a practitioner or believer can help in providing such an understanding of this practice for a non-believer is of course one of the major questions of the study of religion(s), and preparing to answer it requires reflection, study and great care.

It is often helpful to look for comparisons and contrasts in such a situation, and there are forms of puzzlement from other areas of life which have, at least, common roots in the human condition, which as we have already seen is the starting-point for the study of religion(s). We may be a little puzzled if in some tropical swampland we came across someone wearing only a pair of shorts standing quite still by the edge of a pool of water. We may be even more puzzled when we see that he is apparently using his body as live bait for mosquitoes. Now if we ask him why he is standing there, the reply that this is a good place for being bitten by mosquitoes will not remove the question marks which we have set against his behaviour. Indeed it might increase the significance which we attach to them! There are further unanswered questions, which we may have difficulty in formulating clearly, but which are a clear indication of our problem in trying to understand what this man is doing (cf. Kant's problem about a man alone in a room on his knees).

Rather different examples are the difficulties which an American may have in helping an Englishman understand what is going on in a game of American Football, or the parallel but reverse difficulty of explaining what is going on in a game of cricket. If a non-initiate asks a cricket fan, 'Why is the captain asking those fielders to move?', there may be an elaborate but clear answer in terms of strategy. If, however, that was the first of a series of questions which ends up with 'And why should grown men want to spend five days doing that, here, now?', then there surely is a problem which *may* be one of understanding, but may on the other hand be one of taste.

If we compare these two examples with the religious example, a number of points emerge, which might help us appreciate the complexities involved in some of the very general questions which arise about understanding religion. If, in the case of the human mosquito bait, we learn that this man is one member of a research team working on the control of mosquitoes in an area where malaria is a serious problem, and if we learn further that it is necessary to catch and breed from live mosquitoes and that this is the most efficient way of catching them, our puzzlement goes. We no longer doubt the man's sanity and we understand what he is doing. We cease to ask questions about it. It is not perhaps that we understand the fine and important detail of the design of the research, nor of the complex microbiology underlying it. There is, however, a degree of satisfaction and we can 'place' the activity in a larger context. Now many questions about religion(s) are of this sort and answering them requires a broadening of the context and of our knowledge of the context. Careful study of this book will answer, or at least significantly help in answering, such questions. This is one of the central reasons for the variety and range of the book.

There is, however, another feature of the example which is important. We accept as satisfactory a limited answer because we can place the activity, 'standing alone by the edge of the pool wearing only shorts', not only as part of its immediate context, 'facilitating a piece of research', but also as part of a much wider context, namely the diminution of illness and suffering, which we accept as important.

In the case of the cricket match, however, 'standing alone in the outfield clad in white' may well be something which the questioner can see in a wider context, and to that extent 'understand', but may well still leave a sense of dissatisfaction. Thus there may be an appreciation that the tactics of the game, the fact that there is a leg-break specialist bowling from this end, make prudent the presence of Willoughby minor on the boundary, but still no equivalent satisfaction to that marked by the response, 'Ah, I see, you are trying to eliminate malaria from this region'.

Not only is it agreed that there is an ultimate point to standing alone by the edge of the pool wearing only shorts, but there is an understanding of what the point of this is, and also, in this case, that the point is important. In the cricket example, however, one might see that standing alone on the boundary clad in white makes it more likely that the batsman

34

will be caught out, but still not be satisfied that 'there is a point to all this', or that if there is that it has any importance.

In the religious case some of the questions which we ask, and some of the knowledge or understanding which we may seek, is of this wider sort. One may be wanting to know what the point of all this is; 'Very well,' we may say, 'I see that they are praying to Allah, or that he is praying to God, but I am not convinced that this is important, or perhaps even that it ultimately has a point.'

A further variation on the mosquitoes example might help here. Suppose instead of a swampy tropical region we were in a rather cool temperate region by a fast-flowing, rather chilly looking, river. Suppose further we saw not a near-naked mosquito-catcher, but a well-wrapped Englishman wearing thigh-length rubber boots and carrying a fishing-rod. We might well grasp that he is hoping to catch fish rather than mosquitoes and to that extent 'understand' what he is doing. But we might well also shake our heads and say, 'If he wants trout for supper it would be cheaper and much less uncomfortable to buy it from the fish farm down the road.' That is to say, whatever the million or so fishermen in Britain 'see' in this pastime, we do not. Or is it the case that if necessary we might be persuaded to act as mosquito-bait because we see the importance of this, whereas we are not convinced of the importance of acting as assistant to our friend who is quite sane apart from his desire to stand up to his thighs in cold water from time to time? In the one case we might overcome our lack of taste for the activity, whereas in the other we shall not.

This comparison does help highlight some of the features of the religious example of prayer. Now it may be that some disagreements over religion(s) are matters of taste—'you prefer candles and incense, I prefer sermons and metrical psalms'. But in that case there is no disagreement about importance, or possibly about understanding. If, however, the disagreement is of the pattern—'You prefer candles and incense, I prefer going to the theatre, or playing golf'—then not only is there a disagreement about taste, there is also a disagreement about importance, for believers are not inclined to accept that anything is even of equal importance to the practice of religion. Our question must be whether this is properly described as a difference in understanding, and if so whether the study of religion(s) can play any part in removing such a possible lack of understanding. This is an area through which we must tread with great care for it contains many intellectual land-mines.

There are two main ways in which these very general questions about the ultimate importance or 'point' of religion(s) are tackled. Some, including particularly those who belong to the great monotheistic religions, would want to say that the importance of religion derives from the *truth* of the central beliefs involved. If it is not true that we are creatures in a world created by a just and loving God then prayer has neither importance nor 'point'. Others would claim that the argument is not quite so straight-forward. Persuading someone to say, 'Our Father, which art in Heaven', as a believer says it, is first and foremost persuading him that the words have a meaning by showing him what the meaning is.

To appreciate this point is to appreciate that we have moved from the realm of the study of religion(s) as it is variously practised in this book, to the philosophical discussion of the implications of questions raised in and through the study of religion(s). I shall return to these matters briefly in due course.

In brief summary, however, we have seen how the search for knowledge and understanding in the study of religion(s) can take a variety of forms, as can the types of knowledge and understanding to be found in such study. This is the reason for the range of approaches and methods followed in this book. The approach or the method used in any particular section or page will depend upon the particular issue being dis-cussed. Before elaborating on this, however, it would be useful to raise a rather different question.

The Focus of Attention

One of the reassuring things about study rather than speculation or free association is that study is always study *of* something. Study has an object upon which we focus our attention and which helps define the nature of the study. Hence it is reasonable to ask, 'If one seeks knowledge and understand-ing through study where should one focus one's attention?'

We have already spent some time analysing the var-iety of really rather different possibilities which are included under the general heading of 'Knowledge and Understanding', and there is no need to retrace our steps in detail. Rather we should be applying what we have already learned.

We have also noticed the importance of drawing a distinction between the study of religion (singular) and the study of religions (plural). This will be the starting-point for our short excursion into identify-ing the focuses of attention in our study. Again, of course, the variety which we find will depend upon the variety of types of knowledge or understanding which we seek. There are three different types of focuses of attention.

In the first place in setting out to study religion(s) we may be interested in some specific aspect of religion or religions. Two different examples of such study can give some indication of the range of possibilities and the implications of this range.

In a classic work first published at the beginning of the century, *The Protestant Ethic and the Spirit of Capitalism*, Max Weber examined the question of the relation between the development of capitalist civilisation and the type of ethical outlook and practice which he believed lay

36

at the heart of Protestant and in particular Calvinistic religion. This is to focus one's study upon a very specific aspect of one particular religion. It also illustrates the intimate connection between the specific nature of the focus of attention, the type of method used, and determining both of these, the question set about the psychological conditions which made possible the development of capitalist society. Much of what counts as the study of religion(s) will be of this form and since the possible questions are without limit so in one volume, while accepting the constraints of finitude, we must attempt to give some sense of the range of possible specific focuses of attention which are required by the search for answers to specific questions.

The temptation to oversimplify is ever present and, in his foreword to the English translation, R.H. Tawney expresses it well:

It is the temptation of one who expounds a new and fruitful idea to use it as a key to unlock all doors, and to explain by reference to a single principle phenomena which are in reality the result of several converging causes. (p. 7)

Weber is less guilty of this than most, but the danger is inevitably there.

A rather different example of focusing on one aspect of religion is to be found in another classic of the same decade, William James's *The Varieties of Religious Experience*. James's book, subtitled *A Study in Human Nature*, is clearly centred upon close observation of and classification of the variety within one aspect of religion—religious experience. But there is not, as in Weber's case, the organising pressure of a single question. The study is classificatory and extends as widely as this aspect of religion and human nature require. Equally there is not the constraint of a single method brought to bear on a recalcitrant subject matter, and as a study in 'religion' so evidence is produced as it is considered relevant from a variety of 'religions'.

These two examples show how the type of question asked—the sort of knowledge or understanding sought—require a focus upon some aspect of religion which may belong to only one religion, or which may span several religions. The method or methods to be used will vary according to the question asked.

A second general type of focus of attention is not some aspect of religion, but is a particular religion or religious tradition. Here one might be studying—seeking knowledge or understanding of—the religion in question *as a religion*, not for example as a social or anthropological phenomenon. This clearly differs from Weber's interest which is in an aspect of a religious tradition as an explanation of particular social changes. The appropriate form of study here is usually called the History of Religions and is to be distinguished from Comparative Religion which is the comparative study of more than one religion or religious tradition.

It may be that in defining this focus of attention we are on much clearer and firmer ground, but we do run into some of the problems already uncovered in Peter Byrne's essay on 'Religion and Religions'. How do we define what counts as a religion? It is consonant with his arguments there and with the general approach of this volume that there will be borderline cases, and some of the general issues arising out of this are discussed in Anders Jeffner's essays on 'Religion and Ideology' and 'Atheism and Agnosticism'.

The uncertainties there are as nothing, however, when compared with the problems of the third most general focus of attention. What if, as is a fairly widespread desire on the part of many students of religion, one wishes to focus not upon particular traditions, nor particular aspects of religion, but upon religion as such. By now we ought to realise that there is an element of intellectual hubris in such a hope, but perhaps of such things are real scholars made. If our aim is to understand religion, then we ought to aim to do so with the widest possible focus of attention which we can achieve.

The unclarities and uncertainties of such an aim, however, have been documented at some length and I shall not repeat them again. One point of summary and recapitulation will suffice. Attempting to focus one's attention upon 'religion in itself' or 'religion in general' is to focus upon what is diffuse and infinitely varied and it is to do so with a variety of methods which are subject only to the nature and scope of the question being asked.

Methods

The ground which we must briefly cover under this heading has already been well tilled. To the question, 'What methods should one use to increase knowledge or understanding?' the answer must be, 'It depends upon the question being asked.' Some questions, such as those of Weber, required the methods of historical and social analysis. Other questions may require linguistic and archaeological as well as historical skills. It would be impossible to study the forms which religion takes in some cultures without invoking the methods of social anthropology.

In rather different contexts, if for example claims about the Turin Shroud were to be regarded as religious claims, the techniques of chemical analysis would be a precondition of answering some questions. The psychology of religion as a branch of psychology has its own contribution to make, but again always depending upon specific questions being asked. However, there are some general points about method as such which can be illustrated by a brief discussion of one of the most stimulating contributions to the psychology of religion which has been published this century. I refer to Freud's *The Future of an Illusion*.

Freud's writings in this and other essays illustrate well both the strengths and the potential pitfalls of developing and using a specific method and applying it to the study of religion. Freud was clearly intrigued by religious belief and practice and in a number of works including *The Future of an Illusion* set down his reflections on the matter. By that time (1927) he had fully developed his psychoanalytic method of treating illness, and with it a fairly elaborate theory of human nature. His puzzlement about religion was based on his observations of what people do and say. His resolution of that puzzlement was to apply a theory developed in the context of the study and treatment of mental illness to this area of human experience also. Indeed all the indications are that Freud believed his theories to have general application to all areas of human life and his followers have certainly taken this view.

Effectively he regarded religious behaviour as analogous to neurotic behaviour. His characterisation of religion as 'an illusion' is not, he insists, its classification as 'error' (although the onus is firmly on the believer to show that it is not), but it is to claim that religion is based on wish-fulfilment—on what we *want* to be true. Now there is much of interest in such a claim and undoubtedly human beings are prone to believe what, in some sense, they want to believe. The particular twist in Freud's account is that we are not in this case aware of these deep-seated, unconscious, wishes. This is an interesting and important view about which much might be written, but our present task is to focus upon some general features of the application of this method to the study of religious belief and practice.

There is no doubt that there are those whose religious belief and practice are based upon what they want to believe rather than what they have other reason to believe. As such, Freud's observation is clear and accurate. However, what is also true is that Freud may face the same danger as that which Tawney signalled in Weber's case (see p. 36 above)—he seems to want to apply a single method of enquiry and explanation which may well have great significance in one context, as if it were 'a key to unlock all doors'. That is to say, it may well be correct to infer that Mr Enderby's religious belief and Miss Crimpel's religious devotions are, in Freud's sense, 'illusions', without wishing to imply that this is the appropriate account to give of the belief of Thomas Aquinas, or of Franz Jaggerstäter (see *Zahn*) or Billy Graham and so on. Now in each of these cases if there is a clear 'explanation' to be given the explanations will be severally different, but that is just the point. The difficulty and indeed implausibility of Freud's view is that in the end there is only one explanation and that is the same explanation for everyone. This is the greatest single potential pitfall facing the application of specific methods or disciplines to the study of religion(s)—a forced uniformity arising from an illusory universality. Hence the need in this volume to use as many methods as are necessary to answer the variety of questions which arise in the study of religion(s).

The other major point which is illustrated by the example taken from Freud could equally well apply to all such general theories of religion which are derived from the application of a single method of enquiry. In each case, whether we think of Freud, or Marx, or Durkheim, or whomsoever, the method either boasts or conceals a particular theory of human nature. The first and most obvious point is that if we accept Freud's or Marx's respective definitions of religion (and we cannot consistently accept both!) then we are *ipso facto* accepting the correlated theory of human nature which underpins that definition. We should certainly ask for considerable evidence and argument before taking on board such a major intellectual structure. The second point of course is that very often what is offered by religious belief is a theory of human nature which is quite clearly seen as an *alternative* to the non-religious diagnoses of the human condition. We must not allow the adoption of a method in any way to mask or hide that deep point of difference.

Summary and Interim Conclusions

We have surveyed briefly in this essay three interrelated topics, all of which have a central bearing upon the study of religion and religions. The question of the type of knowledge or understanding which we seek in such study clearly has a number of answers, of which we selected three main types. The focus of our attention, and the method of enquiry which we should follow, have equally in each case a number of possible answers. The outcome is a grid of considerable detailed complexity if we were to fill in all possible variables, and which would require at least three dimensions to represent. The point here is not to distract the reader into trying to visualise such a grid, but rather to indicate the reasons for the degree of variety and flexibility of approach which will be necessary in a single volume devoted to the study of *The World's Religions*.

Bibliography

Aquinas, Thomas *Summa Theologiae*, Latin text and English translation in 60 volumes (Eyre & Spottiswoode, London, and McGraw-Hill, New York, 1964ff.)
Barth, Karl *Church Dogmatics*, English translation (T. & T. Clark, Edinburgh, 1936ff.)
Freud, S. *The Future of an Illusion* (Hogarth Press, London, 1928)
James, W. *The Varieties of Religious Experience* (Collins Fontana, London, 1960)
Weber, M. *The Protestant Ethic and The Spirit of Capitalism* (Unwin, London, 1930)
Zahn, G. *In Solitary Witness* (Chapman, London, 1964)

3 | Religion and Ideology

Anders Jeffner

Bertrand Russell, in his *History of Western Philosophy*, claimed that there are many structural similarities between Christianity and Marxism.[1] If we call Marxism a political ideology, this indicates an interesting relationship between a religion and an ideology. If, on the other hand, we accept the Marxist concept of ideology—which is to say false consciousness—then a given religion can be labelled an ideology in contradistinction to Marxism.[2] These examples will perhaps serve to demonstrate that the terms 'religion' and 'ideology' point in different ways to a field in the world of human ideas and reactions that deserves closer examination. It is also obvious, however, that anyone wishing to study the relationship between religion and ideology risks getting stuck in a conceptual bog. The term 'ideology' has acquired a bewildering number of different meanings, while the problems involved in defining the concept of religion are well known. In the following, we will first select and define a useful concept of ideology, and make some remarks on the concept of religion. It will then be possible to point to some relationships between religion and one of its neighbours.

The term 'ideology' is sometimes used in a very wide sense. But since we are interested in a restricted field of human reactions, one in which we can compare such entities as conservatism and Judaism, it will be more useful for our purposes to adopt a more narrow concept. If we go back to Karl Mannheim's distinction between 'total' and 'partial' ideology—as most writers on ideology do—it is clear that the more interesting concept in our context is that of partial ideology. To define a partial ideology, we must first decide how to single out an ideology from other products of human endeavour.

There seems to be a considerable agreement among writers on ideology that ideologies consist of certain interrelated theoretical convictions, evaluations and norms. Various scholars have then tried in

41

different ways to delimit precisely the class of such phenomena that should be labelled 'ideology'. Let us consider, in order, various delimitations relating to truth—value, adherents, function and content.[3]

As I have already mentioned, one influential Marxist concept of ideology restricts the theoretical aspects of ideologies to false convictions. A similar way of thinking is reflected in a modern dictionary in which ideologies are presented as 'selected or distorted ideas about a social system or a class of systems'.[4] Most convictions which we label as ideological may indeed be false, but it is hardly reasonable in our context to include statements as to truth or falsity in the actual definition of an ideology. We have at least to leave the door open for the possibility of true ideological ideas. Can we talk about an ideology embraced by only a single person? This would seem to conflict with all common usages of the term. If we are to call a set of ideas an ideology, they must be held in common by a group of people. This we will therefore accept as one defining characteristic of an ideology.

Ideologies are said to have many important functions for the group of people among whom they prevail. One such function pointed out in the classical literature (Marx and Pareto) is that of justification.[5] Ideologies justify actions and attitudes. They reinforce social rules, and defend a social order that promotes the interests of the group or class. Even certain cognitive structures can be justified by an ideology. Related to the function of justification is the integrating function that has been pointed to by many Marxists. The ideology can be the factor that actually creates the group, as, according to Marx, does the class-consciousness of the proletariat.[6] Many specifically political functions are in fact ascribed to ideologies, such as securing the existence of a political organisation, or a legitimate political authority or leadership. It might well result in all too narrow a concept of ideology were we to select any of these specific functions as defining characteristics: it seems reasonable, however, to stipulate that a set of ideas must have some social and/or political function if it is to be termed an ideology. Let us say that a system of ideas has a socio-political function when it fulfils certain vital needs of a group, and is used in situations that occur with some frequency. A socio-political function is thus a defining characteristic of an ideology, in our sense of the term.

Is it meaningful to point to any given common content of ideologies? E. Schill speaks of ideologies as 'comprehensive patterns of cognitive and moral beliefs about *man, society* and the *universe in relation to man and society*'.[7] This gives us a wide concept of ideology. A more narrow one will be obtained if we see the content of ideologies in C.J. Friedrich's terms, as 'reasonably coherent bodies of ideas concerning practical means of how to change, reform or maintain a political order'.[8] I think the wider concept is to be preferred here, since it allows us to see such interesting ideas as Marx's concept of man, or the various powerful Utopias, as parts of an ideology.

42

In our discussion, we have come across such terms as 'coherent', 'interrelated', and 'system' applied to ideology. This points to an important feature of such systems as Marxism, liberalism and humanism. The theoretical aspects of the system sustain or back the evaluations and norms it contains. Marxist ethics acquires its force from theoretical ideas about nature and society; and what could any liberal political or moral ideal amount to without the theory of the freedom of decision? The relationship can also work in the other direction. Some powerful practical norm or strong evaluative pattern in a society can help to keep alive a given theory. When speaking of the 'interrelatedness' of parts of an ideology, we shall be referring to a relationship between its theoretical and evaluative or normative parts which can be vaguely described as supportive. It seems necessary to include something about interrelatedness in our definition of ideology, in order not to make every theory part of an ideology.

Let us now sum up the discussion, and stipulate a definition of an ideology: an ideology consists of interrelated theories, evaluations and norms about man, society and the universe in relation to man and society, which are held in common by a group and have a socio-political function.

This concept of ideology is vague. To avoid this, a very long discussion resulting in numerous precise concepts would have been necessary, and such an enterprise would not have been worth the effort for our present purposes. The criteria guiding our definition have been usefulness, and the actual usage of the term. Marxism, in our terminology, is an ideology as are conservatism, liberalism and humanism. Existentialism is a borderline case because of its individualistic character, but it often has sufficient of a group function to count as an ideology. In Western societies there exist widespread ideologies, influential among ordinary people, which have no recognised label. One interesting study of such ideologies is to be found in Robert E. Lane's well-known work, *Political Ideology* (1962). The ways of life studied by Charles Morris are also aspects of general, usually unnamed ideologies.[9]

The attentive reader will perhaps already have noticed an apparent problem in our definition. We have selected it to enable us to study the relationship between religion and one of its neighbours, but according to it many religions must count as ideologies. This is a quite deliberate complication, and, as will soon become clear, it has certain advantages.

It is necessary at this point to devote a few words to the concept of religion. We will not, however, enter the great debate about the definition of religion. What we shall point to is a core activity in all religions, namely relating in prayer or meditation to the ultimate power that governs the universe. Every religion, consequently, must contain a theory about the ultimate power, a theory of transcendence. The devotional attitude

43

and practice, and the theories corresponding to it, will here be termed the devotional–transcendent element in religion. Nothing lacking this element will here be regarded as a religion.

We are now in a position to draw up a map that may facilitate our orientation in the common terrain of religion and ideology. This we will do in the form of a cross-table, containing six cells.

The element of an ideology which we have called its socio-political function can be seen as a variable assuming three values, which we will call 'strong', 'weak' and 'lacking'. In the same way, we can think of the devotional–transcendent element as also varying from strong to lacking. The appearance of the table will then be as in Table 3.1.

Table 3.1: Religion and Ideology

The socio-political function of a system of thought	The devotional–transcendent element in a world-view		
	A strong	B weak	C lacking
1. strong			
2. weak			
3. lacking			

When different existing ideologies and religions are placed in this matrix, some interesting relationships become apparent. All the cells will be of interest except C3: an intellectual entity that lacks both a socio-political function and a devotional–transcendent element is by our definitions neither an ideology nor a religion.

Let us start with A1. Many ideologies have both a strong socio-political function and a strong devotional–transcendent element. The most obvious example is perhaps Islam in Iran. Medieval Christianity is another clear example, as are certain forms of present-day Zionism. Christianity can still belong to this cell, as is probably the case among certain South American groups with a liberation theology, or, in another form, in Poland. Ideologies belonging to this group are of equal interest from the political and religious points of view. They are both religions and ideologies, and it can be convenient to label them 'religious ideologies' or 'ideological religions'. It would be a misleading description of an important realm of intellectual reality to isolate doctrines about God, religious practices etc. and call these aspects a religion and the social and political ideas and rules an ideology.

Moving on to B1, we again come across some important ideologies. Take, for example, conservatism. Its theoretical aspects include religious ideas, and religious practices are also considered important even if they do not play a foreground role. The same is true of classical liberalism, and I do not think it unfair to refer to this group the ideology of most parties in present-day Western democracies that call themselves Christian.[10]

The socio-political function of, for example, a conservative ideology is of course a strong one, but we notice an important difference as compared with the A1 systems. In an ideology like political Islam or Zionism, the theoretical aspects of the ideology—theories about the revealed transcendent reality—lend very strong support to the various moral and political rules and practices. In fulfilling a given social practice you are acting as the servant of God, and doing his will. In an ideology like conservatism, the situation is different. Theories relating to the growth of a society, for example, are of importance in the shaping of practical social and political rules. We have here the back-up constituents of an ideology. But the backing they provide does not, for better or worse, lend them the same psychological force. Neither ideological martyrs nor political fanatics are common among the adherents of B1 ideologies. This is an internal difference between the two types of ideology, and it does not mean that B1 ideologies do not have a strong socio-political function. The personalised difference between the two types of ideology is roughly that between Joan of Arc and Margaret Thatcher, or between Ayatollah Khomeini and Ronald Reagan. We will return to this difference when considering type C1.

C1 ideologies are entirely lacking in the devotional–transcendent element. A clear example is Marxism, in its Leninistic form. However, many modern secularised, democratic political ideologies can belong to this group, including liberalism and the social democratic ideologies. Religious elements often play no role whatsoever for the function of these ideologies, and the socio-political function is pronounced. This, however, is not always the case, as has been observed by Bell and in the debate on the 'death of ideologies'.[11] Consequently, modern democratic ideologies with no religious elements are sometimes better classified under B2.

To refer now to the issue of force, we can easily see that there is a difference between the various ideologies belonging to this group. Marxism, in its different forms, possesses a remarkable force of the same type as do the religious ideologies. This is perhaps what people mean when they say that Marxism functions as a religion. But let us try to go a step further, and ask what constitutes this similarity. As we have already said, the transcendent–devotional element of an ideology can back the rules of that ideology by giving them the status of the will of God. But another element can also lend force to a religious ideology. As a rule, a religious ideology offers an integrated, holistic view of the universe. Man acting in society is part of a vast system, and his work is integrated in a meaningful development. To act according to the ideology is to act according to the internal rules of the universe. It is quite possible also for a non-theistic system of religious metaphysics, such as Buddhism, to constitute an element in a forceful ideology. In fact, political Buddhism is gaining in importance on the ideological scene. To return to Marxism, it is obvious that as clearly as it denies the first trait of religious ideologies—theories of a God—it shares the second—an integrated, overall view of the universe. It is a plausible hypothesis that the likeness in force can be explained by this common trait. It also explains structural similarities. Both ideologies contain metaphysical theories of the same general type. The Marxist theory of a socialist society can be compared to Christian eschatology etc. It was similarities of this kind that Bertrand Russell was observing in the passage referred to above. It is perhaps worth making one further observation concerning force. The elements of an ideology that lend force to some of its rules seem to some extent to be independent of the content of those rules. In South Africa, Christian ideas of God seem to be able to strengthen both the apartheid laws, and the struggle against these.

Let us now go on to column A2, and ask whether any ideologies in the defined sense could be characterised in this way. It looks as if the Christian religion in many Western societies is precisely an ideology of this kind. The devotional–transcendent element is strong. It has a socio-political function, and to some extent colours social life. This function, however, is weak and cannot be compared in any way with the political function of the Catholic Church in Poland, or the role of Islam in Arab societies. From the standpoint of the non-religious Western ideologies, religion in its A2 form can be tolerated, actually regarded as positive. The force of religious convictions can even be used to strengthen parts of the non-religious ideology. The secularisation of Western societies seems now partly to involve a movement of Christianity from A2 to B2. The question of whether Christianity in a given society is an ideology of type A2 or B2 is one to be decided by sociological research. Such an enterprise would presuppose operational definitions of 'strong' and 'weak'—a problem we cannot deal with here, but which it is perfectly possible to solve. Secularisation in the direction A2 to B2 is a different process from the movement from A1 to A2, which can also be called secularisation. We can notice, finally, that even if the socio-political function of Christianity as a whole is often weak, the mechanism of force is still at work and can become apparent in certain issues, for example the problem of abortion.

In cell C2 we encounter non-religious political ideologies which function largely as decorative elements in pragmatic political movements. In the history of religions we sometimes speak of a *deus otiosus*. In the same way we could speak about dormant ideologies. When it comes, however, to the empirical question of how far the ideologies in prevailing Western societies have acquired this character, it is wise to be careful. The empirical grounds for generalisation and prognosis are weak.

Moving now to C, we are leaving the realm of ideologies. Nothing, in our definition, can be an ideology without at least some socio-political function. But we are not leaving religion. Some people, indeed, would say that we have now come to the core of it. In C1 we find the 'inner religion', and certain forms of mysticism. The devotional–transcendental element is strong, but the relationship between the religious man and his God does not greatly affect his life in society and has nothing to do with his political convictions, if any. The function of the religious group is devotional, and nothing else. Christianity may perhaps be like this, but hardly a religion such as Islam. The political and social aspects of the Islamic ideology are too firmly tied up with its theology. I have said that Christianity can perhaps exist without a socio-political function. There is reason to emphasise the word 'perhaps'. In most cases a devotional practice seems to have social and political consequences, which takes us back to A2. Let us consider an introvert form of Christianity, like that of the Quakers. It functions, surely, as a forceful political ideology, and not only in questions of war and peace. From the standpoints, however, of the non-religious political ideologies belonging to C1, it sometimes seems as if A3 is regarded as the ideal form of religion. This is the form of religion that can be tolerated in most Marxist societies; and, according to non-religious liberal ideologies, a private religion of this kind can be seen either as a positive source of satisfaction for the individual, or as a form of superstition which must be given the freedom to exist. As we have said above, liberal and, say, social democratic ideologies are of course also open to religions tending towards cell 2, in so far as they have a socio-political function of a non-dominant kind. But when religions are ideologies of the A1 type, embracing in their concept for example civil law, as in the case of Islam, the concept of freedom of religion becomes problematical. In Communist societies like Russia, the Church has officially accepted a role that accords with A3 but in practice seems to function more like A2.

Are there any religions to be referred to B3? This is a question that cannot be answered without a closer discussion of the definition of religion. It is certain, however, that the conventional, disengaged adherence to a traditional church in many Western countries is a mental activity belonging to this type. The devotional–transcendent element is weak. God probably does not exist. There is no harm in sometimes saying a prayer, but it is surely of very little importance. In daily life and in politics, religion plays no role whatsoever. How far this kind of thinking characterises ordinary people in a secularised Christian society is a question that remains to be investigated.

What I hope has become clear from this survey is that the field common to religion and ideology is not easily described. There are no clearly defined entities to be characterised and compared. A religion such as Christianity assumes many different shapes and functions when seen in the context of the political ideologies, and a complex network of similarities and dissimilarities is evident between the doctrines and functions of religions and ideologies. We find patterns of ideas, rules and attitudes that display similarities and dissimilarities in their content and function, and we can describe certain aspects of this intellectual reality by using such concepts as religion and ideology, and by using more specific labels such as humanism and conservatism. Clear comparisons between the content of different ideologies, philosophies, theologies etc. can only be made if we restrict ourselves to specific authors, or to certain normative textbooks. And even such sources require careful analysis. It is not, for example, certain that similar theories in different ideologies and religions are supposed to answer the same questions, or play the same role in the totality of the view. Against this background, I have no desire to offer the usual brief summaries of the more common ideologies and philosophies. In order, however, not entirely to neglect a presentation of the content of different modern views, I will outline some characteristic ideas from ideologies that are sometimes seen as alternatives to religion, and discuss their relation to different religions.

The first of these ideas is taken from existentialism, and it says that an objective, impersonal attitude never gives us any true knowledge regarding the situation of man. We have to be personally concerned, make an unguarded choice, and live ourselves into the reality of human existence. True knowledge is knowledge from the inside. Kierkegaard says

> For an objective reflection the truth becomes an object, something objective, and thought must be pointed away from the subject. For a subjective reflection the truth becomes a matter of appropriation, of inwardness, of subjectivity, and thought must probe more and more deeply into the subject and his subjectivity.[12]

This idea provides to a large extent the basis for subsequent existentialist authors. Kierkegaard was a Christian theologian, and he surely saw it as a Christian idea. It has been greatly used in later Christian theology, but it is also central to such atheist authors as Sartre. To compare existentialism and Christianity is a complicated task. Existentialist ideas like this can in fact be incorporated in the theology of various religions.

Then we have an important ideological standpoint clearly opposed to that just described. According to this view, the only factual basis of private and social actions must be the results of strictly objective empirical science. We are now on the ground of behaviourism, turned into an ideology. Skinner is here the standard example, especially in his programmatic book, *Beyond Freedom and Dignity* (1972). This idea, the implications of which cannot be discussed in this context, is incompatible not only with existentialism but also with most religious standpoints. It can, however, be rendered more precise in such a way as to become compatible with Marxism, even if Skinner would have denied this.

One fundamental Marxist idea which plays a prominent role in many modern discussions is that the socio-economical circumstances of a society are causally primary to its intellectual, cultural and political development. Modified forms of this idea can be combined with religion— both Christianity and Islam—as has also been done both in practical and theoretical terms.[13] In a weak form, involving little more than the assignment of great importance to socio-economical factors in history, it has become commonplace.

The ideologies that we call materialistic have in common the idea that some form of matter is primary, ontologically and causally, in the universe. If something other than matter exists, then it can be causally explained from matter and the laws governing matter. This ideological element has been alive since antiquity, and acquired a powerful form through Marx. It is still a clearly anti-religious element in our culture, but it can be incorporated in various secular ideologies, for instance secular liberalism.[14]

A powerful idea of quite another kind which has been incorporated in modern ideologies, both secular and religious, stems from psychoanalysis. This is that every human being has a powerful unconscious, which to a large extent governs his actions and thoughts.

I think it will now suffice to take one more example, and one from the evaluative field. Let us take the idea that most men live in a corrupted state. This can be found in Marxism, and the reason given for the corruption is the predominance of the class structure of human societies. The actual idea of such corruption, however, is easily recognisable also in different forms in the Christian theology. A clear difference is also evident in this respect between Christian and Muslim anthropology.

This list of isolated ideas in no way negates the possibility of comparing and choosing between overall systems. It is intended simply as a warning against excessively general comparisons, and a reminder of the floating limits of religions and ideologies. This last thesis will be illustrated once again in the next section, when we move on to make some preliminary remarks on the problem of making a reasonable choice between different religions and ideologies. The main aim of this section is not to solve the general problem of such a decision but simply to point out some further traits that can characterise both religion and ideology.

To a certain extent, we grow up into a religion or ideology. Or at least we unconsciously acquire, through our social environment, a certain way of thinking and reacting. This, however, does not contradict the fact that we are able as grown-up, rational human beings to choose between different standpoints in the field of religion and ideology. The problem at this point is that some ideologies and religions affect even the rational standards for such a choice. The rationality is defined by the ideology. This is the case in the moral field, when the good is defined as what is in accordance with the will of God, and his will is regarded as being known only within a given religion. The same situation exists regarding a decision as to the theoretical aspects, if the ability to arrive at the truth is restricted to a given class, or to those in receipt of special gifts from the Holy Spirit. The mere statement that a rational choice is possible—in principle for all men—in the field of religion and ideology seems to involve the repudiation of certain ideologies and religions.[15] For my own part, I regard such a repudiation as reasonable. A rational choice will then involve four steps. The first is to compare the content of the evaluative parts of the ideologies concerned with our own moral convictions and experiences. We may perhaps find that a democratic ideology is to be preferred to a totalitarian one, or that a pessimistic view of man's moral powers is more realistic than an optimistic one. The next step is to look at those theoretical parts of the ideology or religion which can be tested by scientific methods within the disciplines of social, economic or natural science, and historical research. An ideology or religion which is open to scientific research, and does not contradict obvious scientific results, is then to be preferred to one which does. The third step is the most difficult. This is to test the metaphysical aspects of the views entailed—such as theories about transcendental realities, or the ultimate source of order in nature and society. There is no agreement among philosophers whatsoever as to the possibility of a rational metaphysics, or about the rational standards of any possible metaphysics. I cannot deal, here, with this philosophical question. My conviction, however, is that a rational metaphysics exists, but that some basic choices in metaphysics are of a more personal nature than can be contained within scientific reasoning. The final step in the procedure is to study the internal relationships between different parts of the religion or ideology. Do they mutually support each other, or are there tensions—or even contradictions—within the system? Obviously, a choice of the kind now hinted at deserves ideologies and religions that are clearly formulated and explicit. In spite of its obvious dangers, the intellectual comparison we mentioned above therefore has some value.

These brief remarks point to a similar decision-making procedure for religions and ideologies, a fact that again underlines their close relationship. Perhaps, indeed, it is inadequate to call them neighbours. 'Members of the same family' would be more adequate.

Notes

1. Bertrand Russell, *History of Western Philosophy* (New York, 1945), Ch. IV.
2. See for example J. Plamenatz, *Ideology* (London, 1970), pp. 23ff.
3. My way of delimiting the concept ideology here is influenced by discussions

with Professor Robert Heeger of Utrecht. See for example R. Heeger, 'Vad är en ideologi?', *Statsvetenskaplig Tidskrift*, 1972, pp. 307–25.

4. H.M. Johnson in *International Encyclopaedia of the Social Sciences* 7, 1968, p. 77.

5. K. Marx, F. Engels, *Werke XIX*, p. 190 (Berlin, 1969). V. Pareto, *Oeuvres Complètes* (Geneva and Paris, 1956), III § 1043, IV § 2173 and § 2440.

6. See K. Marx, F. Engels, *Werke III* (Geneva and Paris, 1958), p. 70.

7. *International Encyclopaedia of the Social Sciences* 7, 1968, p. 66.

8. C.J. Friedrich, *Man and his Government, an Empirical Theory of Politics* (New York, 1963), p. 90.

9. Charles Morris, *Varieties of Human Value* (Chicago, 1956).

10. Conservatism here means the stream of ideas going back to Edmund Burke (1729–97). Classical liberalism is the political ideology of for instance J. Locke (1632–1704) and J.S. Mill (1806–73).

11. See Daniel Bell, *The End of Ideology* (New York, 1960).

12. S. Kierkegaard, *Samlade Værker*, utg af A.B. Drachmann, J.L. Heidberg og H.O. Lauge, VII:159f. (Copenhagen, 1901–6).

13. The dialogue between Marxists and Christians has resulted in a great number of books and articles which cannot by listed here. See further J. van der Beat, *The Christian–Marxist Dialogue. An annotated bibliography 1959–69*. WCC 1969 and for an analysis Peter Hebblethwaite, *The Christian–Marxist Dialogue and Beyond* (New York, 1977).

14. Different types of materialism will be discussed in the paragraph on atheism below.

15. See my article 'Några problem vid livsåskådningsanalys', *Svensk Teologisk Kvartalskrift*, 46 (1970).

4 | Atheism and Agnosticism

Anders Jeffner

The great Icelandic writer of sagas Snorri Sturluson relates an interesting episode about the Norwegian king, St Olaf. While assembling his army to proceed to Trondheim, he was approached by two brothers from the wilds, Gaukapórir and Afrafasti. They were bigger, stronger and braver than all other warriors. 'Are you Christians?' the king asked. Gaukapórir answered:

> We are neither Christian nor pagan. We and our brothers have no faith, other than in our own strength and skill, and our own fortune in war. This has so far sufficed. Or is there, king, in your army any Christian man who has performed in a day greater deeds than we?[1]

Are we encountering here an articulate atheist, in this obscure time of great religious change in the wilds of northern Europe? In a way, I think it is reasonable to say yes. This is a clear example of a reaction to religion which it makes sense to call atheism. Atheism will then mean a deliberate rejection of all the religious alternatives available at the time. We will take this as the first sense of the term 'atheism' to be considered. As we shall see later on, 'atheism' like so many other terms in the field of religion is used in many different senses.

Atheism in our first sense seems to be an eternal companion to religion. We know that some kind of religion exists in every culture; what is not so frequently observed is that one can also find traces of religious denial and disbelief in practically every religious milieu.[2] The examples from Greece are fairly well known; they can be studied in the numerous legal proceedings against people accused of denying the gods, especially in the fourth century BCE. In early Greek culture we find complaints about asebeía, which means a lack of respect for the rules based on belief in the gods; it also, however, involves a clear theoretical disbelief in all gods. This is atheism in our first sense. In his dialogue The Laws (884–90),

Plato prescribes severe punishment for those who do not respect religion, arguing that a theoretical denial of basic theological assertions is the root of anti-religious behaviour. People who reject religion are also mentioned in texts from ancient Israel and India. Among peoples and tribes without a written language, we find examples of unbelief in the many narratives about men who disregard the gods, and are later struck down by their wrath. It is not my intention here to list such examples of the refutation of religion in different cultures, and I will simply refer the interested reader to the books mentioned in notes 1 and 2.

I hope it has become apparent from what we have already said that it is simply not true that there was a time when all men were religious. The assumption of a religious point of view always seems to involve a personal element which renders it neither intellectually nor socially irresistible. There is always an opening towards atheism in our first sense.

It should be observed that anyone in a Buddhist society who rejects Buddhism as well as other religions is an atheist in our first sense, despite the fact that the Buddhist doctrine itself can be termed atheistic. This last example affords us another meaning of atheism, to which we will now address ourselves.

The term 'atheism' is often used to refer to an argumentative denial of a more specific core-element of religion—the belief in personal gods, or in a personal God. The epithet 'personal' means that the god in question is believed to bear a likeness at least to such human abilities as thinking, willing and communicating. The term 'argumentative' in the definition implies that this view is a theoretical standpoint, adopted on the basis of some kind of reasoning. Atheism in this sense is something more than a dislike of religion, or a neglect of religious practices. A man can, of course, be an atheist in both our first and second senses, as indeed was the Norwegian soldier in our example. He denied a personal God, and he presented a kind of argument. But it is possible to be an atheist in the first sense and not in the second, or in the second and not in the first. An example of the latter is provided by a modern author such as Julian Huxley in his book *Religion Without Revelation* (1957). He offers reasons for not believing in a personal God, while none the less adhering to religious practices and rules. As mentioned above, a Buddhist can belong to this category.

We will discuss here two types of atheism in the sense of an argumentative denial of personal gods or a personal God. The difference between these two forms lies in the argumentative approach. The ground for a repudiation of theism can be a philosophical critique of the doctrine of a personal God in all its forms, as in the philosophy of logical positivism. This is the first type. But atheism can also be based on a positive alternative system of metaphysics, which may be of a religious character (as in the case of Buddhism) or totally non-religious (as in the case of Marxism).

53

It is naturally impossible in our present context to offer any survey of the philosophical arguments for and against the existence of a God. Such surveys can be found in most textbooks on the philosophy of religion.[3] They are often instructive, but a word of warning may well be in place. Short summaries of philosophical arguments can be very misleading without being totally wrong, and all these summaries of 'The five ways of Aquinas' along with the critiques of Kant and Hume seem to me excessively boring. My advice to a reader interested in the critical side of these matters is to study Hume's *Dialogues Concerning Natural Religion* in the original, and without abbreviation. I agree with Hume himself: 'nothing can be . . . more artfully written'.[4] The general warning I have now given can also be applied to the following short summary of the one argument that seems to me to constitute the strongest case against theism. It is inspired by the philosophical tradition known as empiricism, which dates back to Greek philosophy. It flourished in the eighteenth century, and one of its champions was Hume. In our own century it has taken the form of logical empiricism, associated with names like Schlick, Carnap and Russell. The enigmatic Ludwig Wittgenstein also belongs to this tradition.

The argument starts from a very simple principle, which has been called the principle of intellectual morality.[5] It says: 'Do not believe in anything for which you cannot give good reasons.' At first sight, few people would reject this rule. It appears to be the basis of a rational life, and a starting-point for all kinds of scientific and scholarly activity.

The second step in the argument is to try to establish what kinds of reason we can give for the existence of anything whatsoever. In daily life we refer in questions of existence to our common-sense experience. If we together see or hear something, then it must in some way exist in the real world; and if it is possible to experience it, then it is possible that it exists. Many things, however, cannot be familiar to us in this direct way, for example the particles of which physicists speak or various remote astronomical objects. But if the assumption of the existence of an entity is necessary in order to explain what we become acquainted with through our senses, then we have good reasons to believe in it. It is not necessary of course that the 'we' in these sentences should include every human being. One of the basic conditions of human knowledge is that we have to rely on the testimony of others. One single, unprejudiced person can suffice, provided that his judgement is open to control by others. The reasons I have just described can be called empirical reasons. They undoubtedly govern our ordinary lives, and scientific theories as to factual conditions in the real world are based on such reasons. It can now be claimed that there are no other good reasons for the existence of anything, except reasons based on some possible sense-experience. We have to use other tools in exploring reality, such as logic and mathematics, but these tools cannot without any reference to the senses afford us any knowledge about what exists, and what does not exist. We are referred exclusively to our senses. This standpoint is the second premiss of the argument.

The third premiss, of course, is the claim that we cannot offer any empirical reasons for the existence of God. No reliable person has seen or heard a God in a way which is open to control. There was a time when the God-hypothesis seemed necessary in order to explain certain phenomena or regularities in the experiential world, but scientific development has made the God-hypothesis entirely superfluous. The supposition of a personal God has no anchorage in our experience.

From the second and third steps in this argument, the conclusion follows that there are no good reasons for believing in any personal God. Then, according to the maxim contained in the first premiss, we should not believe in a personal God.

This is an example of philosophical atheism. It is a weak form of atheism, since the argument does not claim actually to disprove the existence of a personal God. It seems correct, none the less, to call it atheism. It is a refutation of the belief in God. If the form of atheism is weak, the actual argument, on the other hand, is strong. It does not involve any complex philosophical theories. It is based on common sense and science, without being tied to any given, current scientific theories. As a whole, it reflects an undogmatical attitude. The theist, of course, can deny all the premisses. He can refuse to accept the rule of intellectual morality, but this involves being an irrationalist—which is a difficult and uncomfortable position. It is also possible to try to present empirical reasons for the existence of God, and thus refute the third premiss. I do not, however, know of anyone who has completely succeeded in this. The best approach for the theist, in my view, is to question the second premiss. He can argue that there are more good reasons for existence-claims than references to the senses. It can be claimed, for instance, that religious experiences, or our conscience-reactions, or our I–Thou relations, give us access to reality. Arguments for the existence of a personal God could perhaps be built up on such a ground. It is not my intention to discuss these possibilities further, but I do feel that there is an interesting field here for argumentation between theists and atheists.

Let us now turn to the second type of argumentative denial of a personal God. This is the form of atheism which offers an elaborated metaphysical alternative to theism. The classical example, which is still important, is materialism. Materialism in its various forms is a strong and powerful stream of Western philosophical thought. (One well-known German history of Western materialism covers 1,099 pages.[6])

The most important of the Greek materialists is Democritus, and we can take his theories as a standard example of strict classical materialism. In his philosophy, only matter is existent or real. Even mental states consist of a kind of matter. Democritus introduced the term 'atom' for the smallest constituent of matter. Democritus' ontological

55

materialism was developed in an interesting way by the Roman Epicurean philosopher Lucretius, in his great poem *De Rerum Natura*. It seems evident there that strict materialism is incompatible with belief in a personal God. But this is only true if we also accept the premiss that God is not material. Most materialists have indeed done this, but not all of them. Epicurus, for instance, who based his metaphysics on Democritus, reckoned with the actual existence of gods, even if he thought that we need not bother about them, just as they do not care about us.

If Democritus affords a typical example of classical materialism, the hero of modern materialism is Marx. Some modern materialists, as we shall see later on, would deny this, but he undoubtedly has the greatest influence. Marxist atheism is the strongest atheistic movement of our time.

There are two basic differences in principle between strict, classical materialism and that of Marx, quite apart from the fact that they have emerged against quite disparate cultural and scientific backgrounds. The first is that Marx reckons with the existence of something other than material entities. Mental states are seen as real, although dependent on a material basis which is causally primary. This doctrine is generally called 'epiphenomenalism'. According to the Marxists themselves, the most important difference between Marxist and other forms of materialism is that Marxist materialism is 'dialectical'. According to Marx and Lenin, there exist in the material world certain fundamental dual opposites, which meet and produce a development towards a synthesis of opposing forces. According to Marx, the basic laws governing the development of matter can be clearly formulated and they are termed 'dialectical laws'. One of these, formulated by Engels, is called 'the law of the transformation of quantity into quality and vice versa'. By the help of such laws, Marxist materialism can be applied to social development. It can be explained, for example, in materialist terms how a gradual change in the material basis of a society suddenly gives rise to a qualitatively new kind of society. The application of basic dialectical materialism to human conditions and human societies is called in Marxist philosophical terms 'historical materialism'. Historical materialist theories also explain, according to the Marxists, why and how the false belief in a personal God will disappear in the future. In Leningrad, a former church has been made into a museum for the history of religion and atheism. Those interested in the application of historical materialism to religion will find there many very skilful illustrations.

Apart from strict, classical materialism and Marxist materialism, it may be sufficient to consider one further form, which we can refer to as explanative materialism. Its basic idea is that everything can be explained in terms of matter, or of matter and energy. Many of the results achieved in modern science point in this direction. It is also supposed that matter is always causally primary in relation to everything else. These ideas are compatible with the existence of mind, and epiphenomenalism seems to be a generally accepted theory in most forms of modern materialism. Even if explanative materialism can be included in Marxist materialism, it is a much more modest standpoint. An explanative materialist need not accept the dialectical laws, or the theory of historical materialism *in toto*. A clear example of this form of materialism, in which the atheistic consequences are drawn, is provided by Ernest Nagel, who calls his view 'naturalism'.[7]

Before leaving the subject of materialism, we should underline the fact that we have dealt here only with the theoretical type of materialism. 'Materialism' can also refer to the normative view that owning material things, or possessing economic wealth, is the highest goal of human life. The two forms of materialism need not be combined in any way. On the contrary, theoretical materialists have often been and are idealists in the sense of striving at higher spiritual or moral goals, or sacrificing their own welfare for the benefit of their fellow men.

From materialism, we will now take a step to what may appear to be its absolute opposite—mysticism. As we shall see, however, the great mystical traditions include patterns of thought which allow no room for a personal God. They tend towards atheism in our second sense— an argumentative denial of a personal God. Two traits common to many mystical traditions are of importance here.[8] In the mystical experience, the mystic claims to be in contact with the deepest level of reality. Now for many mystics, both in the Christian and other traditions, experience of this reality means an annihilation of their own personality. 'The visionary is himself One', says Plotinus. This is *Unio Mystica*. St Teresa of Avila, one of the great Christian mystics, wrote 'It is plain enough what unity is—two distinct things becoming one.' This transcendence of the personal 'I', and total unity with something else, is quite a different experience from meeting a person. If such mystics meet God, it is not a personal God. Mystics of this kind have consequently been regarded with great suspicion by the representatives of such religions as Christianity and Islam even to the point of persecution. The condemnation of the great medieval mystic Meister Eckhart ('The knower and the known are one') can serve as an example from Christian history, and from the Muslim world we can mention the mystic Mansur al-Hallaj, who was killed in 922 for his claim of identity with the divine. It must be observed, however, that not all mystical experiences are of this non-personal kind. Nathan Söderblom speaks of a kind of mysticism which he calls 'personal mysticism'.[9] And then we have the great Jewish religious figure Martin Buber: his type of religious experience bears a similarity to mystical experience, but its very kernel is an 'I–Thou' relationship. The mystical tradition seems to move between two poles, from the deep personal encounter to a unity beyond all personal categories.

One further trait in the mystical tradition should be mentioned. What is felt in the mystical experience is impossible to describe, lies outside the reach of human language; it is ineffable. Nearly all mystics are in agreement about this. If, however, the ultimate reality is impossible to describe, then it must be wrong to talk about this reality as a personal God. But it is also a fact that many mystics, despite the doctrine of ineffability, try to say something about their experience with the help of symbols and metaphors. Mystics often balance on the edge of the ineffable, without being totally silent.

Among the many meanings of atheism a third and powerful one may be observed. This involves denial of the existence of a personal God with certain specific attributes: if a personal God is to have such-and-such characteristics, he does not exist. In many religious traditions, including the Jewish and the Christian, God is said to be Almighty and Good. Very early on in our intellectual tradition, people found it difficult to combine this belief with the experience of the factual evils of the world. This gave rise to the so-called problem of theodicy, and if it insoluble it is easy to make it into a proof of the non-existence of a Good and Almighty God. This is a powerful line of thought in both the ancient and modern history of atheism. A pioneer in this field is the Greek philosopher Sextus Empiricus.

We can now conclude this passage on atheism with an interesting observation. For each form of atheism, there are kinds of theism which correspond and come very close to the atheistic position. This I say not in order to blur the demarcation line between the different ideologies, but to point to the possibility that an interesting position may be found at some of the points at which theism and atheism touch each other.

Our first kind of atheism involved the rejection of all currently available religious alternatives. This, however, is also the position of a deeply religious theist like Dietrich Bonhoeffer. He was seeking a God behind the religions, striving towards a non-religious Christianity. We can simply note this for the present, without further discussion. The type of atheism which we defined as the argumentative rejection of a personal God took many different forms. The most interesting relation to theism is to be found in the last of these, namely mystical atheism. But let us first note that the intellectual basis of those theists who wish to fight superstition is the principle of intellectual morality, and interestingly enough this also opens one of the best ways for the theist to combat atheistic metaphysics, such as materialism. It may be possible for the theist and the atheist to travel a long way together when it comes to the question of rational reasons, but at some point they must separate, and the theist has to accept religious experience, for instance, as part of the ground for an existence-claim. The materialist type of atheism lies a long way from theism on the theoretical side but, when in practice, the extent of the views they hold in common can be remarkable, as evident in the dialogue between Marxists, Christians and Muslims. Let us now proceed to mysticism. The reflected forms of belief in a personal God always seem to contain an awareness of the absolute unintelligibility of God. God is seen as transcending all our concepts. Even concepts of a person are used in another sense when applied to God. In the skilfully elaborated doctrine of analogy, St Thomas Aquinas tries to safeguard the otherness of God, without rendering the description of him as a person entirely meaningless. When we come to a modern Christian theologian such as Paul Tillich, one may doubt whether anything whatsoever of the personal character of the Christian God has been preserved. The point, however, is that a deep form of personal theism comes very close to non-personal mysticism. Finally, a word about those who deny the existence of a Good and Almighty God. This denial is part of the constant struggle among Christian and Jewish theists, and its model is the biblical person of Job.

Apart from different forms of theism and atheism, there is also a third position, namely agnosticism. Let us quote directly a famous agnostic, the Greek philosopher Protagoras: 'About the gods I do not know if they exist or do not exist. There are many circumstances which prevent one from knowing that: the obscurity of the matter and the shortness of human life.' Agnosticism can be defined as suspending one's judgement on the question of the existence of God. Let us compare this position with the forms of atheism which we have dealt with. The first form of atheism was a rejection of all available religious alternatives. An agnostic would not reject religion but he would refuse to say yes or no to it. It must then be observed that an agnostic of this kind will often be seen in the same way as an atheist from the religious point of view, following the principle that 'he who is not with me is against me'. The argumentative rejection of belief in a personal God cannot be accepted by an agnostic, although he can come very close to the argument based on the principle of intellectual morality. Some, perhaps, would call this form of atheism a kind of agnosticism. I think, however, that it is better terminology to speak of agnosticism only if the second and third premisses are modified. An agnostic would say that there exist *at present* no rational reasons for believing in God. This, perhaps, is the best example of an agnostic position. An agnostic corresponding to our third kind of atheism has to leave open the possibility of a solution of the theodicy problem, even if he cannot see one.

        An interesting agnostic position is what perhaps can be called 'methodological agnosticism'. This involves not adopting any definite standpoint as to the existence or non-existence of a divine reality, when dealing with a scientific or scholarly problem. In this sense, a high proportion of modern religious studies are agnostic—including the present chapter.

59

Notes

1. This passage from Snorri Sturluson's life of St Olaf in the *Heimskringla* is here translated from a quotation in Tor Andrae, *Die Frage der Religiösen Anlage* (Uppsala Universitets Årsskrift, 1932), p. 32.

2. The article 'Atheism' in the classical *Encyclopaedia of Religion and Ethics* ed. by J. Hastings from 1909 is still a useful introduction to atheism in different cultures.

3. See for instance John Hick, *Philosophy of Religion* (Englewood Cliffs, N.J., 1963). A historical survey of Western atheism is given in Fritz Mauthner, *Der Atheismus und seine Geschichte im Abenland*, 1–4 (1922–4). This work embraces over 2000 pages.

4. *The Letters of David Hume*. Ed. by J.Y.T. Greig, 1932 II, p. 334.

5. My way of formulating the argument is influenced by the Swedish philosopher Ingmar Hedenius.

6. Friedrich Lange, *Geschichte des Materialismus* 9th edn (Leipzig, 1914–15).

7. See for instance his contribution in *Proceedings and Addresses of The Am Philosophical Association* XXVII.

8. For common traits in mystical experiences see for instance W.T. Stace, *Mysticism and Philosophy* (London, 1961).

9. Nathan Söderblom, *Uppenbarelsereligion* (Uppsala, 1903). See also his *The Living God* (London, 1933).

Traditional Religions

5 | Introduction to Traditional Religions

Peter Clarke

The term 'traditional' as used here to refer to the Australian Aboriginal, African, Melanesian, Maori and North, Mesoamerican and South American Indian religions covered in this section of the volume is not meant to suggest that these religions are static and unchanging, but is simply one way of distinguishing them from the major world religions which have spread themselves more widely across many different cultures and which tend to be, therefore, less confined to and by any one specific socio-cultural matrix. Indeed, it is very likely, given that they are, with some exceptions, in a sense non-literate and for that reason among others highly eclectic, that traditional religions have been more flexible and tolerant of change than those excluding, literate religions or religions of the book, the world religions as they are called, whose literary mode of supernatural direction and guidance leaves them in theory at least less room for man-oeuvre. Moreover, while the use of the label *traditional* can be somewhat misleading, it is perhaps less so than *primitive* which has been applied to these religions, not only in the sense of early or primeval, but also in the sense of 'lower' and less 'rational' than the religions of what have often been described as the more 'civilised', 'advanced' societies. This view of traditional religions was based not on empirical data but on a theory of social and intellectual development or evolution current in the nineteenth century. According to this evolutionist approach, the term *primitive* referred on the one hand to a stage low down on the scale of social and intellectual development reached by prehistoric man and on the other to those contemporary, non-literate peoples whom, it was assumed, had remained at this same low social and intellectual level. It is clear that evolutionists of this mind tended to make too close a connection between social structure and thought, making development in the latter totally dependent on development in the former. In this century beginning after the First World War, and increasingly from the 1930s,

63

researchers began to produce convincing evidence that not only undermined the two last mentioned propositions but also the premiss concerning the alleged inferiority of the 'primitive' mind, showing that non-literate peoples, though technologically very far from advanced, had developed, none the less, highly complex systems of thought and belief.[1] One ethnologist, the Austrian, Father Wilhelm Schmidt, went so far as to maintain that the hunting-gathering, forest Pygmies of central Africa, far from being animists or fetishists, later 'degenerations' of religion, were in fact monotheists, and that since they represented the oldest surviving culture on earth this was the earliest form of religion. It hardly needs to be said, however, that any attempt by the ethnologist or any other scholar to trace the earliest form of religion has encountered and will continue to encounter unsurmountable obstacles, the main one being the lack of historical data.

   This has also been a problem for the student of traditional religion and perhaps explains why these religions have come to be regarded not only as static but also the product of and confined to a particular society. The contributions on African and Native American religions in particular show how misleading this view of traditional religion can be. In both instances, as in many other cases, the traditional religions in question spread across numerous political, economic, geographical and cultural boundaries and underwent considerable development and change.

   For the most part, it has been the social scientist and, in particular the social anthropologist, who has provided most of the information we have about these religions, some focusing their attention almost exclusively on the functions of these religions within the social system, others on their symbolic and philosophic content and others (Chapter 6 on Shamanism being an example) on both function and meaning.

   But what about the possible application of other disciplines, such as history, to this subject? Can this discipline, for example, contribute to a deeper understanding of traditional religions? The fact that many of these religions are in a sense non-literate religions not only makes the task of documenting their history extremely difficult but also opens it up to a great deal of speculation and conjecture. But, as several of the contributions to this section show, this should not deter the student from attempting such a study. The kind of written historical document rightly valued so much by the Western-trained historian although of great importance is not everything. The historian can usefully attempt a study of traditional religion by the judicious use of oral tradition and other materials such as those provided by the archaeologist, art historian and linguist among others, as a number of the contributions to this section, and in particular those on African and Native American religion, show. Moreover, in some instances traditional societies have their own 'written' records of their history, as the chapter on Native American religion illustrates. The 'outside world' has also documented, but not always very accurately or objectively as we have seen, something of the beliefs and practices of these religions, and here again we can look to all the contributions to this section for examples. It is both possible and fruitful, then, to attempt the historical study of 'traditional' religions.[2] Moreover, a study such as this might usefully examine these religions in a wider cultural, geographical and religious context. Although their contact with literate cultures and the wider world in general has been uneven it is, however, the case, that for a relatively long time many of the traditional religions, far from existing in a self-contained traditional universe have been part of a complex sphere of relationships that extended to contact with the world religions, and which in varying degrees involved contact with the world of books, most often at first the religious books or scriptures of Christianity and Islam, or the ideas contained in those books. And the result has very often been, not the complete demise of the former but, as the contribution on Melanesian religion illustrates, the development and modification of the beliefs and practices of both the traditional religion and the world religion in question.

But how long can traditional religion survive the impact of these world religions, regarded increasingly by many in traditional societies as religions of progress, and the process of 'modernisation' itself? This question is addressed directly in the contribution on Australian Aboriginal religion. There are examples, as the author of the account on North American Indian religion shows, where in the past forces from outside have brought about the virtual collapse of traditional religion. Moreover, elsewhere in this volume contributors have pointed to the rapid growth of Christianity and Islam over the past one hundred and fifty years in, for example, Africa, and to the fundamental changes brought about by these two world religions in the social and religious life of African societies. Under their impact and that of the forces of modernity all things traditional, including religion, appear to have literally fallen apart.

But changes and developments have not all been in one direction only. As is the case in Melanesian religion, and the same holds for African religion, traditional religion has not only shown in the recent past a remarkable capacity to develop and adapt its own beliefs and practices when confronted by both the world religions and 'modernity' but has also greatly influenced much of the belief and practice of these same world religions and to an extent the direction in which the forces of modernity have sought to steer traditional society. Moreover, there are examples, the Maori religion being one and Afro-Brazilian religion another, where what is in essence a traditional religious life has developed a way of interacting with and settling down alongside a world religion in a modern setting.

Furthermore, although fewer people now refer to themselves as traditional religionists, these religions continue to appeal for a variety of different reasons to many from all walks of life, whether Western-educated or not. In parts of Africa, as one contributor shows, not only have traditional religions 'intermixed with the main movements of twentieth-century change' and 'turned out to be alive and important at the heart of revolutionary movements' but they have also countered new ideas and approaches in a number of fields, including modern medicine and technology, which have not been able to undermine confidence in that important insight at the heart of traditional religion: that solutions to health and environmental problems have an important relational dimension. And we see from the contribution on Australian Aboriginal religion how important Aboriginal myth and ceremony have been in determining Aborigines' legal rights to land. Traditional religions, then, though under threat, continue to be of importance to many both at the level of meaning and function and it would, therefore, be premature to predict their demise.

Notes

1. For an example see E.E. Evans-Pritchard, *The Nuer* (Oxford university Press, Oxford, 1956).

2. In addition to the contributions to this section of the volume see also T.O. Ranger and I.N. Kimambo (eds.), *The Historical Study of African Religion* (University of California Press, Berkeley, 1972).

6 | Shamanism

I.M. Lewis

Shamanism is not, as Weston La Barre comprehensively claims, the origin of *religion*, but rather of *religions* in whose decline and fall it certainly plays a highly significant role. By 'shamanism' we mean the religious activities of inspired priests or shamans who control cosmic spiritual forces and regularly incarnate them. The term *shaman*, more familiar in American and continental than in British ethnography, is generally traced to the language of the Tungus reindeer herders of the Lake Baikal region of the Soviet Union and, according to the great Russian medical ethnographer Shirokogoroff, like its Manchu cognate *saman* means literally 'one who is excited, moved, or raised'. Its first appearance in a major European language seems to have been in seventeenth-century Russian. More particularly among the Tungus, a shaman is a man or woman who has acquired the power of mastering spirits and who knows how to introduce them into his body. Frequently the shaman permanently incarnates his spirits, controlling their manifestations, and going into states of trance on appropriate occasions. As Shirokogoroff expresses it, the shaman's body is thus a 'placing' or receptacle for his spirits, and it is through his power over these incarnate forces that the shaman has the authority to treat and control afflictions caused by malign, pathogenic spirits in other victims. The Tungus shaman is consequently literally a 'master' of spirits, although, as we shall see, the spirits can, at times, overpower their tamer and controller. In this classical arctic setting, shamanism is firmly embedded in the Tungus clan structure. So the shamanistic master of spirits guarantees the well-being of his clansmen, controlling the clan's ancestral spirits which would otherwise wreak havoc amongst his kin. These domesticated spirits can, moreover, be employed to counteract hostile alien spirits and to divine and treat local illnesses and other problems and misfortunes. Here the main diagnostic and therapeutic ritual is the public shamanistic seance in the course of which the shaman seeks to establish

67

contact with the spirits of the upper or lower worlds. Shirokogoroff vividly describes the typical setting:

> The rhythmic music and singing, and later the dancing of the shaman, gradually involve every participant more and more in a collective action. When the audience begins to repeat the refrains together with the assistants, only those who are defective fail to join the chorus. The tempo of the action increases, the shaman with a spirit is no ordinary man or relative, but is a 'placing' (i.e. incarnation of the spirit); the spirit acts together with the audience and this is felt by everyone. The state of many participants is now near to that of the shaman himself, and only a strong belief that when the shaman is there the spirit may only enter him, restrains the participants from being possessed in mass by the spirit. This is a very important condition of shamanizing which does not however reduce mass susceptibility to the suggestion, hallucinations, and unconscious acts produced in a state of mass ecstasy. When the shaman feels that the audience is with him and follows him he becomes still more active and this effect is transmitted to his audience. After shamanizing, the audience recollects various moments of the performance, their great psychophysiological emotion and the hallucinations of sight and hearing which they have experienced. They then have a deep satisfaction—much greater than that from emotions produced by theatrical and musical performances, literature and general artistic phenomena of the European complex, because in shamanizing the audience at the same time acts and participates.

Shamanism, Spirit-Possession and Ecstasy

Mircea Eliade argues that: 'The specific element of shamanism is not the incorporation of spirits by the shaman, but the ecstasy provoked by the ascension to the sky or by the descent to Hell: the incorporation of spirits and possession by them are universally distributed phenomena, but they do not necessarily belong to shamanism in the strict sense.' While we must welcome Eliade's recognition of the link between shamanism and ecstasy, which we shall develop here, it will be clear that his attempt to distinguish between shamanism and possession does not accord with the Tungus primary evidence. This, however, has not deterred the ingenious Belgian structural anthropologist, Luc de Heusch, from taking this supposed distinction between shamanism and possession and making it the corner-stone of his ambitious, formalist theory of religion. Shamanism, de Heusch maintains, is the ascent of man to the gods, possession the reverse. As an 'ascensual metaphysic' the first is, naturally, the opposite of the second which is an 'incarnation'. Where, in the former, man ascends, in the latter the spirits descend. Possession, moreover, according to de Heusch, can itself be divided into two types. The first, characterised as 'inauthentic' assumes the form of an undesired illness, a malign demonic assault which must be treated by the expulsion or *exorcism* of the intrusive demons. The second, a sublime religious experience, is in contrast a 'joyous Dionysian epiphany'. This highly prized state of exaltation is cultivated in what becomes a 'sacred theatre'.

These misleading contrasts, based on the tone of the emotional experience involved, are further confounded by later writers notably by Douglas in her *Natural Symbols*, although Bourguignon, who writes of 'negative' and 'positive' possession, clearly appreciates that the distinction may not have such far-reaching implications. The truth is that, just as there is generally little point in distinguishing between shamanism and possession since both occur together in the arctic *locus classicus* and widely elsewhere, so the distinction between benign and malign possession *experiences* can be highly misleading. In the first place, it is simply not true that what is perceived as a negative or even traumatic event is necessarily interpreted in the same vein as irrefutable evidence of demonic intervention. On the contrary, amongst the Tungus and all over the world, traumatic *episodes*, personal calamities and even physically crippling afflictions regularly serve as the harbingers of the divine call. This is not to say, of course, that where experiences of this kind are actually interpreted as signs of satanic possession they are not treated by exorcism. But, frequently, the situation is far from being as clear-cut as this neat intellectual dichotomy might seem to imply. There is not invariably any direct parallelism between the emotional quality of an experience and its interpretation: what begins as an illness requiring treatment to appease the spirit responsible may gradually develop into a mutual accommodation where, as we would say, 'the patient learns to live with his problem'. In this extended process, which is likely to include intermittent recurrence of the original symptoms, a new and binding relationship develops between the human subject and the spirit with the increasing domestication of the latter. The final step in this long-drawn out initiatory process occurs when, having fully demonstrated his power to control spirits, the ex-patient begins to diagnose and treat similar spiritual affliction in others.

Thus, as St Paul's traumatic experience on the road to Damascus reminds us, what ends in ecstasy may begin in agony. Indeed, those who vainly seek divine inspiration from other shamans may only succeed in achieving it after much self-inflicted mortification. So, in a characteristic account, an Eskimo shaman explained to one observer, Rasmussen, how, after unsuccessfully attempting to learn the shamanistic mysteries from others, he wandered off on his own into the wilderness of the arctic Tundra. There, he explained to Rasmussen,

I soon became melancholy. I would sometimes fall to weeping and feel unhappy without knowing why. Then for no reason all would suddenly be changed, and I felt a great inexplicable joy, a joy so powerful that I could not restrain it, but had to break in to song, a mighty song, with room for only one word: joy, joy! And I had to use the full strength of my voice. And then in the midst of such a fit of mysterious and overwhelming delight I became a shaman, not knowing myself how it came about. But I was a shaman. I could see and hear in a totally different way. I had gained my enlightenment, the shaman's light of brain and body, and this in such a manner that it was not only I who could see through the darkness of life, but the same bright light also shone out from me, imperceptible to human beings but visible to all spirits of earth and sky and sea, and these now came to me to become my helping spirits.

The importance of recognising the ambivalent character of the announcement of the shamanistic vocation cannot be over-estimated. It is precisely for this reason that no absolute value can be attached to displays of reluctance in responding to the call. The universal mystical convention, here, is to protest one's unworthiness, so that the more one does so (e.g. through suffering affliction) the more one asserts the imperative importance of the divine command. Thus, manifest reluctance becomes the conventional mode of signalling the urgency and significance of the divine call. It consequently becomes impossible to attempt to assess the 'authenticity' of inspiration in these terms.

We may conveniently note here, also, that possession and trance do not necessarily always coincide. Trance is a physiological state; but possession is a cultural construct and may be used to interpret the condition of people who are clearly not in any sense in states of trance. Thus, a possessed person may only experience trance from time to time, and especially in shamanistic rituals. Indeed, as Oesterreich acutely observes of the traditional Christian exorcist rituals, as practised, for example, at Loudon, it is frequently only at the climax of the rites designed to expel the spirits that the afflicted victims actually fell into trance!

Shamanism and spirit possession are, then, cultural theories of trance, of states of altered consciousness, and more widely of illness and affliction. The ambivalence which we have been stressing is fully consistent with the fact, well known to mystics of all religions and periods, that religious ecstasy can be readily produced by two apparently diametrically opposed methods: by sensory deprivation (e.g. fasting, wandering alone in the wilderness and so on), and by sensory over-stimulation with hallucinogenic drugs, music, dancing and so on. (Illnesses and other traumas may sometimes include elements of both these extremes.) Since we are now liable to overemphasise the role of drugs, we should note here that even LSD is regarded generally by pharmacologists and psychiatrists as possessing no 'drug-specific' features, being rather as Groff suggests an 'all-powerful, unspecific amplifier and catalyst of mental processes'. We must applaud the painstaking labours of R.G. Wasson and others in attempting to chart the global distribution of hallucinogenic mushrooms, and we must recognise the importance of these powerful stimulants even in some of the classic shamanistic cultures. Thus as Jochelson, who travelled among the shamanistic peoples of Siberia at the turn of the century, reports of the Koryak:

Fly-agaric produces intoxication, hallucinations, and delirium. Light forms of intoxication are accompanied by a certain degree of animation and some spontaneity of movements. Many shamans, previous to their seances, eat fly-agaric to get into ecstatic states … Under strong intoxication the senses become deranged; surrounding objects appear either very large or very small, hallucinations set in, spontaneous movements and convulsions! … attacks of great animation alternate with moments of deep depression.

Yet while acknowledging the significance of drugs here and elsewhere, we must not get things out of proportion as, for instance, John Allegro so manifestly does in his curious book *The Sacred Mushroom and the Cross*. We must not fall into the trap of assuming that shamanism and ecstasy can only be produced with the aid of such powerful pharmacological aids. As we have seen many other well-tried techniques exist in which drugs play no part at all. And from the widest perspective, it is probably in illness and affliction that we find the commonest route to the assumption of the ecstatic vocation.

Cults of Affliction

The shamanistic career, as Siikala has shown, has, characteristically, a tripartite structure, comprising three main phases or episodes. In the first phase, the subject suffers illness or misfortune which is diagnosed as possession by a spiritual power. In the course of treatment by a shaman, the patient is typically induced to behave in a trance-like fashion such that the possessing agency speaks 'in tongues', announcing its reasons for plaguing its victim. In the ensuing dialogue between the shaman and spirit, a bargain is struck, according to which, in return for stated gifts and regular acts of devotion, the spirit consents to allow the patient to recover. This initiation rite removes the immediate affliction at the price of the patient's entry into the ecstatic cult group led by the shaman. The 'cure' is in effect to become a chronic patient. So what began as an involuntary, uncontrolled and unsolicited affliction achieves its apotheosis in regular religious devotion as a cult member where possession is voluntarily solicited (although it may also come at times unbidden). This is the second, longer phase. Here, it is important to note, that once the devotee has learnt the technique of ecstasy, the simplest and lightest of stimuli will regularly succeed in producing trance. So, for example, whenever a cult member hears her spirit-tune being sung or played she is likely to go into trance with the greatest of ease. As M.J. Field points out, in shamanistic cultures, people are conditioned to go into trance at the appropriate time and place much as those in Western Europe are conditioned to fall asleep in a comfortable bed in a dark, quiet room.

With increasing mastery of the spirits, the ex-patient enters the final phase, that of becoming a shaman with the power to cure and control spirit-caused afflictions. This pattern recalls T.S. Eliot's image of the 'Wounded Surgeon' and is remarkably similar to the initiatory 'training analysis' ritual (i.e. simulated illness and cure) by means of which psychoanalysts are recruited and trained. We must not conclude, however, that shamanism is merely an inferior, rustic form of psychoanalysis or psycho-therapy. There are significant parallels in both directions. But we must remember, as Shirokogoroff long ago noted, that if the shaman's therapy only works in the treatment of the psychological aspects of his patients' complaints, his practice is not limited only to psychogenic or psychological illnesses. The range of disorders which he is asked to treat is far wider than that normally encountered in psychiatric practice in Europe or America.

If, consequently, the shaman's role transcends that of the primitive psychiatrist, what of his own mental state? Here the received tradition that shamans are generally mentally unstable, even acute schizophrenics, or at best 'half-healed madmen', requires drastic revision. As Shirokogoroff himself observed amongst the Tungus, 'The shaman may begin his life career with a psychosis, but he cannot carry on his functions if he cannot master himself.' The truth thus is, as we should expect from the range of disorders present in those diagnosed as possessed, that like priests and psychiatrists, the personalities of shamans reveal an equal diversity of types. Indeed, as the uniquely qualified anthropologist and psychiatrist, M.J. Field, has observed of African spirit mediums, effective shamans require strong, stable personalities. Hence the shaman's calling is *not* 'the resort of inadequate maladjusted neurotics and hysterics'. To see these facts in their proper perspective, we should again recall that in shamanistic cultures the initial onset of divine election is highly stereotyped.

We can conveniently begin displaying the utility of our tripartite model of affliction, cure and control by reference to Tarantism as it exists today in the remote and poorer parts of southern Italy. Here, as de Martino shows, entry into the cult is achieved by experiencing an illness or affliction for which the tarantula spider is held responsible. The 'tarantula' has in fact become a composite figure intimately associated with the Apostle Paul. The standard treatment in Salento involves the performance of rituals, with a musical accompaniment (in which the Tarentella is played) at the local chapel, dedicated to the Saint. In these, the Saint is greeted with the extraordinary invocation: 'My St Paul of the Tarantists who pricks the girls in their vaginas; My St Paul of the Serpents who pricks the boys in their testicles.' A typical case-history of a tarantist involves a lovelorn eighteen-year-old orphan girl. This poor creature was prevented from marrying her lover by her poverty, and was 'bitten' at the height of her despair by the deadly tarantula and so forced to join the ranks of the *tarantati*. Later, when she was forcibly abducted by another man, St Paul suddenly appeared before her, commanding her to leave her betrayer and follow him. In the end, a compromise was achieved. The poor girl reluctantly accepted her mortal union as long as she could continue her spiritual adventures with regular participation in the tarantist rites.

Elsewhere, typically, those so recruited into such shamanistic cults are offered the opportunity of eventually becoming shamans themselves. So, in Haitian Voodoo, in the West African *bori* cult, in the north-east African *zar* cult (which has spread from Ethiopia throughout Islamic Africa and along the Persian Gulf coast to Iran), and in countless other similar movements, chronic patients graduate to becoming doctors. Where they exist as underground heretical sects, or Dionysian mystery religions, only tolerated by the male establishment because they masquerade as therapy, such ecstatic cults appeal particularly to women, and the most committed enthusiasts and those most likely to become shamanistic cult leaders tend to have persistent difficulties with men and problems in sustaining the ideal female role. They consequently appeal especially to infertile women, those with gynaeocological disorders, and those who find the burden of male chauvinistic ascendency particularly galling and hard to bear. This gives these marginal shamanistic cults an aura of female militancy and a claim to be regarded as the authentic founders of Women's Liberation. Married women, with generally successful family lives who are less committed adherents, may, nevertheless, occasionally succumb to possession afflictions, requiring costly treatment in the cult. This is particularly likely to happen at times of domestic crisis. So, for example, a husband's opening moves to contract a second marriage in a polygynous society constitute a typical provocation. The treatment in such circumstances can be so costly that the husband is no longer in a position to proceed with his marital negotiations. Wives, consequently, are always potentially vulnerable, and the treatment demanded by their familiars—costly clothes, jewellery, perfumes and other luxuries—can represent a considerable drain on the family budget. Other women, following the manner of Marie of the Incarnation, dedicate themselves to ecstasy when they are widowed, or have completed their child-bearing role and seek relief from menopausal depression and a new career outside the family. The fact that such incomplete women are regarded by the opposite sex as half-men serves to underline the aggressive, masculine tone of these cults and their Liberationist flavour. These sex-war aspects are further highlighted by the frequent hatred which the spirits involved are said to display towards men, and by the flauntingly aggressive sexuality which some leading women shamans display. Moreover, while possessed, many of the women concerned behave like men, and seize weapons and other accoutrements which symbolise masculinity in their rituals. Their rituals and songs may indeed be a complete parody of those of the world of male-dominated establishment religion. Of course, there is conflict between women in relation to men as Wilson maintains; but this occurs in a wider setting of more generalised sexual conflict in which women manifestly chafe at their subordinate position.

Shamanistic Religions

Ecstasy is not, however, a female monopoly and cannot therefore be explained in the biological terms which the etymology of the word hysteria (i.e. 'womb') suggests. In stratified societies men of low socio-economic status join the ranks of the enthusiasts, either in a single, mixed cult, such as that of Dionysus, or, as in the Sudan and Egypt and widely elsewhere, with two parallel cults—one for upper-class women, and the other for the lowest orders irrespective of their sex. As might be anticipated, in the Indian caste system, while priests belong to the highest caste (Brahmin), shamans, who may rival them in power, are drawn from the lowest castes. In this setting shamanism thus offers an important route to power for the lowliest of men. And, of course, when possessed by a divinity shamans of low status become gods who can openly denounce their superiors and treat them with contempt. So, for instance, M.J. Field reports how in Ghana, 'An obscure little rural priest was moved by his spirit to travel a hundred miles to Kumasi where, endowed with the authority of possession, he forced his way into the presence of the Ashantihene and told him some unpalatable truths'. The mighty Ashanti king was forced to listen to him with respect and reverence.

More generally, and as we should expect, those whose social circumstances render them peculiarly receptive to the ecstatic call change as society changes. So, for example, the ex-slave Cuban cult known as *Santeria* has undergone a remarkable sea change in the years since Fidel Castro's rise to power. Despite its lowly origins translated to the Cuban refugee community in Miami, this has become a flourishing middle-class movement appealing to all those who oppose Fidel Castro and desperately seek an alternative Cuban identity. Similar connections appear to exist between the immensely popular *Umbanda* of contemporary urban Brazil and its more rustic, African precursor, *Candomblé*. With its ambiguous relationship to Catholicism, closely paralleling that of Haitian Voodoo, *Umbanda* is increasingly the effective religion of the urban masses. The most intriguing member of its mixed Afro-Indian-American spirit pantheon is that which, with its childlike innocence and uncertain parentage, seems to merge all these elements in a new, uniquely Brazilian identity as Pressel points out. The potential for dynamic developments of this kind seems to be a marked feature even of the ostensibly most conservative of ecstatic cults. Enthusiasm is a volatile force and spirits readily become literally the 'winds of change', being often, indeed, described as 'winds'.

When, under conditions of external pressure (whether of physical or socio-political origin), ecstatic cults develop into fully-fledged main-line shamanistic religions, they repudiate their lower-class connections. Enthusiasm which celebrates the position of the dominant classes in society can scarcely afford to allow itself to be controlled by the lower orders. Under such conditions, ecstasy becomes one of the principle expressions of orthodox, establishment power. This is generally true of classical arctic shamanism among the Eskimos, Tungus and other Siberian peoples and equally the case in the numerous tiny South American Indian communities where hallucinogenic drugs play such an important role. Although it is debatable whether all small hunting and gathering communities live under as acute environmental pressures as the Eskimos, or as precariously, prima facie there does seem to be some connection between this type of economy and central shamanistic religions. The view that the effervescent, shamanistic style of religiosity is a response to acute pressures of one kind or another tends also to find confirmation in the circumstances surrounding the rise and decline of new religions. Strident, new messianic 'religions of the oppressed' are invariably founded by inspired shamanistic prophets and religious dynamism characteristically finds expression in divine possession. The dialectical interplay between this incarnatory prophetism and an established priesthood can indeed be seen in the original and more recent Tungus material collected by Shirokogoroff and Hoppal respectively. The Tungus distinguish between those shamans who hold stable, priestly offices within the clan and their more volatile colleagues who have no fixed position. It is naturally those who are least secure and most ambitious who affect the most florid forms of ecstasy. In much the same way, the wild prophetic founders of the American Indian Ghost Dance subsequently assumed the more sober roles of priestly shamans. In the syncretic Shinto-Buddhistic tradition in Japan, the figure of the ascetic shaman (*shamon*) plays a complementary role to the spirit-inspired medium (*miko*). In feudal Japan, apparently, it was not unusual, as Blacker shows, to find an ascetic husband married to a female medium. Today, however, perhaps as in the Soviet Union with the marginalisation of these beliefs, women shamans seem to be increasingly prevalent in a society which the Japanese scholar K. Sasaki describes as 'a hotbed of spirit possession and shamanism'.

Yet if shamanism seems to thrive in circumstances of constraint and privation which it seeks to evade or transcend, there is also evidence to suggest that exactly the opposite conditions may generate the same response. Thus, as Douglas and others have claimed, formless anarchy or comparable conditions when society relaxes its grip on its members, appear also to promote the emergence of ecstatic shamanistic movements. At this point the Marxist and Durkheimian arguments intersect and, as so often with social phenomena, the extremes meet. This conjunction is, of course, fully consistent with our earlier observation that individuals can achieve states of ecstasy either through over- or under-stimulation. Nor, in this context, should we lose sight of the actual techniques employed to achieve ecstasy. Although the availability of powerful psychedelic drugs is not a necessary and sufficient condition for shamanism, it must influence the ease with which trance states can be achieved.

The Love of the Gods

The ecstatic encounters which shamanism, whether combined with spirit possession or not, always involves are described all over the world and in every period of history in remarkably similar terms. The gods and their devotees may address each other in different countries in different languages, but they all employ the same terms of endearment. The language of spiritual intimacy is truly international, and 'possession' here has strong sexual undertones. In this tradition, St Teresa of Avila speaks of the 'Wound of Love', of 'Rapture', and of 'Union', and Marie of the Incarnation records her experiences with her 'Beloved', 'Dearest Spouse'. Less well-known shamanistic devotees in other cultural settings regularly use the same vocabulary, being 'married' to their celestial 'spouses', even in Haiti to the extent of holding marriage certificates! Amongst the Saora Indian tribesmen of Orissa a shaman is often chosen by the direct intervention of a Hindu spirit who proposes marriage. Here, as elsewhere, such spiritual unions compete with their mortal counterparts, frequently leading to most complex matrimonial arrangements. In the case of the arctic Chukchee, for instance, those shamans who happen to be homosexuals (as some are) may be wedded simultaneously to mortal and immortal husbands. More generally, as in the ancient world, these cosmic love-matches may be blessed with children—as in the case of the Virgin Mary. (The famous nineteenth-century English ecstatic, Joanna Southcott, who died of what has been described as a 'hysterical pregnancy', was less successful.) It is thus not surprising that those ecstatics who love the gods should also regularly describe themselves as their 'children'. This filial idiom compounds the marital metaphor in Christianity where Christ's mother's union with God makes him God's Son. The Tukano Indians of Colombia are even more explicitly oedipal. With the aid of hallucinogenic drugs, Tukano shamans achieve beatific visions which they directly compare to incestuous intercourse. The supreme aim of their visionary quest is actually to be 'suffocated', as they describe it, in a mystic uterine union. The theme of a return to the womb (and of birth and re-birth) is, of course, frequently encountered in psychoanalytic treatment and in experiences with psychedelic drugs in medical and non-medical settings.

Closely connected with this uxorial and filial imagery is the more earthy language of the stables which plays an equally prominent role in the vocabulary of shamans and mystics. In this idiom, the gods regularly 'ride' their human 'mounts' as Apollo straddled the oracle at Delphi, and cult members are consequently widely described as the 'horses', or, as with women in the Hausa *bori*-cult, 'mares' of their familial spirits. The Manchu and Tungus, who also follow this imagery, go so far as placing real (as well as human) horses at the disposal of the spirits. These spirit-mounts are brought into the house and, with silk ribbons attached to their manes, made to stand in front of the ancestor spirit shrines. They may not be ridden by women or clansmen wearing mourning dress.

These equestrian and sexual descriptions of shaman-
istic relations with the gods raise interesting problems. Can the most sublime
religious experience be reduced to erotic fantasy and dreaming? Is it all
simply a matter of sublimation: or is it rather that the human sexual act offers
the most readily available template for transcendent experience and hence the
natural language with which to strive to capture the ineffable?

Further Reading

Basilov, V.N. 'The Study of Shamanism in Soviet ethnography' in M. Hoppal (ed.)
    Shamanism in Eurasia (edition Herodot, Gottingen, 1984), pp. 46–66
Blacker, C. *The Catalpa Bow, a Study of Shamanistic Practices in Japan* (Allen & Unwin,
    London, 1975)
Bourguignon, E. 'World Distribution and Patterns of Possession States', in R. Prince
    (ed.), *Trance and Possession States* (Montreal, 1967)
—— (ed.) *Religion, Altered States of Consciousness and Social Change* (Ohio, 1973)
Douglas, M. *Natural Symbols* (Barrie & Jenkins, London, 1970)
Eliade, Mircea *Shamanism: Archaic Techniques of Ecstasy* (Routledge & Kegan Paul,
    London, 1964)
Field, M.J. 'Spirit Possession in Ghana', in J. Beattie and J. Middleton (eds.) *Spirit
    Mediumship and Society in Africa* (Routledge & Kegan Paul, London, 1969)
Hoppal, M. *Shamanism in Eurasia* (edition Herodot, Gottingen, 1984)
Hori, I. *Folk Religion in Japan* (Chicago University Press, Chicago, 1968)
Jochelson, W.I. *The Koryak. Report of the Jessup Expedition, 1900–1901* (New York,
    1905–8)
La Barre, W. *The Ghost Dance: The Origins of Religion* (New York, 1970)
Lewis, I.M. *Ecstatic Religion* (Penguin, London, 1971)
Metraux, A. *Voodoo in Haiti* (London, 1959)
Pressel, E. 'Umbanda Trance and Possession in Sao Paulo, Brazil', in Goodman,
    F.D., Henney, J.H. and Pressel, E., *Trance, Healing and Hallucination* (New York,
    1974)
Rasmussen, K. *The Intellectual Culture of the Iglulik Eskimos* (Copenhagen, 1929)
Shirokogoroff, S.M. *Psychomental Complex of the Tungus* (London, 1935)
Siikala, A.L. *The Rite Technique of the Siberian Shaman* (FF Communications 220,
    Helsinki, 1978)
Voigt, V. 'Shaman—Person or Word?' in M. Hoppal (ed.), *Shamanism in Eurasia*,
    (edition Herodot, Gottingen, 1984), pp. 13–21
Wasson, R.G. *SOMA. Divine Mushroom of Immortality* (New York, 1968)
Wilson, P.J. 'Status Ambiguity and Spirit Possession', *Man*, 2 (1967)

7 | *Australian Aboriginal Religion*

K. Maddock

The vast island continent of Australia was thinly peopled by a few hundred-thousand dark-skinned hunters and gatherers when British settlement began in 1788. James Cook, who had sailed up the east coast eighteen years earlier, wrote that they might 'appear to some to be the most wretched people upon Earth, but in reality they are far happier than we Europeans'. The ancestors of the Aborigines, as they are now known, probably entered Australia more than 40,000 years ago, but no one knows from where they came or to whom they are biologically or linguistically related.

Today's Aborigines, who comprise one or two per cent of the Australian population, are diverse in character and situation. Many follow an essentially European mode of life, speak only English and biologically are less than half Aboriginal. Others are purely Aboriginal, speak several Aboriginal tongues and pursue a way of life based partly on hunting and gathering. Such diversity results from the forces and pressures exerted through colonisation and from their uneven impact in different areas.

Knowledge of what can loosely be called Aboriginal religion relies on observations since 1788. The Aborigines knew no writing and any earlier sojourners among them left no records, so greater time depth can be obtained only by inference from what has been learned during the past two hundred years. But attempts at reconstruction run into the difficulty that Aboriginal religious practice has greatly changed over that period—vanishing altogether in some areas, showing signs of nativism or Christian influence in others and generally adapting itself to new political and socio-economic circumstances.

For example, our best accounts include those of A.W. Howitt, who worked in south-east Australia late last century, and of his contemporaries Baldwin Spencer and F.J. Gillen, who worked together mainly in the Northern Territory. Howitt wrote detailed descriptions of the Bora (a protracted initiatory ceremony focused on tooth avulsion), but the two performances he attended were inspired by him and carried out by Aborigines who, by that time, were depleted in numbers and much changed in mode of life. Spencer and Gillen wrote comprehensively about the *intichiuma* ceremonies of the central Australian Aranda (these rites were thought to ensure the abundance of plants and animals), but the series they first witnessed was staged in gratitude to Gillen, whose intervention a few years before had put a stop to police terror directed against Aborigines—it seems that the location and some other details of the performance differed from past practice.

No unity of faith or practice existed among Aborigines in a sense comparable to what is found in any of the great divisions of Christianity or Islam. Aboriginal horizons were highly circumscribed—a person's social universe might comprise five hundred or a thousand souls, beyond whom lived people of whom little was known but much might be suspected. Except in more arid parts, an Aboriginal's life would have been largely spent in a tract of a few thousand, or perhaps only a few hundred, square miles. Should we not speak, then, of there being many religions, just as there were hundreds of languages? Perspectives were also very limited in a time sense. Genealogical memory and memories of past events usually ran back no more than two or three generations. Earlier than that, or separated from it by an indefinite lapse of time, lay the creative period when nature and culture were fashioned by a multitude of beings who, commonly half-human and half-animal but with supranormal powers, made a mysterious appearance from beneath the earth or from the sky or from distant horizons before vanishing. This was not creation out of nothing, for something already existed, but it lacked form and active life, being pictured perhaps as a watery expanse or a waste of level ground. It is these beings and their world-formative deeds who are commemorated in the myths and rites of Aboriginal religion. More than that, many are conceived still to exist, in some sense, and, whether existent or not, they have a continuing tangible relevance, for they laid down the rules of the social order and the natural setting is filled with their bodily memorials—here a circular water-hole is the eye of a half-human cockatoo, there the trees lining a watercourse are the tails of half-human snakes and somewhere else a rocky ridge is the backbone of a half-human marsupial.

A paradox can readily be seen in Aboriginal religion (or religions). On the one hand, spatial and temporal perspectives were very restricted, but on the other hand, Aborigines throughout Australia's three million square miles were joined by their shared ancestry and by their long isolation from the rest of the world. We must therefore recognise that chains of connection ran in every direction and back to time immemorial, even if the Aborigines themselves did not know it. So, even granting that it is more accurate to speak of *religions* than of *religion*, we can reasonably expect common religious features. Also we can expect that divergent features will, in many cases, prove to be historical variations on indigenous themes.

E.A. Worms, a Roman Catholic priest, has made the most determined modern effort to distil the essence of Aboriginal religious belief and practice. He sees the religions of the continent as forming an organic whole, characterised by eight common features:

1. Absence of esoteric doctrine;
2. Belief in a personal sky-being;
3. Belief in auxiliary spirits, often the sons of the sky-being, who taught sacred rites and gave sacred instruments;
4. Belief in holy objects left behind by the sky-being, in which his power is contained;
5. The use of liturgical drama to renew and symbolise the sky-being's creative acts;
6. The practice of initiation, including tests of hardship;
7. Traces of sacrifice and prayer, in the wildest senses of those words;
8. The existence (presumably within each community) of a leading liturgist or medicine-man.

Considered in the light of all the fieldwork carried out in Australia, Worms's list is too specific to be accepted as valid, though Worms himself might have defended it as an enumeration of the shared features of the religious complex out of which the present-day Aboriginal religions have developed. A personal sky-being, for example, is known in many areas, most notably in the south-east, where he is depicted as an All-Father, human in form, mighty in power and continuing to take an interest in life on earth, even though he has withdrawn to the sky. In particular, he was associated with the Bora ceremonies, at which he might make a personal appearance. But in other areas no such outstanding being is known or else the most obvious counterpart is female (the All-Mother of some northern areas) and is associated more with the earth or the water than with the sky (she may, for example, be identified as a rainbow serpent who admittedly appears in the sky—as a rainbow—but more usually dwells in fresh water).

To take another example, Worms is right to recognise the importance of spirits who gave sacred instruments or taught sacred rituals (the intimate connection between the two is shown in the fact that the name of a ceremony is often the name of the instrument used in it, such as gong or bullroarer). But they cannot always be seen as relatives of the sky-being (or his counterpart). Thus myths of the Gunabibi, a major northern ceremony, credit it in some areas to a human-like father and son and to a pair of snakes, while in other areas the leading mythical figures are a pair of human-like sisters and a snake. None of these beings has any special association with the sky.

Worms allowed for the obvious differences among Aboriginal religions by distinguishing what he called 'incidental accretions'. They include such features as the prevalence of secondary spirits and of snake and other animal symbolism and the exclusion of women from much of the men's ritual. When one considers the reports now available on various northern and central ceremonies it is hard to escape the conclusion that some 'incidents' are as essential as any of the suggested common features. Of the eight, one can be confident of the universality (or near universality) only of the third, fourth, fifth and sixth—and even they must be modified so that a sky-being is no longer insisted upon.

Worms's approach has been little emulated, though the time is now ripe for fresh attempts making use of the mountain of information collected by fieldworkers over the last two decades. So far the more usual approach has been in accord with W.E.H. Stanner's view that the best avenue for the understanding of Aboriginal religion is through the study of the surviving regional cults (or ceremonies). In them we see religion in action.

The rich perspectives opened by this approach are well shown in W. Lloyd Warner's classic monograph on the Murngin of north-east Arnhem Land. In the late 1920s, the time of his study, they were performing these major ceremonies (as well as a number of others of lesser scope):

1. Djungguan;
2. Gunabibi;
3. Ulmark;
4. Marndiella;
5. Dua moiety's Narra;
6. Yiritja moiety's Narra.

Each ceremony is a complex whole, including a series of ritual acts and dances, a series of songs and a set of ritual paraphernalia. It is performed at grounds constructed for the purpose and is associated with a body of myth—and hence with the world-formative deeds of the creative period. Religious performance cannot be isolated from the social system, for the roles which actors play are allocated according to important social divisions—of sex, for example, or of moiety.

To speak of Murngin religion as comprising a number of ceremonies may leave the impression that it lacks overall system. In fact, Warner sees unity as coming especially from myths, which provide a symbolic underpinning for the ceremonies. Thus the first four of the six ceremonies listed above belong to the myth cycle of the Wawilak sisters and the last two to that of the Djunkgao sisters. Each myth is in effect an organising focus for two or more cults, providing not only their charter, in Malinowski's sense, but an interpretative rationale through which many ceremonial episodes can be understood as present-day re-enactments of events occurring in the creative period.

The Wawilak myth, for example, tells of two sisters who set off from the interior on a northwards journey to the sea after committing incest. As they travelled they named the plants they gathered and the animals they killed; they also named places and countries and, from time to time, changed language to that now associated with the area through which they were passing. When the younger sister felt a child within her (the fruit of incest) she told the elder, and they hurried on to a water-hole associated with the rock python. There they made a fire and began to cook the plants and animals collected on their journey, but each sprang from the fire and ran like a man to the water, into which it dived. Next the elder sister gathered bark for a bed for the younger, but in doing so she menstruated into the water. The pollution aroused the python. He rose to the surface, the water level also rose to flood the surrounding country and soon rain began to pour down. Hastily the sisters built a house. They fell asleep within it, but were soon awoken by the rain, which was becoming heavier and heavier.

In a vain effort to stop the rain the sisters sang the songs of the Gunabibi, Djungguan, Marndiella and Ulmark. Then in desperation they sang of rock python and menstrual blood. At this the python made them fall asleep by magic, after which he swallowed them. He regurgitated them, swallowed them again and finally regurgitated them a second time. Later the spirits of the sisters appeared in a dream to two men, to whom they taught the four ceremonies.

The Wawilak myth is more than an original tale. It enables symbolic sense to be made of what is done in the ceremonies associated with it. In the Gunabibi, for example, the bullroarer (one of the 'holy objects' of Worms) is identified with the python, the various animals referred to in songs or mimed in dances are among those the sisters saw and named on their journey and a structure of forked sticks, erected at a late stage and serving as a focus of action for both men and women, is the house in which the sisters took shelter. We can also see the myth as rationalising the religious division of labour and responsibility between the sexes—a theme elaborated in a different way by the myth of the Djunkgao sisters.

It would be a mistake to explain the ceremonies as having been derived from the myths. Rather the ceremonies, as large-scale collective actions of stereotyped form, could more plausibly be invoked to explain the myths, for the latter are not learned in word-perfect fashion and can vary a good deal in the telling. But, when Murngin religion is looked upon as a more or less functioning whole, myth and ceremony are best seen as complementary variables.

Many of the cults described in the literature are not confined to one locality. Those of the Murngin, for example, are performed by other Arnhem Land peoples. The Gunabibi, in particular, enjoys a wide distribution, being known over many tens of thousands of square miles of northern Australia. But, as is to be expected from the lack of an overarching 'church', considerable variations can occur in details of performance from one locality to another, and the associated myths can be quite different. Thus, to the south-west of the Murngin, the Gunabibi is explained by a myth about a father and son, both properly married, who set off on a journey inland from the sea after a water-dwelling monster swallowed ceremonial performers and regurgitated them as bone.

In addition, there can be important differences in the purposes fulfilled by ceremonial performances. Emphasis may be laid especially on the passage of youths into manhood and on the separation of masculine from feminine elements in society—certainly that is how Warner depicted Murngin religion. But ceremonies may also be understood as a means to transform spirits of the dead from a wandering state to a state in which they may enter ancestral waters—and from which, in the belief of some areas, they may undergo reincarnation. Ceremonies may be centred on the disposal of the bodily remains of the dead, or they may aim to ensure the perpetuation of plant and animal species. Invariably they incorporate a division of labour and responsibility, for which reason it is by no means fanciful to see them as occasions on which Aborigines colourfully and dramatically map out their social structure. And, because the associated myths and songs are located at known places, or lines of places, in the landscape, the ceremonies are also a kind of geographical mapping. Some of these functions— the social and geographical mapping, for example—probably pertain to all ceremonies, but others are contingent and can change from one area to the next even as regards the 'same' ceremony. Thus assisting in the transformation of spirits of the dead provides some of the purposive core of the Gunabibi south-west of the Murngin, but it is no part of the Gunabibi among the Murngin themselves. They secure that end through other ritual observances.

These considerations suggest that the future development of the study of Aboriginal religions will do well to follow two complementary paths. On the one hand, we need to elucidate the system of ceremonies (understood as complex wholes) of particular peoples. On the other hand, we must aim to trace the chains of connection between the systems of different peoples. In ascertaining the relations of transformation between different ceremonies in the same locality or between the 'same' ceremony in different localities, we may hope to reach more or less plausible conclusions about processes of religious growth, change and decay on the continent. Given the shared ancestry of the Aborigines and their long isolation from the rest of the world, it might well turn out that these processes could best be understood on the analogy of the incessant dealing and re-dealing of a pack of cards.

But have Aboriginal religions (as distinct from the study of them) a future? They have vanished from parts of Australia, and where they survive the context of performance—and therefore the significance of performance—is by no means what it would have been in pre-colonial times. Formerly, for example, most Aborigines spent much of the year on the move in small groups in a quest for food. Performances of major ceremonies were occasions of heightened social life, when perhaps a few hundred people would come together for a few weeks. Disputes might be settled and marriages arranged, as well as ceremonies performed. The switch to a largely sedentary existence and to assured food supplies has changed all that. The social order in which Aborigines live can no longer be wholly explained by the deeds of the spirit beings of the creative period. Greatly improved communications have exposed Aborigines not only to profound differences in attitude and belief among Europeans but to considerable variations in Aboriginal practice according to location or region. Not all influences are corrosive. Thus the definition of Aboriginal land rights in South Australia and the Northern Territory has incorporated the mythic and ceremonial aspects of traditional relations to land. Accordingly it would be premature to foretell the demise of Aboriginal religions. The likelier outcome, at least in the near future, is the emergence of very widespread religious movements based on a selection of themes and elements from the more detailed but spatially more restricted cults of the immediate past.

Further Reading

Charlesworth, M., Morphy, H., Bell, D. and Maddock, K. (eds.) *Religion in Aboriginal Australia: An Anthology* (University of Queensland Press, St Lucia, 1984)

Howitt, A.W. *The Native Tribes of South-East Australia* (Macmillan, London, 1904)

Spencer, B. and Gillen, F.J. *The Native Tribes of Central Australia* (Macmillan, London, 1899)

Stanner, W.E.H. *On Aboriginal Religion* (Oceania Monographs, Sydney, 1964)

—— 'Religion, Totemism and Symbolism', in R.M. and C.H. Berndt (eds.) *Aboriginal Man in Australia* (Angus and Robertson, Sydney, 1965)

Warner, W.L. *A Black Civilization* (Harper, New York, 1937)

Worms, E.A. 'Religion', in H. Shiels (ed.) *Australian Aboriginal Studies* (Oxford University Press, Melbourne, 1963)

8 | *Melanesian Religions*

V. Lanternari

The inhabitants of Melanesia traditionally gain their livelihood mainly by horticulture, with gardens of yams and taro, and in the coastal areas by fishing. Pig-raising is also practised in a number of isles and in the interior region of New Guinea. As in practically all sedentary societies who take their livelihood from cultivated plants, a fundamental feature of the native Melanesian religion is the cult of ancestors. Belief in the deceased persons' spirits gives rise to a number of ceremonies, which are carried out by the members of each clan in honour of their ancestors. The ancestors' cult is a means to control individual behaviour and to preserve the moral code. It also helps to strengthen social cohesion and to maintain the cosmic order. Finally, it re-establishes symbolically, on each occasion, continuity between past generations and the living, that is to say between tradition and the present life.

Knowledge of the necessary rituals is often passed on from father to son or, in matrilineal societies, from maternal uncle to nephew. In the Fiji group there was a class of hereditary priests who officiated at ancestor cult ceremonies and became possessed. In this state they spoke with the voice of the spirit and were consulted as oracles. Sometimes, as in the Solomon Islands, ancestral spirits are believed to inhabit fish or other animals. Among some tribes, they are believed to inhabit their skulls which are recovered some time after death. They are moulded with coloured resins and clays, then they are collected in men's houses or placed on a figure modelled in clay and fibre (*malekula*), or in a special model-hut (New Georgia). The skulls actually represent the deceased persons. Their power is considered to be favourable or harmful according to the proper or improper fulfilling of ethical and ritual duties by their clan heirs.

On the northern coastal region of Irian the *korwar* figures are a notable form of religious art production. *Korwar* is the wooden or stone statue of a deceased forefather. Some time after death a statuette is made by the relatives of the deceased, into which his soul is then lured. The very skull of the departed person may be placed on a headless *korwar* statue. Among the Fly River and Purari River tribes and in New Britain the frontal portion of the skull was modelled in the form of a mask. Generally speaking, masks are worn by initiates during sacred ceremonies, particularly in the initiation rites. Actually, the uninitiated believe that the masked performers are spirits and regard them with awe and terror. The initiates, though conscious of the deception, nevertheless feel a sort of identification with the spirits they represent.

Sometimes the cult of the dead, together with the males' initiation rites and the New Year fertility feast, merges into one single multivalent ceremony, in which an atmosphere of symbolic death-regeneration is produced. This ceremony is more generally concerned with the adolescent life crisis of puberty, with the growing of crops and with propitiation for the whole tribe's destiny in its relationship with the cosmic order. The *Nanga* ceremony of Fiji is an example of this kind of complex ritual. On this occasion, the young novices are led to the sacred stone platform in the centre of the village. Here they meet an awesome group of actors whose arrival is announced by the sound of sacred flutes representing the ghosts' voices. The actors-initiates are masked and disguised in frightening apparel; they threaten the novices in terrifying mimes. Frightened by the scene, the novices ritually die; but after some time they are reborn and collectively recognised as adult members of the society. Thus the return of the dead is dramatically represented as a symbolic rite of human and cosmic regeneration. Offerings of crops and meat are produced for the spirits from the heaps of yams and the swine which have been prepared for the celebration. Prayers are said to obtain the spirits' co-operation in fostering prosperity and general well-being.

Another and somewhat different example of the merging of initiation rites with mortuary ceremonies and with a general regeneration feast is the *Malanggan* ritual in New Ireland. The name itself, *Malanggan*, is also shared by special kinds of ceremonial objects of great artistic interest. The *Malanggans* are either intricate, wide horizontal carvings, or meticulously executed multifigured, vertical carved poles. Both types are embellished by printed patterns of a stylistically impressive effect. The *Malanggan* carvings are solemnly presented by adult initiates to the novices during the initiation rites, which are performed on the occasion of the great *Malanggan* celebrations in memory of the departed.

In Melanesia, the spirits of recently deceased persons are believed to exercise individually a direct influence on the living, while the spirits of those who died in the more remote past are collectively evoked on the occasion of periodical rituals. On these occasions they are honoured with food offerings and particularly the first-fruits. Then they are formally and vigorously expelled and invited to go back to their abode. The inhabitants of many of the Melanesian islands believe that the ghosts have their dwelling on a smaller isle in the west.

This belief becomes relevant with reference to the newer development of syncretistic movements generally called Cargo-cults. They have emerged among the inhabitants of a great number of islands, in response to the arrival of the white peoples' boats with their surprising products (cargo), so different from anything the natives had ever seen. The initial identification of the white people with the spirits of the dead was favoured by the traditional mythical belief concerning the western abode of the ghosts and their maritime journeys. People were easily induced to mythologise about the cargo and to ascribe its creation to a spiritual world with which the white man was in contact. Thus, since the white man brought the goods, the cargo was a gift from the dead. The occurrence of Cargo-cults in myriads of societies or groups, independently of one another, in response to similar events such as the encounter with an unknown kind of human being and new material objects, demonstrates the creative potentiality inherent in the traditional system of beliefs and myths. It also proves that the cult of the dead is a fundamental component of the structure of Melanesian religion. This cult is centred on the widespread belief that the spirits or ghosts are the original givers of wealth, of prestige and of mastery to the natives.

As for the traditional ceremonies, in which the spirits of the deceased are honoured with every kind of offering, we conclude that through the ritual activity a profitable psychic equilibrium is fostered by the people for themselves. Through the rite, in fact, a mutual giving-receiving relationship is established between the living and the supernatural powers. Further, by paying homage to the spirits people hope to obtain the practical reward of good fortune for themselves.

On the whole, ritual activity in Melanesia generally revolves around three main critical moments of the individual's or community's life: death, initiation and the New Year. Initiation rites are of two main types: initiation of all boys into adult status, which is typical of New Guinea, Bismarck Archipelago, the Solomon Islands and New Caledonia; and initiation into age-grades or secret societies (the 'degree-taking' rites), which are common in New Britain (*Duk-duk*), New Ireland (*Igiet*), Florida (*Matambala*), Banks Islands (*Tamate*) and northern New Hebrides (*Qatu*). The initiated are ritually and collectively instructed by the elders on their moral duties, myths, ancestors' deeds, the general prescriptions and taboos and sometimes also magical rites. They are supposed to communicate, during the rituals, with the spirits through the voice of the sacred flutes or of the bull-roarer. In the north-eastern region of New Guinea a monster, called Balum, symbolically swallows the new initiate, as a symbol of death and rebirth and also as a test of courage. The novice, in general, is subjected to a period of segregation, and to physical proofs of pain-tolerance, in many cases through such sexual mutilations as penis-incision or circumcision. While the initiation to adulthood is shared by all young men, the initiation into secret societies is reserved for men who can afford the expense. They get, from the initiation, special privileges of a political and judicial kind. The women's initiation to adulthood is also widespread, but it has an individual character as opposed to the collective character of the men's initiation. Furthermore, the female initiation is reduced to a feast in which the girl receives some gifts, changes her clothes and is instructed about her impending duties as wife and mother. In fact, this type of initiation corresponds to the celebration of her first menstruation. Both men and women are supposed to marry only after initiation.

For initiated men the revelation of cult secrets to women or to the uninitiated is regarded as a serious breach of tradition. Since the observance of the general moral code is imposed on the initiated men, an outstanding function of the initiation rites is to ensure a correct and harmonious proceeding of the social life. Contraventions meet not only with human blame and censure, but also with automatic spiritual punishment such as sickness and misfortune, attributed to the intervention of the spirits.

In recent times European contact has brought about a decline of the traditional ways of life, mostly in the religious, socio-ethical and economic spheres. Christian missionaries have intervened against initiation rituals and other feasts, which they regarded as unacceptable manifestations of paganism. The forced abandonment of customary ritual activities, the attraction of modern cultural models, the diffusion of alcoholic beverages and the changes in the old value orientations caused by the new forms of economic enterprise introduced by the Europeans, have produced the collapse of old spiritual sanctions, and the deterioration of moral standards. The uneasiness and the feeling of frustration caused by these factors underlie the spreading of the Cargo-cults which clearly express a deep yearning for the renewal of the traditional way of life. Significantly, the Cargo-cults are promoted by native prophets under charismatic inspiration. Following dreams and visions, they become the spokesmen of widely shared aspirations and sentiments.

So far we have considered Melanesian religion mostly in the phenomenological contexts of death and initiation. Both are tightly interwoven with a third mythico-ritual context: the religion of the New Year. A very well-known example of the New Year feast in traditional Melanesian societies is the *Milamala* feast of the Trobriand Islanders, as it is described by Malinowski in his classical work, *Coral Gardens*. The Trobrianders celebrate the *Milamala* after the principal harvest of the yam crop has been completed, in August. The celebration lasts one lunar month; its name is shared by the month itself, and contains the notion of abundance (*malia*). On this occasion heaps of yams are ostentatiously distributed in the village, while the store-huts are full of the new tubers. *Milamala* is primarily a joyful celebration of the products of cultivation. Nevertheless, the newly produced yam crop is taboo. It cannot be eaten before the end of the ceremony. A fundamental aspect of the ceremony, in fact, is the return of the spirits of the dead (*baloma*) to the village, *en masse*. The hungry spirits are welcomed and an offering of the first-fruits is given to them. Heaps of yams are prepared on special platforms along the paths of the village, which the spirits are supposed to visit every night. They eat the essence of the yams. And only then, when the offerings have been accepted, is the consumption of the new food permitted.

This ritual symbolically underlines the acknowledgement of the spirits' ownership of the cultivated plants and of food in general. The offering of the first-fruits to them, together with the imposing of the food taboo on the living, clearly signifies the restitution of property to its spiritual owners and the symbolic annulment of the yearly work of cultivation and of the product itself, as if a sacrilege had been perpetrated against the supernatural powers, particularly the spirits of the dead. In the final part of the feast—which is at the same time a feast of the crops and of the dead—the *baloma* spirits are ritually expelled by a solemn declaration, and people then indulge in eating, dancing and sexual licence.

This ritual behaviour—the celebration of crops, the food taboo, the ceremonial return of the dead, the first-fruits offering to them and the final expulsion of the spirits and the orgy—is observable, in more or less the same forms, among the majority of the Melanesian peoples, whose belief systems and culture have been examined by scholars. Moreover, from a more general point of view, it is worth pointing out here that among practically all societies of primitive or archaic cultivators, a structural interplay can be observed between the ideological sphere pertinent to cultivation and production, and the one pertinent to the world of the dead. Among these societies the cult of the dead is of great significance and in one particular form this cult is represented by the eschatological complex of the return of the dead viewed as the forerunners of a general regeneration.

Further, it is reasonable to assume that the New Year feast of the Melanesians can be interpreted as the ritualised expression of the feeling of a link between the tilling of the earth—mother of plants—and the violation of the ancestors' seat—the earth itself where the dead are buried—so that the rites of the temporary food taboo, of welcoming the *baloma* spirits once a year, of the first-fruits offering to them, reveal the significance of a symbolic and articulate action viewed as expiating the inevitable guilt committed. In this way the fear that in the future food production may fail is overcome. The final feasting, the joyful and frantic indulging in eating and dancing and in the sexual orgy after the expiatory role of the previous rites and after the expulsion of the spirits, play the complementary role of clearing the way for the community to proceed trustfully and joyfully towards the new cycle of life and of agricultural activity. The Melanesian New Year feast, therefore, can be regarded as paradigmatic of how an eschatological worldview is expressed by a ritual drama in which the resurrection of the dead is represented in its living and sensible reality.

By way of contrast, among those tribes who practise pig-raising, ritual life centres on a solemn pig festival, which is carried out at intervals of several years. The pig festival is substantially a rite of social promotion, within the context of the dynamic competition between individuals who aim to acquire social prestige and to emerge as leaders ('big men'), or who wish to maintain the role and power they have previously acquired. Ambitious men gain or maintain personal power by arranging and managing a great pig festival. The procedure is based, firstly, on the ability of wives to procure and rear as many pigs as possible, within a period of several years. It is also based on the ability to mobilise kin, friends and clients of the candidate for leadership, in order to obtain their co-operation in the rearing of a great number of pigs. When the candidate or 'big man' believes that the right moment has arrived to display his riches, in the form of all the pigs amassed by himself and by his clients, the pig festival begins. It takes the form of a tremendous fight to kill the animals, and of a huge sacrifice of hundreds of swine. This sacrifice has a number of mythical references. For example, according to a Kiwai myth in New Guinea, man and pig are identified and the killing of a pig is at the basis of death for humankind. That is the reason why the pigs are not killed by their personal owners, but by others. The religious character of the feast is also marked by the ritual dedication of the animals to the spirits or to mythical beings as the culture-heroes, or (among the Marind-anim of New Guinea) to the swine-Dema. The Dema are mythical beings of the Marind-anim; all natural objects, plants, animals and humankind itself derive from the Dema.

The social function of the pig festival is to create or to re-establish the special rank of 'big men' who exercise religious, social and political power within the federation of the affiliated kin, friends and clients who have co-operated with them. The principle of reciprocity is central to the relationship between leader and co-operators. The former is supposed and is even obliged to return the favours he received from the latter. Where he is unable to fulfil his obligations, he loses his power and rank. On the other hand, each 'big man' has also to face competition from every other ambitious individual who may at any time try to rise in rank and status by arranging his own pig festival. We see from the Melanesian pig festival that myth and ritual are interwoven with the dynamics of the social structure. The pig festival includes in its structure also some of the same rites as the New Year festival, such as the offerings to the spirits, the initiation of young men and such beliefs as the return of the dead.

A final observation is worth adding: the sacrificial massacre of hundreds of pigs is followed by what amounts to a frenetic bout of eating. The excessive consumption of meat on this occasion can only be understood and rationalised if seen within the framework of a dialectical relationship between ordinary and extraordinary behaviour, and particularly between profane time and sacred time, that is to say between daily life and feast. Actually, the waste of goods and food in the feast is one of its structural rules, since the purpose of the feast is to express the reversal of ordinary everyday conditions, relationships and situations. Thus daily poverty and hardship are denied—in strongly symbolic language—by the exaggerated consumption of food in the feast.

A concept widely diffused in Melanesia is *mana*. According to classical authorities such as Rivers, Hocart and Codrington, it is at the very heart of most religious beliefs and practices, and also of the world of magic. *Mana* is a supernatural and impersonal power or influence, which operates in and influences all the events or phenomena which remain outside the ordinary competence or domain of men. Though impersonal, *mana* is always activated and directed by certain kinds of people. Originally it belonged to all kinds of spirits and ghosts, and to certain individuals. Even some inanimate objects possess *mana* because they are inhabited by a spirit. These objects are characterised by unusual and strange forms. In New Britain the sorcerers have power from *mana* to cause illness and even death. In Guadalcanal (Solomon Islands) a sorcerer may obtain *mana* from a ghost (*tindalo*) inhabiting a special bird, *naroha*. The sorcerer goes to a place where that bird can be found and asks him for *mana*. Among the Fijians the *mana* is associated with ghosts, spirits, chiefs and medicines. In many tribes all around Melanesia the spirits of the dead are held to be the principal sources of *mana*. Bones of deceased persons, for instance, are employed to build arrows in Lepers Island. The effect should be to bestow *mana* on the arrow and to get success in striking the prey. Bones or teeth are also employed to make charms. In New Guinea the belief in *mana* exists only among the south-western and Papua-Gulf tribes.

Since a rigid distinction between magic and religion is fundamentally doubtful, we can consider here some of the so-called magical practices that are common almost everywhere in Melanesia. As is well known, magic is aimed at preventing individual or collective calamities of every kind. Malinowski's idea was that magic intervenes in those circumstances and situations regarded as being beyond human control. He underlined a series of magical operations of the Trobrianders in the preparation of canoes for their *kula* expeditions, in order to ensure the success of the expedition itself. Magical practices are also carried out, he wrote, on yam farms, in order to ensure that the plants grow well, and to protect the plantations from the intrusions of wild pigs.

A number of traditional practices, of magico-religious significance, especially head-hunting, cannibalism and human sacrifice, were suppressed after the arrival of Europeans. Head-hunting was originally practised for the purpose of acquiring and displaying skulls, a mark of warriors' virtue. Among the Marind-anim of New Guinea, once a year a head-hunting expedition was organised against the enemy. All the able-bodied members of the tribe participated in it. A special hut was prepared where the skulls were placed as glorious trophies and as bringers of new force to the tribe. The heads were also used in the fertility rites, as a magical source of vitality.

Cannibalism was practised by some of the tribes inhabiting the smaller Melanesian islands and New Guinea, mainly in the initiation ceremonies. Among the Kiwai people a ritual prescription for novices in the initiation rituals was to kill an enemy as a test of courage. Cannibalism followed on this occasion, the principal purpose of it being to seize the force and vitality of the victim. Human sacrifice occurred sporadically, mainly in the Solomon group, on such occasions as the launching of a canoe.

The suppression of certain traditional customs after contact with Europeans, the introduction of new cultural models from the Whites and the appearance of the European ships off the coasts from the end of the last century, profoundly affected the world-view of the indigenous inhabitants and the same disturbing effect was produced by the arrival of the first planes in the open glades of the forest in New Guinea. A messianic and millenarian atmosphere soon began to pervade all parts of the region. Ancient mythological topics, particularly those of the periodical return of the dead, were revived, reshaped and adjusted to new configurations. What was traditionally, in the yearly feast of the dead, simply the periodic expectation of the return of the dead and of a temporary renewal of life, now, in the new cults, became the enthusiastic expectation of a definitive and eschatological regeneration of the world.

This happened on a great number of islands and among many peoples, and it gave rise to a completely new process in the local history: the rise of millenarian Cargo-cults. In other instances the myth of a culture-hero of the past was revived, for instance in the case of Manseren Manggundi in the Schouten Islands of New Guinea. In every case, both the spirits of the dead and the culture-hero were held up as messianic heralds of a new era of good fortune and blessing. According to the myth, Manggundi was a beneficent, popular hero reputed to have access to the source of all riches and foods. He also had power to lead men to the threshold of the Golden Era by bestowing on them the riches he controlled. But the myth also narrated that men did not acknowledge him when he first came among them, so that, hurt and discouraged, the hero departed, promising none the less to return. The myth is a clear 'rationalised' representation of the poor conditions of life of the aborigines, and also an expression of a longing for a better future.

The myth of Manggundi was revived more recently, when in 1938 a number of prophets established millenarian movements. They announced the regeneration of the world, combining in their teachings the traditional ideas of abundance and immortality with the new idea of emancipation from colonialism. Inspired by dreams, they preached the advent of a Utopia (*koreri*) marked by liberty and riches.

In Dutch New Guinea another prophetic cult was created among the Muju people in 1913 by Karoem. This prophet was visited by a spirit, who showed him how to lead the Maju out of their backward condition to one of wealth, well-being and fulfilment. All taxes and tributes imposed by the administration, and all contributions to mission churches, would be abolished. A great city would rise up, including a factory, a mint and shops. A huge ship laden with goods for the inhabitants would arrive at the port. The dead would come to life. Karoem was arrested by order of the Dutch government, but his prophecies spread far and wide among the Muju people who tried, in public assemblies, to contact the spirits in order to prepare for the advent of the New Day. In many cases, as one can see from the examples we give, these movements pave the way for the more or less organised expressions of socio-political ferment and discontent. Always, they are a response to the critical experience of culture shock, derived from the encounter with 'modern' and attractive but frustrating forms of civilisation.

One of the best-known examples of Cargo-cults is the so-called 'Vailala Madness' of the Orokolo tribes on the Gulf of Papua. It arose soon after the First World War in response to European influence and missionary preaching. The founder, Evara, was visited by the spirits. In a state of trance, characterised by frantic excitement which very quickly affected the assembled crowd, and which the whites viewed as manifestations of collective hysteria, Evara prophesied the arrival of a ship guided by spirits of the ancestors. They would bring the cargo of rice, meal, tobacco and guns for the people. The cargo, the prophet said, did not belong to the whites but to the Melanesians. The former, in fact, would be miraculously expelled from the island and their cargo would then pass into local hands. The psychic and physical excitement which spread among the prophet's followers is one very typical feature of this cult, and another is its millenarian notion of the return of the dead. This concept, while based on traditional belief, was developed and revived in new ways after Evara had heard a white missionary deliver a sermon on the resurrection of the dead. Thus we can see the direct influence of Christianity on the rise of the Melanesian messianic cults in modern times. It is important to note, however, that European Christianity as it was and still is preached by missionaries was modified in the light of local needs and hopes. For example, in this case the biblical concept of the Resurrection was reinterpreted, adapted and made relevant to expectations and material requirements of the indigenous population.

Furthermore, the founder, Evara, introduced special rituals and insisted on the observance of certain ethical and moral norms. He commanded his followers to attend the feasts in honour of the departed; he ordered them not to steal, not to commit adultery and to observe Sunday rest. Special 'temples' were erected for worship, the main purpose of which was to facilitate the speedy arrival of the cargo, and the regeneration of the

93

world. Some followers called themselves 'men of Jesus Christ', and were at least nominal Christians. Meanwhile so great was their faith in the immediate arrival of the miraculous cargo and in the dispensation of goods in the Golden Age that they abandoned all those agricultural and commercial pursuits which traditionally gave them a livelihood. Although desirous of the material benefits that Europeans had to offer, Evara and his followers were totally opposed to white domination. After a number of incidents, the colonial administration intervened and arrested several chiefs of the movement. As Peter Worsley points out, Vailala Madness expressed both the eagerness of these people to possess European goods and at the same time their desire to expel the whites. The followers of the Cargo-cults not only abandoned work, but sometimes even destroyed their gardens and killed their pigs, indulging in dancing and feasting. They placed offerings on the graves of the dead, and in some cases they constructed roads for the spirits of the dead who were supposed to come from the sea.

Some recent experiences from the Second World War were also incorporated into some cults. For instance the members of the Marching Rule, a Cargo-cult which spread in the Solomon Islands, came to expect the arrival of the Americans whom they viewed as the heralds of a this-worldly 'paradise'. Other prophets took rational initiatives of a social and reformative character. Among these were Yali in the Madang District of New Guinea (1946–50), and Paliau in Manus Island, Great Admiralty Islands (1946–54).

Generally speaking, then, in the Cargo-cults we can see the adaptation and development of traditional myths and rituals found in the great yam feasts and elsewhere: the idea of the return of the dead, of the boat of the dead, the ritual suspension of work and the offerings to the spirits. The socio-culture crisis brought about by the disturbing presence of the Europeans, the expectations of the periodic return of the dead and of renewal of life, typical of the yearly traditional feasts, becomes in the new cults the expectation and the symbolic foundation of a definitive and eschatological renewal of the world. Nevertheless, in spite of their mythico–ritual basis, which is taken as their starting-point, the cargo-movements are often vehicles of modernisation and social improvement.

Further Reading

Burridge, K.O. *Mambu, a Melanesian Millenium* (Methuen, London, 1960)
—— *New Heaven, New Earth* (Basil Blackwell, Oxford, 1971)
Brunton, R. 'Misconstrued Order in Melanesian Religion', *Man*, 1 (1980), pp. 112–28
Lanternari, V. 'Origini storiche dei culti profetici melanesiani', *Studi e Materiali di Storia delle Religioni* (1956), pp. 31–86
—— *The Religions of the Oppressed. A Study of Modern Messianic Cults* (Alfred Knopf, New York, 1963)

—— *La Grande Festa. Vita rituale e sistemi di produzione nelle società traditional* (Liguori Editore, Bari, 1976)

Lawrence, P. *Road Belong Cargo* (Manchester University Press, Manchester, 1964)

Sahlins, M. 'Poor man, rich man, big-man, chief. Political Types in Melanesia and Polynesia', *Comparative Studies in Society and History*, no. 5 (1953)

Worsley, P. *The Trumpet Shall Sound. A Study on Cargo-cults in Melanesia* (MacGibbon and Kee, London, 1957)

Wagner, R. 'Ritual as Communication: Order, Meaning and Secrecy in Melanesian Initiation Rites', *Annual Review of Anthropology*, XIII (1984)

9 | *Maori Religion*

T.P. Tawhai

If you ask a Maori in, for example, a settlement such as Ruatoria where Maoris constitute a majority of the population, what he understands by religion, expect him to scratch his head in thought, before at length replying 'Whose religion?' Religion and Christianity may be synonymous words for him, but what they mean will vary between 'a human recognition of a superhuman controlling power', on the one hand, and 'the preaching of one thing and too often the doing of something else', on the other. It was religion in the latter sense that the Christians who 'brought Jesus to civilise the natives' in earlier days seemed to follow, showing up their God in an adverse light in the eyes of the ancestors, whose traditional gods acted swiftly and usually harshly. For all that, the ancestors were well able, soon after their contact with Christianity, to distinguish the Message from the messengers. The Maori of Ruatoria will accept that Christianity is an integral part of his fellow Maori's life, but that each will also have his own brand of religion, for historic and other reasons; for instance Maoris have the same religion as their forebears. While the Christian God provides Maoridom with its first Redeemer, he appears mostly to ignore needs at the temporal and profane level, leaving this domain to the ancestral gods who continue to cater for those needs. The *tohunga*, formally trained experts in various academic disciplines, say that in the 'long ago' the gods took an active interest in the affairs of humans, and interaction among them and the ancestors was the norm rather than the exception. Thus, in the long ago, marvellous events occurred, which would account, at least in part, for a past which today sounds more like fable than anything else.

Such issues as whether there was at some stage an entity that can be said to be the origin or architect of creation, and whether such an origin or architect had a single material form, if any, were and continue to be subjects of much speculation. Our typical Maori's tribal upbringing makes him familiar with the capacity of superhuman controlling powers to exist as they choose—in a single form, or transformed at will into numerous manifestations.

What immediately concerns him are such issues as the effectiveness of the relationship between a person and a superhuman controlling power in magnifying that person's capacity to work his will; or the constraints and obligations upon that person in order to sustain the relationship. The ability to accommodate these issues rests a great deal upon knowledge based in turn upon *korero tahito* (ancient explanations). These may be called 'myths', if that word refers to material the main purpose of which is to express the beliefs and values of people.

That the *korero tahito* persist in influencing the Maori's mind is evident during *hui* (large social gatherings). Whether it is the occasion of a *huritau* (birthday), or *tangi* (a gathering to deal with a bereavement), each elder present uses the forum. Gazing around in assessment of those present, he rises in his turn to his feet and with measured dignity expounds in solemn rhetoric. To make his points he invokes the imagery of the tribal myths, with apt gesture, and with references to the symbolism, for example of the art and carving of the meeting-house.

The following passage is transcribed and translated from a speech by a *tohunga* Arnold Reedy, recorded in 1966. It conveys something of the way in which biblical ideas and *korero tahito* continue to interact, in the Maori way of thinking.

Should I happen to meet with [the Apostle] Paul I would probably say to him, 'By Gosh, Paul, those thoughts conflict greatly in my mind.'

The reason is that Adam is the ancestor of the Hebrews and of the Israelites. Whereas ours is this other: Io the Parent. That's ours. From Him/Her are Papa and Rangi and then the Tamariki. Such is the Maori *whakapapa*, right from Tikitiki-o-rangi.

There, then is the difference between our God and the God of the Hebrews. The God of the Hebrews and Israelites they say has His residence in Heaven. Ours, and the God of our ancestors, resides there too. But they know that Tikitiki-o-rangi is the name of the residence of Io; it's there. Io has a house there, Matangireia by name. It has its own forecourt. All those sorts of things are there.

What er . . . Paul is saying looks, to use an English term, very much confused, in my view.

Because, take Adam: Then said the God of the Hebrews, 'Let us create man after our image.' And so the God of the Hebrews created Adam. But when that Adam was born into this world, others resided there too, and he considered them: 'What an ineffectual state of affairs.' For sexual organs simply dangled there with nowhere to go, nowhere.

Let us observe the formalities in our discussion! [an elder's (female) voice] . . .

People were born. What Paul is telling us here is that nobody was born. How did he manage it? He took hold of one of his ribs and yanked it out, and then said, 'This is Eve.' They had union and Cain and his younger brothers were born, the generations of whom Paul speaks; these are the Hebrews and the Israelites.

Look here, ours, not so; ours goes this other way. The *tamariki* of Papa and Rangi resided, but that God continued to reside above, the beginning and the ending. The visaged one, the faceless one. Io, Io the Parent, he is the beginning, he is the ending.

But the *tamariki* of this couple [Papa and Rangi] resided between them. Gradually, eventually, a stifled sense overwhelmed them; they of course being all male, there were no female ones. Some began to say, 'Let us kick our parents into separating, so that we may emerge into the ordinary world of light.' Others spoke. Tu Matauenga began to say, 'Let us slay our *matua*, slay them.' And others were saying, 'No, that is too shameful.' From that time hence, Tu Matauenga is god of war, of bloodshed.

Some began to say, 'How shall we proceed?' Tane lay down and raised his feet. Hmm! He began to kick, causing gradual separation, and hence was called by that name of his, Tane-toko-Rangi [Tane sunderer of the sky]—and so, there is separation, there is separation.

But at the separation of Papa, I of course do not agree with what Paul says; there is strong conflict in my mind, the matter is this other way. They were separated and the *tamariki* emerged.

Rongomaraeroa was guardian of fern; that's the Minister of Agriculture. Is it not so? Tu Matauenga, Minister of War—War Department. Er ..., Tane-nui-a-rangi: that was god of the forests.

Minister of Forests ...

Tangaroa, Tangaroa of the Marine Department. They now have these posts, they have. (Money had not been invented at that time.)

But here is the problem. These people were all male; there was no female. These people considered their situation: 'By golly, comrades, this is a distressing state! Just us, wherever you look it's the same.' Each one with his (male) sexual appendages. Gradually they became highly distressed by their own company. They began to ponder, 'What shall we do, what shall we do?'

'It is well!', Tane-nui-a-rangi informs them, 'it is well. I have the prescription for our disorder.' He, Tane-nui-a-rangi, proceeded to the beach at Kurawaka and arrived. He began to heap up sand, more sand. He pondered his appearance, and began to mould (the heap) into shape similar to his own. But he added length to the hair ... etc.

'O Ropi [the female elder, Mrs Ngaropi White], these are the words of Wi-o-te-rangi, O Ropi.'

The Maori on the street of Ruatoria, nowadays at least, is content with the knowledge that he has access to the expertise of *tohunga* like Arnold Reedy. To outsiders he is inclined to present a front of learning, as a defence against anything that might question the worth of his tribal culture; the treasures transmitted to him by his ancestors.

Before turning to the main task I will note something about myself. The aim is to indicate some of the traditional constraints under which I write, and also to provide some data concerning the reliability of individual sources. I am of Ngati Uepohatu, a tribe whose unextinguished fires, lit by our explorer ancestor Maui, burn in the Waiapu valley near East Cape. The continuously burning fires refer to the state of being unconquered, and in turn refer to the tribe's unsullied prestige; that is the purity, *inter alia*, of its *korero tahito*. Maui is the legendary Maui Tikitiki a Taranga (Maui of the topknot of Taranga, his mother) who as our *korero tahito* explains discovered and settled Aotearoa (New Zealand). The name Aotearoa means 'long twilight', unlike the brief equatorial ones Maui and his crew were used to. Maui had voyaged out and Mount Hikurangi of Aotearoa had seemed to thrust up out of the sea as he sailed toward shore. Noah on the other hand had waited patiently and it was the waters which subsided thereby exposing Mount Ararat. (I think this reflects something of the philosophies of the two peoples. The Maori view is that things come to those with the courage to get them. The Judaic view is that things come to those who can wait.)

My understanding is that each tribe has its own system of ancient explanations. The apparently permanent migration of some Maori into the tribal territories of other Maori has complicated the picture in some ways. And in relation to that and other matters, I recall an often quoted precept of the ancestors which goes: if you must speak, speak of your own. I speak of *korero tahito* and accordingly speak of Ngati Uepohatu ones. Our *korero tahito* have in the telling more or less depended in the past upon such factors as the appropriateness of the emotional climate in which it is told, the messages stated by the surroundings on the occasion, the body language of the narrator and the attributes that the human voice lends to words. Written presentation takes these things away. More than that, it tends to rigidify what has and should remain pliant. Flexibility in our *korero tahito* enables them to accommodate the capacity of the narrator to render them more relevant to the issues of the day. It is therefore with misgivings and a sense of danger that I must explain that this telling is only for this time, and that tomorrow I would tell it another way.

Te Po

Te Kore evolved through aeons into *Te Po*. *Te Po* also evolved through generations countless to man to the stage of *Te Ata* (the Dawn). From *Te Ata* evolved *Te Aoturoa* (familiar daytime) out of which in turn evolved *Te Aomarama* (comprehended creation). The state of *Whaitua* emerges (the present tense is used to animate the narrative) with the recognition of space. There are several entities present. Among these are Rangi potiki and Papa who proceed to have offspring namely: Tane, Tu Matauenga (Tu for short), Rongomatane (Rongo for short) and Haumie tiketike (Haumie for short). The *korero tahito* ends.

In the Maori conception the creation is a great kin unit, and thus is thought of as having a genealogical structure. The genealogy begins with Te Kore. In the dialect of the Maori on the street of Ruatoria, the article *te* has both negative and positive meaning, rendering Te Kore as an ambiguous name or title. Te Kore can mean either 'The Nothing' or 'Not The Nothing', and in the Maori's thinking ambiguity is a trait of the super-being and superior things. For reasons I have been unable to ascertain, Te Kore is hardly mentioned, and the common reference is instead to Te Po. The *tohunga* Arnold Reedy when asked what Te Po was, replied: 'The never-ending beginning.'

Te Po is not thought of as object, or as context. It is said that Te Po is oneness, meaning among other things that Te Po is both object and context.

The employment of the genealogical framework means that to reach Te Po would take a journey in mind, and a return in spirit to former times. During such former times the awareness of our pre-human ancestors operated at the intuitive level only. The situation is sometimes likened to that of a person who is in the grip of sleep, and in that unconsciousness nevertheless senses that although it is night now, dawn is at hand.

Reproduction occurs at the intuitive level. Te Po logically would be the forebear of the Maori on the street in Ruatoria. However the Maori has a strong impression that Te Po is not subject to logic, that Te Po is remote not only on account of the lapse of time but probably more importantly on account of magnitude. It is such as to appear to him to render it fanciful and perhaps even dangerous for him to contemplate Te Po as one of his pre-human ancestors. (The danger is not from Te Po whose magnitude and remoteness put in doubt an interest by Te Po in earthly activities and their performers. An assertion as to genealogical connection has the effect of boosting one spiritually, the boost being dependent on the spiritual level of the one being connected to genealogically. The danger is that at higher spiritual levels, different laws of nature operate and may not necessarily contribute to human survival.)

While Te Po is recognised as a superhuman controlling power, Te Po is not invoked as are some younger superhuman controlling powers. As far as the Maori is concerned the controlling power of Te Po is indirect, controlling those superpowers to whom we can relate directly.

The Tamariki of Rangi and of Papa

The *tamariki* [*Tamariki* translates as 'children'. The word in fact refers to persons of the group who belong in the generational category to which one's natural children do or would have belonged. The group can be as large a one as the tribe] named are Tane, Tu, Rongo, Haumie and Tawhiri matea (Tawhiri for short). Tawhiri, son of Rangi, is half-brother to the others and is eldest. The *tamariki* perceive it is dark, their world consisting as it does of the valleys and hollows between the bodies of Rangi and Papa who are in close embrace. The feeling of cramp and a longing for light is general. There does not seem to be any prospect of change. Except for Tawhiri, the *tamariki* agree to a proposal to separate Rangi and Papa, the former to be removed afar off and the latter to be retained as nurturing parent. [Rangi potiki and Papa, supported by Tawhiri, resist separation. This is the first time in the *korero tahito* that there is opposition to differentiation or expansion, and the intervening factor is *aroha* (love, sympathy). The separation is physical only. Rangi sends his *aroha* down in the rains, which are his tears, to Papa, who responds by sending up her greetings at dawn in the rising mists. Although physically apart they are united in spirit, their *aroha* binding them as one. The saying that '*aroha* is the one great thing' may have originated here, and it is tempting to suppose that some ancestors appreciated the process of condensation without which life on this planet as we know it would not exist.] The retention of one parent is the idea of Tane, as is also the advice that force only adequate to accomplish separation and no more should be applied. All four brothers in turn attempt to bring about separation but it is Tane's effort alone that brings success and in that role he gains the title of Tane-toko-Rangi (Tane who sets Rangi asunder). [Tane, Tane mahuta, Tane-toko-Rangi and so on is similar to Dad, Mr Chairman at the Rugby Club meeting, Major in the army and so on: the same individual wearing different hats.] With the change in role the name of Rangi becomes Rangi nui (the sky) and that of Papa becomes Papa tuanuku (the earth).

Tawhiri brooding over the maltreatment of Rangi and of Papa projects thoughts that assume material form as the clouds, rains, sleet, storms. In the spirit of revenge Tawhiri unleashes these upon his brothers. They wreak havoc with all except Tu who withstands their assault. Tu, who had urged the others to present a united front against the assault, and who had been ignored, now turns upon his brothers and uses them for food and for his other needs. The *korero tahito* ends.

The addition to intuitive perception of sensory perception proves expansive and the plot of complex interrelationships is seen to thicken. Expression of experiences now requires physical terms such as cramp, but also emotional terms such as *aroha* (sympathy, love) and the feelings that make for the spirit of revenge. Possession by the *tamariki* of human attributes provides a basis for assuming that, exalted as they are, they are sufficiently human as to be approachable by the Maori. Sometimes as themselves, but more often in their forms as manifestations, the *tamariki* are recognised superhuman controlling powers. Thus Tane manifest as Tane mahuta (trees and birds) is invoked by those who have business in the forest. Rongo manifest as Rongomaraeroa (sweet potato) is invoked during the cropping season.

The purpose of religious activity here is to seek to enter the domain of the superbeing and do violence with impunity: to enter the forest and do some milling for building purposes, to husband the plant and then to dig up the tubers to feed one's guests. Thus that activity neither reaches for redemption and salvation, nor conveys messages of praise and thanksgiving, but seeks permission and offers placation.

From this *korero tahito* together with the Te Po one we see that humans consist of a tangible and an intangible part. Implicitly both originate in Te Po. The intangible part is *wairua* (soul). There is also the *mauri* (essence or potential) but how it relates to *wairua* is unclear. The word 'essence' is appropriate in that it conveys the idea of that which cannot be analysed further. The word 'potential' is appropriate in so far as it refers to the unrealised. *Mauri* construed very briefly in terms of power is *mana*. The privileges and constraints that accompany the possession of *mana* is the *tapu*. And the dread or awe that surrounds the possession of *mana* is the *wehi*. A chief is often welcomed with the words: *haere mai te mana te tapu me te wehi*.

'Welcome to the powerful, the privileged and the awesome.' The Maori on the street of Ruatoria speaks of the *mauri* of carving, the *mauri* of oratory and so on. And by that he means the spiritual climate that surrounds the carver and his carving, especially during the creative process, the spiritual climate that surrounds the orator and his words, especially during the moments of delivery.

Tane and Hine-ahu-one (Earth Maiden)

Tane observed that the *tamariki* without exception were male and so set about redressing the imbalance. Using the female substance, the earth, Tane formed the first anthropomorphic female and mediated the spirit into her through his breath. He called this manageable female Hine-ahu-one and begat from her a daughter called Hine-titama. Tane took her to wife. One day she asked him who her father was, and his reply was that she might ask the walls of the house. [The walls of the house were of timber and Tane was referring to his many roles: the father, husband, giver of shelter and so on.] When she learned the answer she fled in shame and eventually arrived at Rarohenga, the underworld. [The shame did not, as is sometimes supposed, spring from the incest but from a violation by Tane of a fundamental principle of social relations, namely sharing. So long as there was only one woman Tane was entitled to her exclusively. As soon as there were more than one under his jurisdiction he was bound to share. This he failed to do.] Tane followed and implored her to return with him to the world of light. She declined, saying that she would remain to welcome their descendants into her bosom after the completion of their lives in the world of light and that he should return there and welcome them into it. Tane tearfully agreed. In her new role Hine-titama is called Hine-nui-i-te-po (Great lady of te po). The *korero tahito* ends.

The *tamariki* lack the generative power and on this account there is some sense of failure. The Maori on the street of Ruatoria has only vague notions about the whole thing. The power that the *tamariki* lack is possessed by Hine-ahu-one who transmits it to her daughter Hine-titama. Hine-titama bears children for whom it is clear for the first time that this life has an end. Henceforth it may be said that people are born only to die and because of this the womb has sometimes been referred to as *te whare o te mate* (the house of death). The Maori on the street of Ruatoria is disinclined to subscribe to this piece of inverted logic. As descendant of Maui he knows the myth that tells how his ancestor met his end: strangled while attempting to enter the womb of the slumbering Hine-titama in her role as Hine-nui-i-te-po. In his view it is an ignominious end. Some say Maui wished to return to the pre-born state and others that he wanted to obtain immortality. But the *korero tahito* about Ruaumoko tells us of man's innate wish to be born, and as for immortality, the *wairua* (soul) lives forever.

At the end of this life the physical part of the dead return, rather than proceed, to the bosom of the ancestress Hine-nui-i-te-po. The *po* in her name has made for an interpretation such as the 'grand lady of the night'. I wonder whether the reference is not Te Po—the 'grand lady of Te Po'? If this is so then the boundaries of Te Po lie on the other side of conception and through the doorway that is death. This interpretation of that part of her name seems to be borne out in the addresses made to the dead in the form of farewells and travelling directions: *haere atu ki ou tipuna te hanga tamoko kei Te Po* ('precede us to your ancestors, the tattooed ones at Te Po').

Tane and Tu

These two had contrasting personalities. Tane was peaceable and philosophic while his younger brother was aggressive and a man of action. The brothers clashed. For his part in that affair Tane was given the lordship of Tikitiki-nui-a-rangi—the fourth heaven—and with the role the title Tane-nui-a-rangi. [The creation includes many heavens and also basement levels. The numbers are in question; mention is made of twelve heavens and at least four basement levels. The higher the level the more spiritual the environment.] Tu for his part lost the power to travel to the different heavens. The *korero tahito* ends.

In retrospect we can trace the growth of expansion and can say that it is a propensity in the creation. It was present at the level of awareness or consciousness and then extended into the physical level; more specifically into the realm of bodily experience and of geographic realms.

In the Tane and Tu *korero tahito* the field of expansion is *mana*. The *mana* of Tu is in the temporal field; that of Tane-nui-a-rangi is in the divine field, with one foot nevertheless in the temporal field. This situation has not, however, been taken to mean that the flow of *mana* from the realm of Tane into that of Tu is more fluid than vice versa. This expansion is not expressed as a feeling or reaching toward a God or origin at this stage or for a long time to come. Emphasis is sometimes placed upon the element of confrontation, the situation that appears to have developed when the two *mana* came into contact. However this *korero tahito* is not mentioned among explanations of the rites invoked when different *mana* are brought together; as for example, the rites invoked when visitor and host come together on the occasion of a *hui*.

Tane-nui-a-rangi

An information release from Naherangi—the eleventh heaven—reached Tane-nui-a-rangi; that three baskets of knowledge had been made available at Naherangi for the taking. Competition would be intense. The chances that Tane-nui-a-rangi would win the baskets appeared slight indeed, but of those closely associated with man's genealogical tree he was the one with the greatest chances of success in that venture. It transpired that Tane-nui-a-rangi was successful notwithstanding fierce harassment by Whiro, lord of one of the infernal regions. Tane-nui-a-rangi has the three baskets with him at the moment in his fourth heaven. The ancient explanation ends.

The source of much knowledge, the difficulties that were faced in order to obtain it, the willingness of no less than Tane-nui-a-rangi to face those difficulties, the high motivations required of students before they are considered fit persons to come in contact with knowledge of a superior kind, all these are indications that knowledge should be prized.

(I had thought that the significance of the number three—the number of baskets—would have struck people not in a numerical sense but as representing a balance of knowledge to enable one to live a balanced life. Like the three-fingered hands on many carvings, the three represents a useful, because balanced, piece of anatomy.)

Maui Tikitiki a Taranga

Taranga has a miscarriage and miscarriages are normally born dead. There was a social role for the dead foetus, and that was to provide the focal point for the rites to appease the soul thought to have been angered by this denial of the opportunity to live life. But this miscarriage has been born alive, and of course society has no role and therefore no place for the person whose time of arrival is not yet.

Taranga cut off her tikitiki—topknot—wrapped the foetus in it and flung the bundle into the sea. This is washed ashore in due course and morning finds the bundle entangled in kelp upon the beach. Sunshine causes the placenta encasing the foetus to shrink and strangulation is averted when a seagull pecks away the placenta. More dead than alive the foetus is espied by Tane-nui-a-rangi who removes it to Tikitiki-nui-a-rangi. The foetus survives as the child Maui-tikitiki-a-Taranga—Maui of the topknot of Taranga. Among other activities Maui delves into the three baskets of knowledge. When Maui is capable of deciding whether to remain in Tikitiki-nui-a-rangi or to return to the world of men he opts for the latter. The ancient explanation ends.

The abnormal circumstances in which Maui first sees light singles him out as unusual. The apparent withholding of his mother's personality to prop up his own during the first hours of life precludes him from being a social being. He is then denied a place on the breast of Papa tuanuku—a right of every human. Thus the gates opened to humans into this life have been shut in his face.

Physically too, the chances of enjoying life are waning. Nature itself seems to have reversed its function. The protecting placenta is threatening to strangle him, and the energy-giving rays of Tama-nui-te-ra (the sun) is threatening to deprive him of what scarce energy remains to him. Starved as well, it appears he is being discouraged from this life and forced to turn his face to the next. The reference to him as *my mokopuna*, by Tane-nui-a-rangi, confirms that Maui is indeed more of the next world than of this. One with such a disposition is ready to delve into the baskets of knowledge.

Conclusion

Sir Apirana Ngata, considering in 1930 doing a doctorate in Maori social organisation, left as the introductory part of rough notes the following:

> The thesis is that after 140 years contact with the kind of civilisation the English brought to these islands there are indications that the Maori is settling down to a regime under which he finds he can exist side by side with the Pakeha [European] or at some distance from the Pakeha, not merely physically but rather socially, economically, morally and religiously so as to make the Maori communal life possible in the same country.

This chapter bears out Ngata's thesis, in respect at least of the Ngati Uepohatus during the 1980s.

Further Reading

Alpers, A. *Maori Myths and Tribal Legends* (John Murray, London, 1964)

Best, E. *Maori Religion and Mythology* (2 parts) (Government Printer, Wellington, 1976 and 1982) (first published in 1924)

Binney, J., Chaplin, G. and Wallace, C. *Mihaia—the Prophet Rua Kenana and His Community at Maungapohatu* (Oxford University Press, Wellington, 1979)

Metge, J. *The Maoris of New Zealand* (rev. edn) (Routledge & Kegan Paul, London, 1976)

Reed, A.W. *Maori Myth and Legend* (Reed, Wellington, 1972)

Salmond, A. *Hui—A Study of Maori Ceremonial Gatherings* (Reed, Wellington, 1975)

Schimmer, E. *The World of the Maori* (Reed, Wellington, 1966)

Simmons, D. *The Great New Zealand Myth: a Study of the Discovery and Origin Traditions of the Maori* (Reed, Wellington, 1976)

10 | *African Traditional Religion*

T.O. Ranger

African religion has been much misunderstood, and misunderstood in ways which have made it very difficult to treat historically. Those who have been hostile to African religion have called it primitive; those who have been favourable to it have called it primal. Both words imply an unchanging continuity with the earliest times. African religion has been contrasted, both unfavourably and favourably, with the dynamic 'religions of the book', with their belief in a divinely ordained historical process and their assertion of the primacy of man over nature. Critics of African religion have said that its collective character has constituted a tyranny over individuals and that its conservative character has acted as a brake on progress. Admirers of African religion have praised its contributions to solidarity, stability and community. Critics have depicted African religion as the product of human fear in the face of an all-powerful and arbitrary nature. Admirers have praised its humility and ecological sensitivity. Yet these opposing evaluations arise from essentially the same analysis of African religion which both critics and admirers have seen as having escaped the blessing, or the curse, of historical development.

The Protestant missionaries of the nineteenth century were men committed to modernising change—to the trinity of Christianity, Commerce and Civilisation. They saw African religion as a powerful force holding Africans locked into an impoverished past. To many of them it hardly deserved to be called a religion at all, and if it were to be considered as a religion then it was only a very primitive and immature one. These missionaries ran together every sort of African belief and practice, confusing religion and witchcraft belief under the general heading of 'superstition', and describing every African ritual practitioner as a 'witch-doctor'. Missionaries were confident that revealed Christianity could lead Africans into a dynamic and progressive future. Ironically, though, their picture of African religion was made use of by evolutionary anthropologists who often sought to discredit all religion by revealing its irrational beginnings. Such anthropologists used data on African religion as evidence for the beliefs of the earliest human societies, out of which the historical religions had evolved.

In the twentieth century both missionary and anthropological assumptions changed but not in the direction of treating African religion more historically. Indeed, in reaction against the bogus history of the evolutionists most anthropologists ceased to ask historical questions at all. They produced instead subtle and illuminating studies of how African religion functioned to maintain the organic stability and coherence of traditional African societies. Functionalist anthropologists were often sharply critical of missionaries, whom they saw as ignorantly interfering with, and sometimes destroying, age-old and delicate mechanisms of social balance.

Many missionaries, however, also came to be much more sympathetic towards African religiosity and many of them sought to learn from functionalist anthropological studies. These missionaries came to admire precisely those qualities in African religion on which the anthropologists laid most emphasis. They liked, and hoped to reproduce within an 'adapted' Christianity, the communal values and social stabilities which they thought were guaranteed by African religion. It was no coincidence that these attitudes were most widespread and influential when colonial economies ran out of steam in the 1930s and when stable African rural communities were the ideal of both missionaries and administrators. Since Western historical 'progress' seemed to have led to disaster, African a-historicity began to look much more attractive. Many people's models of African religion were built up at this time by bringing together a collection of opposites to contemporary European beliefs rather than by any objective study of African religion itself.

Such models were taken over by a number of other groups who became particularly interested in African religion. One of these was the Pan-Africanist school, which argued for a single, common African consciousness arising from a fundamental religion of 'soul-force'. Pan-African consciousness, which it was believed had been preserved by Afro-Americans also, was contrasted with the technological aridity and competitive individualism of Europe. Another group which took over an a-historic model of African religion was the comparative religionists. Anxious to treat with respect all religious traditions of the world, they coined such terms as 'the primals' to describe the oral religions of the Third World. In books about religions in Africa such scholars set out to pay as much attention to African religion as they did to Christianity and Islam. The ways in which they treated these different religions, however, varied greatly. Christianity and Islam in Africa were treated very historically, with relatively little said about the imaginative experience of African Muslims or Christians. African religion, on the other hand, was not treated historically at all, but described entirely in experiential terms. This mode of treatment did as much injustice to African religion as it did to African Christianity and Islam.

Finally, African theologians writing in the last twenty years have offered the same a-historical picture of African religion. One of these, John Mbiti, has published the most widely influential studies of African religion. In these he has emphasised that African religion knew no future tense and possessed no founders, converts or prophets. African religion was coexistent with African societies; every member of a society was born into its religion. Mbiti regards this total integration of religion and society as wholly admirable and laments that it could not survive the rate of change and scale of interaction which have characterised modern Africa. He looks to national and indigenised African Christian churches to play the same role in the future.

It may well be asked whether so many different scholars, writing from so many different perspectives, can have been mistaken in their shared view about the a-historicity of African religion. The view clearly has a foundation in real contrasts between African religion and the historic religions of the book. But to say that African religions have not been historical in the same way as Islam and Christianity is not to say that they have no history at all. Intellectual developments of the last twenty years have led to at least an initial understanding of what that history has been.

One of these intellectual developments, of course, has been the general rise of historical studies of Africa. Thirty years ago most people doubted whether it was possible to write the history of any aspect of pre-colonial African societies, let alone of their religion. Today there is a vast body of historical literature about Africa, though it remains true that African religious history is the least fully developed. Nevertheless, it is now the case that we know that most African societies have undergone such profound economic, social and political changes that if African religion were coexistent with society it must also have changed profoundly. Moreover, the whole notion of an African 'society' has come under question. Many historians argue, for instance, that the tribal units into which twentieth-century Africa seems to be divided are of relatively recent origin. If this is the case, then it makes no historical sense to talk of 'Kamba religion' or 'Zulu religion' prior to the nineteenth century. Such constructs have their own and very recent history.

It seems clear, then, that African religion has a history—or perhaps more accurately that African religions have a history. The problem is to discover how to document and describe that history. Here African religious historians are able to draw on the whole battery of skills and methods which have been developed by African historiography as a whole. One of these is the collection and assessment of oral traditions. It turns out that some types of African religious institution—cults which possess shrines and priesthoods—have their own mechanisms for transmitting oral traditions. It also turns out that many bodies of oral tradition refer back to key religious figures, and especially to prophets and to bodies of prophecy.

In assessing this material, historians are greatly helped by intellectual developments within anthropology. Anthropologists have become interested in process and in transformation, and especially in cultural and ideological processes and transformations. Many of them draw a distinction between the 'imageless discourse' in which Europeans talk about change and an African 'argument of images' in which change is expressed and facilitated. In short, in Africa the metaphorical and ritual language of religion, so far from reiterating changelessness, is the very form which change takes.

Finally, there has been an increased interest in African religious history because it has become obvious that African religion is still playing a dynamic role in many parts of contemporary Africa. One example of this was the crucial influence exerted by spirit mediums in the Zimbabwean guerrilla war of the 1970s. These men and women, believed to be the mediums for spirits of founding heroes, 'made history' in two ways. They mediated between peasants and guerrillas so as to produce a single ideology of resistance. And they creatively restated oral tradition and re-defined traditional history so as to integrate the guerrillas into the past as well as the present. In this case, then, African religious figures commanded history as process. Any historian of the Zimbabwean war has to take African religion into account whether he is a historian of religion or not.

What, then, can we begin to say about African religious history? We have to start off with a different model of African religion. For much of pre-colonial Africa we have to replace the idea of bounded tribal entities, each with its own 'religion', by a much more open and complex pattern. We have to think of broad regions of interaction between village-based agricultural peoples. Across these regions there flowed movements of hunters, and traders, and people in search of salt, and pilgrims to shrines. There were, therefore, many different levels of relationship between people. There were relationships with kin and neighbours but also relationships with other hunters and traders and pilgrims. There were relationships with the cultivated land, but also with the hunting bush and forests. African religious ideas were very much ideas about relationships, whether with other living people, or with the spirits of the dead, or with animals, or with cleared land, or with the bush. In many parts of Africa, though not invariably, all such relationships were thought of as relationships with spirits—spirits of ancestors, spirits of the land or the water or the bush, spirits of dead foreigners. The idiom of spirit was an idiom of personification, dramatising the personal rather than the merely metaphorical content of relationships. What Europeans have come to think of as absolutely impersonal phenomena—such as epidemic diseases—were also personified in African religious thought, and were represented by named spirits. All these spirits could manifest themselves by taking possession of living men or women.

These ideas—of relationship, spirit and possession—helped to make possible ordered interactions between people and helped to establish codes of conduct. Thus cults of the land enforced ecological rules—determining where and when fire could be used, when planting could begin, what crops should be grown. Cults of ancestors legitimated ideas of inheritance and laid down who could marry whom. Cults of alien or a-social spirits helped to establish rules of communication between traders and the communities through whom they passed. At the same time, the idea of relationships expressed through the idiom of spirits allowed for explanations of misfortune. Misfortunes were understood in terms of breach of relationships, either deliberate or inadvertent. Normality could be restored by determining to which spirit reparation was to be made.

So far this model has no doubt seemed a very functionalist one and, with its emphasis on rules, a very conservative one. But a number of points can at once be added. First, religious ideas were by no means restricted to personifying and policing relationships. There was speculation about the moral character of power; about the nature of personal identity; about what constituted 'good' and what 'evil'; about whether one could reasonably expect good fortune to be the norm or whether life was intrinsically ambivalent or even tragic. There was plenty of room for divinities as well as personifying spirits, and often the most important relationships were themselves thought of as involving divinities, so that some cults of the land addressed themselves to the spirit of a Creator God, as controller of rain and fertility. Second, the regions so far described, and the flows of people and ideas across them, were themselves the product of long historical processes and were constantly subject to change. The introduction of new crops, the rise of a trade in ivory, the emergence of strong polities which could exact tribute, and the development of new religious ideas and cults, could all significantly change the pattern. Thirdly, these systems of regional flows could not and did not produce a single, common, coherent religion, coexistent with 'society'. Each set of relationships involved different people at different levels and scales of interaction. So, recent historians of African religion have often talked about 'cults'—a territorial cult, concerned with relationships with the land; hunting guilds, concerned with relationships to other hunters and to wild animals; ancestral cults; so-called 'cults of affliction', bringing together strangers believed to be affected by the same spirit of disease and hence often emerging in zones of extensive trading. The geographical areas in which each of these cults operates vary greatly; so too does their personnel. Cults overlap each other and quite often compete with each other. Some esoteric cults initiate selected elders in a special, tragic or fatalistic understanding of the world, while the majority of people are engaged in less demanding and more optimistic rituals.

Hence there is great scope for innovation in this model. Contrary to Mbiti's propositions, there can be founders and prophets and converts. The presiding spirits of some territorial cults are remembered as having been in life historical prophetic figures, martyred by jealous rivals or arbitrary chiefs. A stranger could enter a region with a message about a hitherto unknown spirit of affliction or about a hitherto unknown means of eliminating the evil of witchcraft. New religious movements spread across whole regions with surprising regularity and rapidity. Often the founders or emissaries of such movements claimed a special authority given to them by God; they had died and returned to life with a special commission from God. Often this special commission was to restore old rules which had been broken, but even such conservative prophets could in effect produce change. Other prophets articulated new messages which called for change or legitimated it. In such a religious situation there was great dynamism rather than stasis; pluralism rather than a single, collective religion.

Of course, this open set of regional flows was often radically modified by the emergence of strong political units, whch sought to define their boundaries and to give a distinct identity to their subjects. This sometimes happened because of an unusual environment which gave special opportunity for co-ordinated exploitation, so that a ruler could advance claims to 'own' and control the land in a very particular way. In such a case, the rulers could take over a territorial cult completely, replacing the original presiding spirits, and turning it into a cult of dead kings. This happened, for instance, in the kingdom of Barotseland, on the flood plain of the Zambezi. Or the rulers could claim a special, privileged relationship with the territorial spirits, so that only they could be possessed by them or come to embody them, as happened in the kingdom of the Kuba in north-eastern Zaire, where a state-induced 'agricultural revolution' took place. Sometimes, on the other hand, a powerful kingdom emerged because its rulers could control the flow of trade, in which case territorial cults were much less significant to the state. Other polities depended on control of great cattle herds. Yet others depended on the development of a new military strength, either because of new techniques and weapons or new forms of social organisation. In such cases, cults of authoritarian militarism grew up.

In some cases, the ruling classes of African states became so powerful that they exerted control over most levels of religious association. Thus, the ancestral cult could become centralised so that at its apex were the spirits of dead kings; cults of initiation could be centralised so that young men and women were only inducted at the command and under the supervision of the king; trade flows could be so commanded by the state that cults of possession by alien spirits were set aside; new ideologies of military power could develop, bringing with them a prestige which made people strive to become identified solely as members of the state. All this could happen, though such a degree of control over all religious layers was

111

rarely achieved even by the most powerful state. But even where it did happen the result was not simply one all-dominant consensus religion. Recently, for example, students of the Asante state have been revising views of the nature and function of Asante religion.

Hitherto the myths and rituals of Asante religion had been seen as ensuring an absolute consensus and submission to the divinely ordained authority of the king of Asante. But recent studies have shown that precisely because state power made rebellion or political opposition almost impossible, dissent within the Asante state took the form of counter-myth and counter-ritual. The Asante state was one of the most powerful in Africa. Elsewhere, even strong states had to coexist with long-established regional cults whose zones of influence overlapped with that of the state. And throughout Bantu-speaking Central Africa, abuses of chiefly power were regularly countered by the rise of prophets, whose role was to expose the corruption of rulers and to restore a right political order.

This picture of the variety, scale and dynamism of African religion not only contrasts sharply with older models of static, small-scale 'tribal' religions, but also means that historians have had to change their ideas about what happened when African religion encountered mission Christianity and colonial capitalism. Hitherto it had been thought that small-scale and stable religions could not handle the challenge of large-scale rapid change. In some remote places African religion 'survived'; elsewhere, bits and pieces of it continued to operate. But essentially, it was thought, African religion had become archaic, incapable of change or growth and fated to decay. The historic religions, with their sense of the future, their gift of literacy, and—in the case of mission Christianity—their commitment to the values of capitalist enterprise, were manifestly bound to triumph in the modern period. Now that we know more about the pre-colonial vitality of African religion, however, we have to question this sort of interpretation.

In its place a very different picture has begun to emerge. To begin with, we are coming to understand that African religion responded to the crises of the nineteenth century with a variety of thoughtful innovations. Economic crises—the rise of the slave trade in East Africa and its collapse in West Africa; political crises—the collapse of many long-established states and the emergence of new polities led by military adventurers; ecological crises—the spread of human and animal epidemics; the increasing awareness that powerful outsiders were pressing in upon Africa: all these meant that 'intellectuals' within African religious systems endeavoured to develop new ideas and forms that made more sense and gave more control of the world. In some cases they developed the idea and role of the High God, whose 'macrocosmic' authority seemed appropriate to the greatly increasing scale of societal interaction. In other cases, though, cults of possession by minor spirits became more widespread and influential, as a means of linking people together over wide regions.

112

In many places there was a sense of an almost millenial moment so that there were attempts to cleanse society by means of movements of witchcraft eradication, with public confession and destruction of charms, whether protective or malevolent. Throughout East, Central and Southern Africa great prophets emerged whose names and pronouncements are still vividly remembered today. These prophets were bearers of truth from God and only incidentally predictors; their lives and sayings allowed African peoples to feel that colonial conquest and capitalist transformation were not inexplicably imposed from outside but were events taking place in an indigenous drama.

It seems clear that many nineteenth-century missionaries were received by African societies as part of this complex movement of reinterpretation. Some missionaries were received as witchcraft eradicators, to whom people flocked to throw their charms on bonfires; others are remembered to this day as prophets. Others were accepted as knowing important things about the High God, even if they were ignorant about other spirits and about witches. From this moment on it becomes almost impossible to write about any of the religions of Africa—African religion itself, Islam, mission Christianity, independent African Christianity—in isolation from each other. There has been great religious pluralism in twentieth-century Africa, but, as we have seen, there was much religious pluralism in pre-colonial Africa too.

It also seems clear that African religion has not turned out to be incompatible with 'modern' societies. Certainly, African religious leaders were often prominent in armed resistances against European invasion and conquest. But their relation to the colonial world was not merely one of conservative repudiation, with the result that African religion remained influential only in the most remote communities. Instead the twentieth century has seen the same ferment of religious speculation and innovation as the nineteenth. Some scholars have shown how African religion could adapt to people becoming peasants; others have shown how it could adapt to people becoming migrant labourers. Cults of affliction and witchcraft eradication movements have been as vital under colonialism as they were before it. African cults of chiefship have often been supported by colonial powers who supported chiefs in what was called Indirect Rule. And colonially-backed chiefs have often been denounced by prophets at the head of popular movements. So-called 'secret societies' have formed the basis for self-help associations of urban migrants.

The variety of forms of African religion have thus proved relevant to colonial Africa. So also has the underlying and fundamental realisation of African religion—that morality is a matter of relationships, and relationships not only with living persons. The rise of Western medicine has certainly not undercut this insight; nor has the rise of scientific agricultural expertise. Crises of health and crises of environment demand relational

113

rather than merely technological solutions. Moreover, the modes of communication of African religion—its argument of images—retain their power, enabling African rural communities to generate powerful metaphors for comprehending and operating within their world.

In conclusion, therefore, not only historians of religion but historians of social, cultural and economic change in Africa have come to realise that they must understand the idioms and history of African rural religion. So far from being set aside from, it has been intermixed with the main movements of twentieth-century change. African religion has turned out to be alive and important at the heart of revolutionary liberation movements. More than ever it needs to be understood historically and dynamically as well as experientially.

Further Reading

Binsbergen, W.M.J. van *Religious Change in Zambia. Exploratory Studies* (Routledge & Kegan Paul, London, 1981) (for an examination of twentieth-century African religious change by a historically conscious anthropologist)

Fernandez, J. *Bwiti: An Ethnography of the Religious Imagination in Africa* (Princeton University Press, New Jersey, 1982) (for an analysis of the argument of images in an innovatory African cult)

Lan, D. *Guns and Rain* (Heinemann Educational, London, 1985) (for an account of how spirit mediums made history during the Zimbabwean guerrilla war of the 1970s)

Mbiti, J.S. *African Religions and Philosophy* (Heinemann Educational, London, 1970) (for a non-historical account by an African theologian)

Parrinder, G. *Religion in Africa* (Penguin, Harmondsworth, 1969) (for a non-historical account by a distinguished comparative religionist)

Ranger, T.O. and Kimambo, I.N. (eds.), *The Historical Study of African Religion* (Heinemann Educational, London, 1972) (for a statement of the possibility and importance of a historical approach)

Ray, B.C. *African Religions. Symbol, Ritual and Community* (Prentice-Hall, New Jersey, 1976) (the most useful general introduction, which summarises the major anthropological works on African religion and is aware of the historical questions)

11 | North American Traditional Religion

G. Cooper

The majority of the original inhabitants of the North American continent migrated there from north-east Asia across the Bering Straits, over a time-span of perhaps 12,000 to 60,000 years ago. Arriving as hunters, the movement of peoples across North America (and further south into Central and South America) led to the development of numerous tribes, displaying a wide variety of languages and lifestyles. Most tribes continued to rely primarily on hunting and gathering, but in certain areas, notably the east and south-west, tribes became more sedentary as they learned to grow crops, mainly maize, squash and beans. The most densely populated areas in aboriginal America lay along the eastern and western seaboards, where food supplies were most plentiful.

Particular tribal religions thus result from a development of some thousands of years in varying ecological, economic and cultural conditions. Furthermore, systematic investigation into native American religions did not begin on any major scale until the end of the nineteenth century, when all tribes had been affected in some degree by white culture. Consequently it becomes almost impossible to make generalisations about North American native religions, for we are dealing with many different and distinct religions and not one homogenous system.

There are none the less certain common elements underlying North American indigenous religions. No tribe has a word for 'religion' as a separate sphere of existence. Religion permeates the whole of life, including economic activities, arts, crafts and ways of living. This is particularly true of nature, with which native Americans have traditionally a close and sacred relationship. Animals, birds, natural phenomena, even the land itself, have religious significance to native Americans: all are involved in a web of reciprocal relationships, which are sustained through behaviour and

115

ritual in a state of harmony. Distinctions between natural and supernatural are often difficult to make when assessing native American concepts.

Conceptions of time among native Americans are cyclical and concerned with reciprocal relationships, such that ritual becomes not mere re-enactment of mythic events, but rather the mythic event re-occurs in the present. Linked to this is the power of names and words: songs, prayers and myth-telling are viewed as spiritual forces which directly affect the world, giving it form and meaning and effecting changes.

Conceptions of the world derive from mythology. Hultkrantz has noted four major types of myth in North America. Firstly the cosmological myths, describing the cosmos, its origins and the interrelation-ships of its phenomena. This of course includes the Creation myths, of which there are a number of types. The most widespread is the Earth Diver, in which animals dive for mud in the primeval sea. Other major types are creation by world parents (the Father-Sky and Mother-Earth symbol being pervasive in North America), by Spider, from conflict between two beings, and the Emergence myth, which, strictly speaking, is more an account of human origins from worlds below the present one than a pure creation myth. Secondly there are institutional myths, which account for the existence of cultural and religious institutions. Thirdly there are ritual myths, which serve as 'texts' for ritual and ceremony and, finally, myths of entertainment or mythic tales, which are subject to elaboration and invention by the raconteur and are thus not of the same sacred character as other myths, but which, none the less, have important religious significance.

A distinction should be made between myth, which deals with the activities of deities and mythic beings in primordial times, and legend, where activities occur in historic times between humans and super-naturals. In North America, such a distinction is often difficult to make, since the two often merge. The Oglala Sioux account of the acquisition of the sacred pipe, for example, is, strictly speaking, a legend, but has the same sanctioning power as myth. A major function of mythology is to highlight the correct relationships between the phenomena of the world, thus provid-ing not only sanction and explanation, but also moral and educational guidance. A greater elaboration and precision in myth and a closer correlation of myth with ritual is to be found among the horticulturalists, notably in the south-western USA. This closer relationship of myth and ritual allows not only greater precision of myth, but also of cosmology. In the horticultural societies, there is a more clearly defined three-layered world of heaven-earth-underworld than generally occurs among the hunting peoples, whose concepts of the underworld are vaguer. In the south-west, many more worlds are described, since here the myth of Emergence from previous worlds predominates. The concept of the world tree or pole is wide-spread, as are symbols of the cross, representing the four directions, and the circle.

Some variation is to be found in the notion of a Supreme Being. Despite a conviction by many early Western scholars that such a conception did not exist in North America, it has been clear for some time that this was erroneous. One reason for the confusion may well be that the Supreme Being is often only vaguely outlined and plays little role in immediate religious concerns. As such, the Supreme Being exists as a *deus otiosus*, remote from everyday affairs. This is not to suggest that conceptions of the Supreme Being necessarily lack sophistication. The Supreme Being of the Oglala Sioux, for example, involves aspects of transcendence and immanence of great subtlety. None the less, the Supreme Being usually remains remote, being prayed to at times of particular criticality, and other sacred beings play more prominent roles in everyday religious activity; in cultic activity the Supreme Being generally has an inconspicuous role. Even in mythology the Supreme Being does not, with the exception of certain cosmogonic myths, play a major role. The most prominent role in native American mythology generally is filled by the Trickster-transformer-culture-hero.

This latter figure reflects a widespread native American interest in the process whereby the world has been fashioned into its present nature, rather than in the original creation. The Trickster-transformer-culture-hero is a mythological character combining three different roles in one and is to be found throughout North America in different guises, being Coyote in the Plains, Basin, south-west and California areas, Raven or Mink on the north-west coast, Hare in the south-east and Bluejay in the Plateau area. Among hunting peoples, he tends to display the full range of roles—Trickster, a prankster or fool, whose activities provide the source for numerous and widespread 'Trickster tales'; Transformer, whose activities transformed the basic 'stuff' of the world into the present condition; and Culture-Hero, who, through daring adventures, provided numerous benefits (fire, water, daylight etc.) and cultural skills and customs to human beings, rendering the earth safe for human habitation. Among tribes where agriculture is prominent, it is often the Trickster elements alone that are found, cultural benefits being due to other beings. The 'Trickster tales', found throughout North America, provide one of the most entertaining series of myths and are extremely popular. Even though such myths can be considered as entertainment tales, being subject to elaboration and invention and therefore not having the same sanctioning power as other myths, which are sacred and hence unalterable, these tales none the less have important instructive and explanatory purposes and have significant religious value.

There are other mythological beings of importance, although many are regionally specific. Among the more widespread are the Thunderbird, which produces thunder and lightning, and the Hero Twins, culture-heroes who, in some areas, are associated with warfare.

Without doing injustice to native American concepts, it is possible to make a distinction between the sacred beings of myth and those of everyday life. There are exceptions such as the Thunderbird, which attracts significant cultic attention on the Plains, but generally mythological beings, whilst providing sanction for the cosmos and affecting the nature of the world, are often not so prominent in everyday religious concerns. Here we find, especially among the hunting peoples, where the close correlation between myth and ritual found among agriculturalists is lacking, that other sacred beings figure more prominently. Chief among these is the Master or Mistress of Animals, the divine leader and protector of game. He or she exercises stewardship over wild animals, especially those hunted by humans, and ensures that correct ritual is carried out by humans when hunting and burying the bones of animals. The Master or Mistress of Animals varies in character. Among the Eskimo, there is a female deity, Sedna, who controls sea animals from a home beneath the sea and, at times of game shortage, must be placated by a shaman, who makes a trance journey to her home. Elsewhere there may be a guardian animal for each of a number of species, often in hierarchical order, or there may be one for all species, as, for example, buffalo on the Plains. Among the Kwakiutl of the north-west coast, there are two guardians, one for land and one for sea, representing a wider cosmic dualism. In some hunting societies, the Master/Mistress of Animals can virtually be identified with the Supreme Being, reflecting the importance of game in hunting societies.

The seeking of a personal relationship with the sacred through vision is one of the most distinguishing features of many tribes. Deliberate 'vision quests' occurred throughout much of North America, typically involving a period of purification and prayer, followed by seclusion in a remote place for a period of days, during which time the supplicant fasts and prays until a vision is attained. Among the Eastern Woodlands and Prairie tribes, boys were expected to undertake the quest at puberty and acquire a guardian spirit, usually in animal form, which would lend supernatural power, usually throughout the individual's life. Among the Plains tribes such activity was observed by men, who regarded the vision quest as a means of gaining and renewing spiritual power. Visions were also associated with mourning, supplication, success in hunting and warfare and in curing. On the north-west coast, the vision became more a form of spirit possession, occurring during the winter ceremonial initiation rites. Unsought or spontaneous visions were generally regarded as more powerful than sought visions, but occurred more rarely and were the prerogative of the few, generally those who became shamans.

The acquisition of a guardian spirit was a practice found in all areas of North America, except the south-west. The most common way of acquiring one was through vision, but in some areas it was possible to inherit or purchase a guardian spirit, although the spirit involved had to agree to the transfer. Taken as a whole, the nature of guardian spirits seems limitless, varying from mythic beings to demons, the weather, even kettles, although by far the most common were animals and birds, occasionally appearing in anthropomorphic guise. Usually different spirits had different degrees of power or possessed different kinds of specialised power. Through the acquisition of a guardian spirit, an individual gained access to power, the nature of such power varying with the spirit, such as to lend either general power, giving aid in hunting or warfare, or a more specific, perhaps greater, power, such as the ability to cure illness or to prophesy. The relationship to the spirit was sustained through following instructions given by the spirit, including the use of certain songs and prayers, the observation of various taboos and the preparation of a 'medicine bundle', containing objects relating to the particular spirit. Spirits could be demanding and argumentative and the strong relationship between an individual and the guardian spirit in some cases amounted almost to a personal religion. On the Plains, individuals having the same guardian spirit formed societies, occasionally engaging in competitive demonstrations of power.

Individuals acquiring a guardian spirit which gave the power of curing generally formed a distinct group. Those who acquired this power through an unsought vision were regarded as particularly powerful and usually became shamans—those who entered trance to perform a variety of tasks, of which curing was the most important. True shamans and shamanism proper were to be found in the Arctic and north-west coast areas, although shamanism demonstrates its influence throughout the continent and many individuals displayed power derived from visionary experience who cannot be termed shamans in the strict sense. Unfortunately, the wide variety of individuals and activities centred around curing and the lack of an adequate morphology of such specialists means that they can only be referred to by the imprecise term 'medicine-men'. They can, nevertheless, be clearly distinguished from the more priestly figures, found in the south-west among the Navajo and Pueblo tribes, whose power is derived from the learning of traditional rites, rather than personal contacts with spirits.

Disease concepts traditionally rested on notions of soul-loss, taboo-violation or witchcraft, the latter two often resulting in the idea of object-intrusion—the lodging of an object in the patient's body. Curing rituals thus involved soul-retrieval, characteristic of shamanism, or object-extraction, all requiring the assistance of spirits to lend power. In the Eastern Woodlands and Plains there developed a curing ritual referred to as the 'Spirit Lodge' or 'Shaking Tent', in which a bound medicine-man attracted spirits to a darkened lodge or tepee to effect his release and cure the sick. Underlying all curing rituals is the basic notion of restoration of harmony.

One other sacred specialist deserves mention—the sacred clown. Found predominantly in the Plains, south-west, California and north-west coast areas, the clown displayed varying regional characteristics. In the Plains, he observed backward or contrary behaviour; among the Sioux this resulted from a vision of the Thunderbird. In the south-west, among the Pueblos, clown groups engaged in sexual, social and ceremonial satire. Although such behaviour occasionally appeared to have more entertainment than religious value, the clown was regarded as being a particularly powerful and sacred figure, displaying links with fertility as well as having psycho-social functions.

Women's participation in religious affairs was generally more limited. In some tribes women attained visions, although this was not common, and whilst medicine-women could be found, especially in Oregon and California, as a whole they were not as numerous as men. Child-bearing and rearing was considered their primary role. The ability to bear children gave women a singular power of their own, which, particularly among the hunters, was considered antithetical to power wielded by men. Female power was manifested most obviously in menstruation and women were normally isolated during this time for fear of 'polluting' sacred objects and ritual activity. Among the Athapascans especially, the girl's first menses was marked by an important puberty ceremony.

Ritual and ceremonial life demonstrates great richness and diversity. A brief summary of selected tribes in different areas must necessarily suffice to give some indication of this richness.

The Ojibwa of the north-east lived by hunting, fishing and gathering in a relatively harsh environment. In common with other hunting tribes in many parts of North America, individual rites predominated, centring round visions, attention to dreams and the acquisition of guardian spirits, termed *manitos*, which inhabited trees, rocks, birds, animals and other natural phenomena. Most rites involved the use of tobacco, regarded as a sacred plant. The largest ceremony was the *Midewiwin* (literally 'mystic doings'), a society of medicine-men which held an annual ceremony for the purposes of initiating new members and curing illness. Initiates, on payment of the requisite fees, could progress through a number of initiatory levels. The ceremony culminated in a public performance in a specially constructed medicine-lodge, in which the initiates were shot with *migis* (small white clam shells), which drove out sickness and renewed life.

On the Plains, the Oglala Sioux, whose traditional culture as we know it developed with the introduction of the horse in the early eighteenth century, likewise derived their living from hunting, predominantly buffalo, and here again individual rites predominated. Seven rituals associated with the use of the sacred pipe, originally given to the Sioux by the sacred White Buffalo Calf Woman, constituted the bulk of Sioux rituals. Whilst they included individual rituals, such as the purificatory Sweat Lodge and the Vision Quest, one in particular—the Sun Dance—was a major communal ceremony. This ceremony was held annually during the summer and involved the construction of a special lodge, at the centre of which was raised a cottonwood tree, representing the world pillar. The ceremony took place over four days and provided an opportunity for individual sacrifice as well as renewal of the relationship of the whole tribe to the sacred, being in essence a world-renewal ceremony.

Some of the richest, most dramatic ceremonialism occurred on the north-west coast, where stable and plentiful food supplies and sedentary living patterns in villages on the beaches allowed the development of rich material and ceremonial cultures. Among the Kwakiutl tribe, clans traced their ancestry to mythical animals who, in primordial times, became humans and founded the different lineages. There was a strong emphasis on status and rank and, through inherited rights, individuals were initiated into religious societies during a long winter ceremonial period. Pre-eminent among these societies was the *hamatsa* cult, relating to the great deity *Baxbakualanuxsiwae* (Great Man-eater). Initiation involved seclusion in the woods, spirit possession and public ritual with the appearance of dancers wearing elaborate masks and costumes and representing supernatural beings. The potlatch ceremony was a ceremonial distribution of wealth, related to rank and, like all Kwakiutl ceremonialism, reflected underlying motifs of transformation, death and rebirth.

Agricultural ceremonialism was found in some form wherever crops were grown. The most prominent forms occurred among the Pueblos of the south-west, particularly the Hopi of Arizona. Relying on scanty rainfall for the growing of maize and other crops, Hopi ceremonialism is linked to both myth and the agricultural cycle. Social, political and ceremonial organisation was traditionally interlinked and a number of different religious societies perform ceremonies at particular times of the year from November (the start of the New Year) onwards. Involving secret rituals in ceremonial chambers, called *kivas*, and with public dances on the concluding days, ceremonies incorporate rituals of recreation, initiation and the attraction of *kachinas*—spirits who bring rain and other blessings to the tribe. Masked dancers appear as *kachinas* in both private and public rituals. Other Pueblo groups to the east, whilst stressing fertility, show stronger emphasis on curing ceremonies, carried out by organisations of medicine-men. Although these practices show clear shamanic influences, Pueblo religious specialists rely solely on learned traditions as the basis of their power and not on visionary experience.

The Navajo, pastoralist neighbours of the Pueblos, likewise rely on the learning of word-perfect ritual as the basis of their ceremonialism. Arriving in the south-west around 1500 CE as small hunting bands, this tribe provides a good example of a people who have adopted more elaborate religious conceptions and practices (in this case from the Pueblos) and, in so doing, have developed basic shamanic curing rituals into complex and lengthy ceremonials for the curing of illness, which constitute virtually the whole of Navajo ceremonial practice. During these ceremonials, some of which last nine days and nights, the patient is identified with holy people through prayer, song and the use of dry-paintings or sand-paintings, which depict mythic events associated with the particular ceremonial; in fact each ceremonial is a reoccurrence of a myth, the patient being identified with the hero and original patient, who, through exorcising of evil and identification with holy people, is restored to a state of harmony.

These brief examples can only suggest the richness and diversity of native American ceremonial life, which tends to be almost exclusively concerned with this life. Native American religious life generally displays little concern with eschatology. The afterlife was commonly seen as a happier continuation of this life, behaviour in this life having little effect on one's fate after death. In all of North America, bar the south-west, the belief occurs in one form or another that human beings are equipped with two kinds of soul: a bodily soul, granting life and movement and consciousness to the body, and a dream or free soul, identical to the person, which can leave the body and visit far-away places, including the land of the dead. This free soul can be directed at will by shamans and indeed the general belief can be traced to the pervasive influence of shamanism. The dead, with few exceptions, were feared in varying degrees and it was considered important to maintain a clear separation between living and dead.

The traditional religious life of the native Americans is the result of development over many thousands of years. Even before the arrival of the Europeans, ecological, economic and cultural factors meant that native American religions have never been static systems of belief and practice. However, the incoming Europeans had a radically different and more overwhelming influence on traditional cultures. Policies towards the native Americans varied, but the net result was the introduction of diseases and military conquest, which killed millions and led to the extinction of numerous tribes, the taking of land and the suppression of traditional culture and religion. The loss of land and traditional lifestyles has affected different tribes in different ways. Little remains of traditional religious culture in some areas, whereas other areas (for example in the south-west, where the desert land was of little interest to whites) retain strong traditional religions.

The south-west was the initial area of penetration by Europeans into North America when the Spaniards arrived in the sixteenth century and proceeded to impose political and religious domination on the Pueblos. Despite nominal conversion to Catholicism, traditional ceremonialism survived virtually intact and today the two systems of belief coexist with relatively little friction. Elsewhere, missionary activity, coupled with the banning of traditional ritual in the 1880s, has led to the nominal conversion of most native Americans to Christianity. I say nominal because it is in fact often impossible to make clear distinctions between Christians and traditionalists. Whilst there are strict adherents to both of these belief systems, they are not necessarily mutually exclusive, many native Americans fluctuating between the two, depending on circumstances. Of overriding importance is their sense of identity as, firstly, members of a particular tribe and, secondly, as native Americans.

In this regard, two religious responses by native Americans to encroaching white culture and religion are of importance. The first is the Ghost Dance movement of the late nineteenth century, which originated with the Piaute prophet, Wovoka, who beheld God in a vision. He was told that the old life would return and the dead come back to life, provided that the Indians regularly performed dances. This millenarian movement, combining Christian and indigenous elements, swept across the Great Basin and Plains areas in 1889–90, assuming a distinctly anti-white tendency among the more warlike tribes, particularly the Sioux, who introduced 'Ghost Dance shirts', said to offer protection against bullets. The movement culminated in military action against the Sioux, ending with the murder of Chief Sitting Bull and the massacre of a large band of Sioux at Wounded Knee in 1890. With this defeat and the failure of the millenium to materialise, the movem. died away. It was, none the less, a significant attempt to posit a positi future for peoples whose ways of life were being destroyed.

A more successful syncretic response is the Peyote Cult. The ritual taking of peyote, an hallucinogenic cactus, developed in Mexico and spread northwards into the Plains during the latter part of the nineteenth century. It is now firmly established in a number of tribes and, although its spread was vigorously opposed by both Christians and traditionalists, it clearly provides a means of gaining power for the dispirited and, by combining Christian (the use of the Bible, Christian prayers and ethics) and traditional (singing, drumming, visions and the incorporation of indigenous spirits) elements, it provides a new ritual form which is distinctly Indian, but which allows accommodation to a changing world.

It has often been assumed that, with the overwhelming influence of white culture and the corresponding destruction of traditional native American ways of life, that the traditional religions have become virtually extinct. This is an inadequate and erroneous conception. Whilst traditions often display outward signs of collapse, native American religions have always been dynamic, incorporating historical changes and disruptive elements within them. The effects of white culture have been especially dramatic and severe, but the persistence and survival of the basic identity of so many Indian tribes is a testament to their ability to withstand change and adapt new situations to the essential characteristics of their own traditions.

Currently, therefore, native American societies display a variety of religious beliefs and practices, ranging from the purely traditional, through syncretic forms such as peyotism, to Christianity. One important recent factor has been the rise of what has been termed 'red power', reflecting a widespread determination by native Americans to pursue more forcibly such issues as land rights and sovereignty, guided by an increased concern with arresting the erosion of their traditional cultures and religions. This is resulting in much resurgence and revitalisation of traditional religions. These religions are thus by no means extinct, indeed they continue to give strength and meaning to native Americans and offer scholars of religion a rich source of revealing and significant insights into the religious life of human beings.

Further Reading

Beck, P. and Walters, A. (eds.) *The Sacred* (Navajo Community College, Tsaile, 1977)

Brown, J.E. *The Sacred Pipe* (University of Oklahoma Press, Norman, 1953)

Cooper, G.H. *Development and Stress in Navajo Religion* (Almqvist and Wiksell, Stockholm, 1984)

Feraca, S.E. *Wakinyan: Contemporary Teton Dakota Religion* (Museum of the Plains Indian, Browning, 1963)

Gill, S.D. *Songs of Life: an Introduction to Navajo Religious Culture* (E.J. Brill, Leiden, 1979)

—— *Native American Religions: an Introduction* (Wadsworth, Belmont, 1982)

Goldman, I. *The Mouth of Heaven: an Introduction to Kwakiutl Religious Thought* (Wiley, New York, 1975)

Hultkrantz, A. 'Spirit Lodge, a North American Shamanistic Seance' in C-M. Edsman (ed.), *Studies in Shamanism* (Almqvist and Wiksell, Stockholm, 1967), pp. 32–68

—— *The Religions of the American Indians* (University of California Press, Berkeley, 1979)

—— 'Myths in Native American Religions' in E.H. Waugh and K.D. Prithipaul (eds.), *Native Religious Traditions* (Wilfred Laurier University Press, Waterloo, 1979), pp. 77–97

LaBarre, W. 'The Peyote Cult', *Yale University Publications in Anthropology* (Yale University Press, New Haven, 1938), vol. 19

Landes, R. *Ojibwa Religion and the Midewiwin* (University of Wisconsin Press, Madison, 1968)

MacNeish, R.F. *Early Man in America* (W.H. Freeman, Oxford, 1973)

Mooney, J. *The Ghost Dance and the Sioux Outbreak of 1890* (University of Chicago, Chicago, 1965; originally pub. 1896)

Slotkin, J.S. *The Peyote Religion: a Study in Indian–White Relations* (Free Press, Glencoe, 1956)

Waters, F. *Book of the Hopi* (Viking, New York, 1963)

12 | *Latin American Traditional Religion:* Three Orders of Service

Gordon Brotherston

In the native New World, as anywhere else, religion responds to geography, economics and language, phenomena which over that continent prove to be extremely varied. Yet underlying a diversity of local cults and practices, certain doctrines or 'orders of service', proper in the first instance to religion, may be discerned as nothing less than paradigmatic. A clear case is the trance journey, typified by a visit to the nether world: prevalent in cosmogony throughout North America, including Mexico and parts of Central America, this other-worldly quest has been widely instituted as a principle of religious initiation in such traditional priesthoods as that of the Midewiwin, on the uppermost Mississippi. Noting the tests, rhythms and astronomical correlatives of the trance journey takes us into what may be considered a true shamanist substratum of the whole northern sub-continent, comparable with that analysed by Mircea Eliade, and by Ake Hultkranz in his study of the North American Orpheus motif.

Other such paradigms appear rather to confine themselves to cultural areas already established in scholarship, and indeed stand as a privileged diagnostic of those areas. Examples come from greater Mexico or Mesoamerica, and from South America. In the teeming pantheons of the former, an area which owes its very definition to the existence of pre-Columbian scripts, iconographic and hieroglyphic, as well as screenfold books of paper and parchment that deal pre-eminently with religion, we find a remarkable triple pattern which holds good over great distances and time-depths and which corresponds intimately with the particular agricultural and urban development of the area. Further south, we find rather a monotheistic emphasis, in the cult of Viracocha, the chief deity of the vast empire of the Inca known as Tahuantinsuyu or 'Four Districts' in Quechua: stretching

125

down the Andes from present-day Colombia to Chile, this area forms a highly distinct world within South America. This is due not least to the pastoral economy unique to it in America and hallowed by Viracocha, which in its own way transformed the myriad cults, beliefs and myths of the surrounding lowlands that have provided the main focus for the four monumental volumes of Lévi-Strauss's *Mythologiques.*

In considering these three cases, we may appeal to a wide range of evidence not least from the disciplines of archaeology, anthropology and history. Here the guiding principle has been above all literary: throughout the emphasis is on native texts, that is, on statements made by native Americans themselves and where possible recorded in their language and by their means and media. In sheer technical terms, such an approach has been facilitated by the growing scholarly attention to the whole issue of script and visual language in the New World, from the scrolls of the Midewiwin, through the great bibliographical heartland of Mesoamerica, to the *quipu* or knotted-string records of the Inca. Acknowledging these original sources helps to validate the deeper coherences of native American religion, as these are evinced for example in a comparison between the pages of a pre-Columbian screenfold book and sand-paintings used in Navajo ceremonial today. It also helps to make up for some of the grosser distortions of the past, which arose in the main from Christianity's perceived need to justify, in religious terms, the invasion and expropriation of native America that began with Columbus.

The Shaman's Trance Journey

A striking introduction to all that concerns the trance journey is provided by the Ottawa-Algonkin shaman Chusco (Muskrat). Born a few years after Pontiac's rising in the early 1760s, Chusco bargained with General Wayne at Greenville (1793); he was prominent in the Midewiwin but his wife's involvement with the Christian mission at Mackinac led to his apostasy in the last ten years of his life (1828–38), during which time he divulged Mide secrets to Henry Rowe Schoolcraft. In this way he came to contribute to the one-verse epic of Indian America in English, Longfellow's *Hiawatha* (i.e. Manabozho), a work which draws heavily on Schoolcraft.

In Schoolcraft's *Algic Researches* (1839), Chusco's narrative bears the title 'Iosco or a visit to the sun and moon: a tale of Indian cosmogony, from the Ottawa'. The opening incorporates tales told by Indians who by one means or another had visited the Old World: travelling east, Iosco and five companions first cross the sea and end up in a gilded European capital. Still determined to encounter the sun and the true source of life, the six press on with their journey, and only from this point does the cosmogony proper begin. Changing entirely, the landscape becomes subterranean, and after three days which 'were really three years' the six meet the rattle-wielding Manabozho. In conversation he offers them guidance and notes that on arriving they had passed over three-fourths of their way and that they are to spend the remaining time with him, a day which also is really a year, making four in all. Before setting off again, in twos, each of the three pairs makes a wish about how long they should live, with the result that only the humblest pair, Iosco and his companion, succeed in crossing a chasm that then opens before them.

On the other side these two meet the moon, a woman in white 'approaching as from behind a hill'. She tells them that they are now half-way to her brother's (the sun) and that from the earth to her abode was half the distance; and she promises in due time to lead them to her brother then absent on his 'daily course'. In this half-way position they stay with her until the 'proper time' arrives to meet the sun. The story goes on:

> When the proper time arrived, she said to them, 'My brother is now rising from below, and we shall see his light as he comes over the distant edge: 'come,' said she, 'I will lead you up.' They went forward, but in some mysterious way, they hardly knew how, they rose almost directly up, as if they had ascended steps.

At a point 'half-way' between the edge of the earth and 'midday', Iosco then converses directly with the sun, being in effect blessed by him. Then, having reached the point of plenitude, the 'Heart of Heaven' or midday, they set off down again, making the last half of the descent 'as if they had been let down by ropes'.

With its references to Europe and the Old World, Iosco's solar quest was no doubt Chusco's own, and reflects the struggle he felt in himself between Mide and Christian teaching. In any case, the tale lives up to its cosmogonical epithet; it leads us up from the lower to the upper paths of the solar walk. For in time and space Iosco follows the apparent course of the sun and moon; and the 4+4 day-years he spends between west and east evoke the four-year leap day span of the sun, each year acquiring the quarter-day later defined between east and west; and they evoke as well the utas and the eight-year octaeteris over which the yearly sun and the moon again get back in step with one another (8 years equal 99 moons). As for Manabozho, the third figure in the story encountered prior to the moon in the underworld, he has been equated with the Nanabush of the Lenape *Walam Olum* and the great Hare or Rabbit Michabo. Just this identity is widely attributed to the Morning Star Venus in North America, among the Sioux, where as a hunter he steps over the eastern horizon before the sun (by rising heliacally), and in Mexico, where the sign for Venus is equivalent ritually to the sign Rabbit. Along the solar walk of the northern Blackfeet Algonkin, the Morning Star, together with his parents sun and moon, makes up the 'big three', the trio of the brightest bodies in the sky; and it is the case astronomically that the octaeteris experienced by Iosco includes Venus (over 5 synodic periods) just as much as the moon and sun, a point developed below.

127

The moral concerns implicit in Iosco's quest were anticipated in a famous story recounted by Pontiac, likewise an Ottawa and a Mide shaman, as well of course as the great military opponent of the English. Faced with the task of closely uniting his diverse forces he described a pilgrimage similar to Iosco's, undertaken by a member of the 'grandfather' tribe of the Algonkin nations and the Huron alike, a Lenape (Delaware) of the Wolf clan. The only record that survives of Pontiac's words stems from the inimical pen of Robert Navarre who, witnessing the narrative, deplores it as 'the principal of the blackest of crimes against the English nation, (i.e. Pontiac's rising) and perhaps against the French, had not God in his grace ordered it otherwise'. Despite Navarre's hostility as interpreter, the outline of the narrative comes through clearly and suggests the same paradigm of native religion and cosmogony. It is also perhaps significant that the day chosen by Pontiac to relate it, 27 April 1763, was reported as the fifteenth of the moon, i.e. full moon.

Anxious to know the 'Master of life', the Lenape sets out on his journey, making much the same preparations as Iosco does. Overall this again lasts eight 'days', and it leads to a choice between three paths that grow strangely luminous in the twilight of the eighth day. This motif conjoins the two lots of three paths evoked in Iosco: those of the bright trio on the solar walk (sun, moon, Venus), and those chosen respectively by the three pairs of travellers, only one of which led to midday in the sky (that of the sun). This reading is strengthened by the fact that again only one path, the third, takes the Lenape hero the whole way through the day; the other two go only 'half-way' and issue into a large fire 'coming from underground', which is where Iosco encounters Venus and the moon and where the unsuccessful pairs of his companions go no further. Having travelled the right path, the Lenape is shown the way to his goal by the moon, who likewise appears on a mountain as a white woman.

Several details in Pontiac's narrative, notably the instructions given to the Lenape by the Master of life, are quite possibly Christian in origin and were perhaps inserted to win over the evangelised Huron and even the French to his cause. Yet there can be little doubt about its adherence to the solar-walk paradigm of Chusco's story, and hence about its indigenous spirituality.

In literary-historical terms Chusco's and Pontiac's narratives are best understood as products of the Midewiwin, the predominantly Algonkin priesthood that had and has its heartland in Ojibway territory at the sources of the Mississippi, the Great Lakes and Hudson Bay. For they both invoke doctrines basic to that body, notably those relating to the hunt and to the initiation of novices by degrees, which feature Manabozho as guide, intermediary and instructor of the Mide, the moon and its phases, and the quest for life's sources in the noon sun. Mide charts on birchbark graphically record the novice's path through a series of degrees which like the 'days' of the solar walk conform to an ideal total of 4 (+4), while certain chronological symbols specify fast and feast periods each of four actual days. More graphically still, symbols recording antiphonal verses intoned during initiation, which also normally fall into stanzas of four, depict both the physical course of the solar walk which the candidate aspires to make and the celestial travellers along it, sun, moon and Venus.

Hence pictographic texts copied and interpreted by Sikassige, Little Frenchman, Kweweshiash and other Mide shamans begin with the entry into the Mide lodge, the collecting of fees, and preparatory activities like taking a sweat bath and digging down into the earth for 'medicine' with which to enhance perception for the journey itself. This may start 'below' and follow the course, for example, of the otter sacred to Manabozho, or the beaver renowned for his capacity to travel great distances before resurfacing. Or it can be celestial: the candidate rises up on and into the arch of the sky by steps or like a bird and there encounters the Great Spirit (Gitche Manito) depicted as the sun. To a figure mounting the celestial arch from the east like 'the sun pursuing his diurnal course till noon', and like Iosco and the Lenape traveller, correspond the words: 'I walk upon half the sky'; similarly the moment of plenitude at noon or midday is registered by a figure atop the arch, to which Sikassige puts the words: 'The spirit has given me power to see'. (See Figure 12.1a, b.)

Figure 12.1: Mide Symbols for the Solar Walk

(a) half arch to noon   (b) whole arch   (c) above and below

The lower and upper courses of the solar walk are epitomised as such at their 'half-way' moments, in paired or double-headed symbols: arms 'taking life' from down in the earth or up in the sky; trees with foliage at crown and root and that walk; upright and inverted heads which rotate through the walk and to which attach the words: 'I come up from below, I come down from above—I see the spirit, I see beavers' (Figure 12.1c). In a single-stanza song 'for beaver hunting and the Metai Mide' collected by Tanner, the down-up opposition occurs in the first and last symbols, a subterranean lodge and a flying eagle. This text is also notable for the chronology encoded in its second symbol, which depicts the four 'day-years' familiar from Chusco and Pontiac. Referring to marks drawn on a fasting figure, on chest (2) and legs (4), come the words: 'Two days must you sit fast, my friend; four days must you sit fast'. 'Binding' the legs the four lines mean actually sitting fast for four days but as far as the candidate's inner devotion goes Tanner's informant assured him that they are understood simultaneously to mean four years.

A definite link between these Mide texts and the extended alphabetic narratives of Chusco and Pontiac is provided by Catherine Wabose, an apostate like Chusco, who described her first solar walk both verbally and in a pictographic Mide chart. Prepared by a ritual fast of four days, she sets off on a mysterious path stretching down between the setting sun and the new moon at the western horizon; having passed figures equivalent to the full moon and Venus (see Figure 12.2b, d), she rises to the heart of the sky, the climax of the vision, before again descending, on a snake. The importance of the moon's phases is clear from Wabose's and one of Little Frenchman's symbols (see Figure 12.2c) while moon and Venus, in the posture of the guide Manabozho, are similarly conjoined in single stanza of

Figure 12.2: Mide Symbols for the Three Travellers

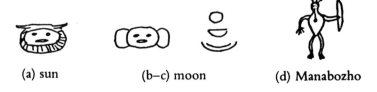

(a) sun (b–c) moon (d) Manabozho

hunter's pictographs also recorded by Schoolcraft. The accompanying words read:

> I am rising (like the sun)
> I take the sky, I take the earth (at the horizon)
> I walk through the sky (like the moon)
> Venus guides me.

As Sioux living on the southern border of the Mide heartland, the Winnebago offer insights of their own into the meaning and function of the solar-walk paradigm. For though he scarcely comments on the fact, it has paramount importance in Winnebago funeral rituals meticulously recorded early in this century by Paul Radin, a friend and collaborator of C.G. Jung. Here, the solar walk is unequivocally revealed as the route to true life followed not just by the initiate shaman but by the soul after death.

Instructed by a great-grandmother figure, the Winnebago soul sets off on a path that takes him past the underworld fire of the Lucifer-like Herucgunina, leads him step by step over the eastern horizon, and brings him up to the circle of his relatives in the heart of the sky. He (or she) is told:

> My grandchild, Earthmaker is waiting for you in great expectation. There is the door to the setting sun. On your way stands the lodge of Herecgunina, and his fire.

Those who have come [the souls of brave men] from the land of the souls to take you back will touch you. There the road will branch off towards your right and you will see the footprints of the day on the blue sky before you. These footprints represent the footprints of those who have passed into life again. Step into the places where they have stepped and plant your feet into their footprints, but be careful you do not miss any. Before you have gone very far, you will come into a forest broken by open prairies here and there. Here, in this beautiful country, these souls whose duty it is to gather other souls will come to meet you. Walking on each side of you they will take you safely home. As you enter the lodge of the Earthmaker you must hand to him the sacrificial offerings. Here the inquiry that took place in the first lodge will be repeated and answered in the same manner. Then he will say to you, 'All that your grandmother had told you is true. Your relatives are waiting for you in great expectation. Your home is waiting for you. Its door will be facing the mid-day sun. Here you will find your relatives gathered.

Texts such as this bring together the Mide tradition (compare the 'footsteps' with Iosco's) with the Plains Ghost Dance of the 1890s, in which Sioux and Algonkin alike re-enacted the circular dance of their relatives in the heart of the sky.

Besides this, the Winnebago ritual observed by Radin touches on the matter of the 4+4 day-years experienced by Iosco and other travellers along the solar walk. For the Winnebago wake lasts four days, during which period the mourners concentrate on helping the soul on his way beyond death, until he has passed the critical half-way encounter with Herucgunina. Indeed, what the mourners say and do, whether or not they exaggerate or lie about their own capacity to help, directly affects the soul's passage. For his or her part, the traveller enters another type of time, the 'ancient' time of the spirits, in which the true period of mourning is said to be not four days but four years. Similarly, sacrificial victims among the Aztecs contemplated a journey to the underworld with the words: 'over four years we shall be carried on the wind'. In other words, as in Tanner's fasting symbol, it is a question of two dimensions of time, earthly and spirit, days and years, which run concurrently, correlated by means of an astonomically significant cipher. (For the shamans not far north of the northern Algonkin a day *is* a year.)

Geographically, the solar-walk paradigm may be understood as part of a larger tradition of native American ritual and chronology whose coherence is especially marked in the northern half of the continent, extending from the Atlantic coast and the south-east, across the Plains to the south-west and Mexico. For in Mexico and Mesoamerica, the walk is clearly mapped out in native script, hieroglyphic and iconographic, in the screenfold books of ritual. On the *mappa mundi* pages of the Fejervary and Laud screenfolds, for example, it may be traced through the cardinal stations of native astronomy in the tropics, the east and west horizons, with zenith and nadir each half-way between; such is the case too with the Venus tables in the hieroglyphic Dresden screenfold. For this is the route followed by the

culture-heroes of Mesoamerican cosmogonies implicit on those pages and
written out alphabetically in such works as the Nahua 'Cuauhtitlan Annals'
and 'Legend of the Suns', the Quiche-Maya *Popul vuh*, and the lowland Maya
Books of Chilam Balam. True to the astronomical analogue, these travellers
pass through the underworld (Mictlan, Xibalba), rise again at the eastern
horizon, and reach the moment of plenitude in the heart of the sky.

In the 'Legend of the Suns' the 'feathered serpent'
Quetzalcoatl descends to Mictlan to acquire the bones from which to make
woman and man; on his way back up east, this Venus-figure faces a strange
hazard, one astoundingly reminiscent of that faced at the same astronomical
position by the Morning Star of the Blackfeet Algonkin: he is set upon and
pecked at by birds. In the *Popul vuh*, whose underworld 'test-theme' has
been fruitfully compared with that in the cosmogonies of the south-west, the
hero Twins descend to Xibalba to avenge their father who had been mur-
dered there and got no further than this half-way station; they themselves
pass through and like their Mide counterparts step up into the eastern sky,
where they actually become sun and moon:

And thus they took their leave,
  Having completely conquered all of Hell (Xibalba)
And then they walked back up
  Here amid the light,
And at once
  They walked into the sky.
And one is the sun,
  And the other of them is the moon.
Then it grew light in the sky,
  And on the earth.
They are still in the sky.

(tr. M. Edmonson)

This same stepping up past the eastern horizon
recurs in the far more esoteric lowland Maya version of what is basically the
same cosmogony in the Chumayel Book of Chilam Balam. In a long and
complex chapter of that book (pages 42–63), levels of reality are successively
claimed through the establishment of the basic sets of Mesoamerican ritual
themselves, the midwife's 9, the augur's 13, and finally the 'alphabet' of
Twenty Signs, against each of which a tenet of Christian dogma is critically
examined. Embodied as the *uinal*, this last set begins his cosmic journey
under a great-grandmother's tutelage, exactly as in Winnebago ritual which
indeed is echoed with surprising closeness when it comes to 'getting into step'
at the eastern horizon (here also a pun and an Eleatic paradox):

He started up from his inherent motion alone.
His mother's mother and her mother, his mother's sister and his sister-in-law, they
  all said:
How shall we say, how shall we see, that man is on the road?
These are the words they spoke as they moved along, where there was no man.

When they arrived in the east they began to say:
Who has been here? These are footprints. Get the rhythm of his step.
So said the Lady of the world,
And our Father, Dios, measured his step.
This is why the count by footstep of the whole world, xoc lah cab oc was called lahca oc 12 Oc.
This was the order born through 13 Oc,
When the one foot joined its counter print to make the moment of the eastern horizon,
Then he spoke its name when the day had no name.
as he moved along with his mother's mother and her mother, his mother's sister and his sister-in-law
The uinal born, the day so named, the sky and earth,
the stairway of water, earth, stone and wood, the things of sea and earth realized.

1 Chuen, the day he rose to be a day-ity and made the sky and earth.
2 Eb he made the first stairway. It ebbs from heaven's heart
the heart of water, before there was earth, stone and wood

It is on reaching the 'heaven's heart' that the *uinal* completed his journey and himself: the twenty constituent Signs join hands to form a circle of relatives reminiscent alike of the centre of the Aztec Sunstone and the Ghost Dance songs.

In all, the Mesoamerican texts lend a truly epic dimension to the solar-walk paradigm and relate it specifically to the emergence of man in the grand evolutionary scheme of multiple creation or suns. And in so doing they enrich our astronomical reading of the 4+4 cipher, further developing the day-year time-shift noted in texts from further north; compare, too, the lots of 4 day-years in the lives of the Navajo Sun's children in the same world-age context. Duly observed in the Aztec Atamale ceremony the 4+4 years of the octaeteris are formally embedded in the very mechanism of the Mesoamerican calendar, which groups years into leap-day spans of four recurrent Signs and in which the second burial ceremony occurred after four years. For their part the Dresden Venus tables take the octaeteris (of 2920 days) as their base; and they clearly establish the much cited eight days of the solar walk as the official length of that planet's inferior conjunction or underworld passage from west to east. This fact strongly corroborates our previous detections of Venus figures in Mide and related texts. The principle of the Dresden tables is Venus's subsequent ascension in the east, its heliacal rising as Morning Star. Detailed in the iconographic screenfolds, this dramatic moment is ritually acknowledged in the Nine-night chants of the south-west and on the Plains, and appears for example in the Sioux story of the rabbit hunter who manages to outpace the sun. It also dominates the 'Cuauhtitlan Annals' version of One-Reed Quetzalcoatl's self-incineration in 895 CE and his apotheosis as Venus, for prior to his heliacal rising, the passage through the underworld falls into two lots of 4 days, the official length of inferior conjunction either side of Mictlan. In a passage of great beauty, adapted by D.H. Lawrence in his novel *The Plumed Serpent*, we learn how Quetzalcoatl's heart makes the same journey, having burned to incandescence:

> So that where Quetzalcoatl burnt himself is called the place of Incineration.
>
> And it is said that when he burned, his ashes rose up and every kind of precious bird appeared and could be seen rising up to the sky: roseate spoonbill, cotinga, trogon, blue heron, yellow-headed parrot, macaw, white-fronted parrot, and all other precious birds. And after he had become ash the quetzal bird's heart rose up; it could be seen and was known to enter the sky. The old men would say he had become Venus; and it is told that when the star appeared Quetzalcoatl died. From now on he was called the Lord of the Dawn.
>
> Only for four days he did not appear, so it is told, and dwelt in Mictlan. And for another four days he sharpened himself. After eight days the great star appeared called Quetzalcoatl on his ruler's throne. And they knew, on his rising, which people, according to Sign, he penetrates, shoots into and loathes.

In conclusion here it may be fairly claimed that the solar walk was and is a paradigm in native North American religion. Integral to it are a pattern of days and years of astronomical significance and the principle of the time-shift itself. With Chusco this leads further into the inner dimensions of the day, forenoon and afternoon; in Mesoamerica it leads outwards towards a vast evolutionary story recorded at length in the *Popul vuh* and counted by aeons, hundreds of millions of years, in the hieroglyphic inscriptions.

Mesoamerica's Priests, Farmers and Warriors

When rejecting Franciscan efforts to Christianise them in 1524, in the Aztec capital Tenochtitlan (today Mexico City), the priesthood of that place pointed out that they already had a religion of their own, one with roots deep through the vast extent of the Aztec tribute empire, and Mesoamerica itself. Rather than insist on this point, the Aztecs preferred, as they put it, to open the treasure casket just a little, to allow a glimpse of their indigenous tradition. And they did so in a finely structured piece of rhetoric, which touches in turn on the three gifts of their gods, each being allotted a stanza that begins with the words '*They* gave' or '*give*' (*yehuan-maca-*) and ends with the question 'where?' (*in canin*). This part of their speech is worth quoting in full, because of its precise detail, and because it has not been widely published in direct English translation:

> They gave us
> their law
> and they believed,
> they served, and they taught the honour among gods;
> they taught the whole service.
> That's why we eat earth before them;

that's why we draw our blood and do penance;
and that's why we burn copal and kill the living.
They were the Lifelord
and they became our only subject.
When and where?—In the eldest Darkness.

They give us
our supper and our breakfast,
all things to drink and eat,
maize and beans, purslane and sage.
And we beg them
for thunder-Rain and Water
on which the earth thrives.
They are the rich ones
and they have more than simply what it takes;
they are the ones with the stuff,
all ways and all means, forever,
the greenness of growth.
Where and how?—In Tlalocan
hunger is not their experience
nor sickness, and not poverty.

They give also
the inner manliness, kingly valour
and the acquisitions of the hunt:
the insignia of the lip, the knotting of the mantle,
the loin-cloth, the mantle itself;
Flower and aromatic leaf, jade,
quetzal plumes, and the godshit you call gold.
When and where?—It is a long tradition.
Do you know
when the emplacement of Tula was, of Uapalcalco,
of Xuchatlappan, of Tamoanchan,
of Yoalli ichan, of Teotihuacan?
They were the world-makers who founded
the mat of power, the seat of rule.
They gave
authority and entity
fame and honour.
And should we now destroy the old law,
the Toltec law,
the Chichimec law,
the Colhua law,
the Tepanec law,
on which the heart of being flows,
from which we animate ourselves
through which we pass to adulthood,
from which flows our cosmology
and the manner of our prayer?

In each of the three stanzas, the divine gift in question
achieves meaning in human and sociological practice, which in turn is distinguished as that of the priest, the farmer and the warrior. The first of these

groups or classes, the priests, draw their power from self-denial and penitence, a shamanist way which goes back to the palaeolithic and the eldest darkness (*inoc yoayan*). In the Mesoamerican cosmogony and system of world-ages recorded in the *Popul vuh*, this is the time when humans were first distinguished from animals by their capacity in principle to worship 'Heart of the Sky', with the copal incense that the Maya riddle in the Book of Chumayel and the Fire-god on the Fejervary title-page together identify as the 'brains of the sky'. At the start of this world-age or 5,200-year Era, the high priest of its first city, the lowland Tula named below, is characteristically shown holding a copal incense-burner, as he is in the Rios Codex of Tenochtitlan (page 9). Evocative of the native American theory of evolution, with its lowly reptiles and iridescent birds, his name Quetzalcoatl (feather-snake or plumed-serpent) is the one by which the Aztec priests referred to themselves. This is the figure whose underworld trance journey, discussed above, made possible the creation of the human beings of this world-age.

After the priests come the farmers, the American agriculturalists who, after their economic success with gourds, manioc, chillis and other millennial crops, surpassed themselves with the invention of maize, probably not long after 3000 BCE, the staple highly adaptable to altitude and soil type whose protein value is much increased when paired with beans. The space-time of this invention is the rain-god's lush abode at midday or zenith, Tlalocan: with his goggle-eyes and toothy mouth (like the rain-god of the Hopi further to the north), Tlaloc enjoys the power to bring down the waters above, as in the Flood which ended the first world-age. In his role as the ninth of the midwife's night or lunar figures, which served as year-guardians, the rain-god Tlaloc was also the most propitious protector of the annual maize crop, as the Fejervary screenfold confirms (see Figure 12.3). Maize and beans with their respective flours, purslane and sage, are the primary agricultural produce shown to be due annually in the Mendoza

Figure 12.3: The Rain-god and the Maize Plant

136

Codex and the tribute accounts of the Aztecs, while the staple maize becomes the very substance of mankind in the *Popul vuh* cosmogony. In the religion of the Toltecs, and even more in that of the Aztecs, Tlaloc's rain was not freely given. It was bargained for, in exchange for the blood of sacrificed victims whose flowing tears would simulate and so stimulate the flow of rain: before dying, the victim would imagine his journey up to Tlalocan, the 'house of quetzal plumes', Tlaloc's abode at the heart of the sky, passing on the way through the 'place of the unfleshed', the abode of 'the frightening prince' or Lord of the Underworld—once again the trance journey.

Third come the hunter-warriors, the founders of empire, whose first impulse is to acquire and enhance the urban centre with luxury goods of clothing, incense and jewellery, likewise listed in the tribute books, in the same sequence. Indeed, with this third group political history begins, in a series of emplacements whose whereabouts the Franciscans could not have been expected to know any more than they are likely to have cared to. The roll-call of six particular cities begins with Tula or Tollan, the great lowland metropolis which stands as the first named city in a wide range of Mesoamerican texts, including the *Popul vuh* from highland Guatemala, and the Rios Codex of Tenochtitlan where its appearance (page 9) is synonymous with the start of the present 5,200-year Era. And the list ends with Teotihuacan, which our archaeology is now confirming flourished up to no later than the end of the classic era, that is, about 800 CE. The hunter-warrior profession is shown also to have been at the origins of four laws or calendrical usages diagnostic of four of the principal imperial traditions of western Mesoamerica: the Toltec which goes back ultimately to the first city Tula, probably on the Gulf Coast; the Chichimec, which includes the Aztec themselves and other Valley of Mexico tribes; the Colhua which possibly linked Texcoco, to the east of theValley, with Tilantongo and the Mixteca; and the Tepanec, Otomi-speaking and to the west, the demise of whose capital Azcapotzalco led to the rise of Tenochtitlan. Whatever may one day prove to be a full and correct reading of this concise historical scheme, there can be no doubt about the warrior's role in it, or about his opposition in principle to the sedentary farmer, under the initial and primary aegis of the priesthood, representatives of which were after all delivering the speech in question.

Of considerable interest in itself, and distinguished by initial verb tense in the speech, this last typal opposition between planter and hunter-warrior recurs elsewhere in Tenochtitlan literature. Written in Aztec or Nahuatl like the Priests' Speech and the depository of an extensive collection of poetry from the tribute empire of that city, the *Cantares Mexicanos* manuscript distinguishes the *xopancuicatl* or 'burgeoning song' of the planter from the *yaocuicatl* or war-song of the warrior; written in native or iconographic script, the Boturini screenfold when depicting the Aztec migration into the Valley of Mexico appeals to the same division, in order to characterise the separation of the eastern agriculturalists of Huexotzinco with their *milpas* and the western hunters of Malinalco with their arrows and nets. In architecture, it was emblemised in the twin temples atop Tenochtitlan's main pyramid, the one dedicated to the rain-god Tlaloc, the other to the war-god Huitzilopochtli.

Modelled on Tezcatlipoca ('smoking mirror'), who with the priestly Quetzalcoatl and the agricultural Tlaloc completes the 'trinity' of major Mesoamerican gods, this Huitzilopochtli of the Aztecs deserves a brief commentary in his own right. For in the Aztecs' account of their migrations from Aztlan (somewhere in northern Mexico or the southern United States), when they were poor and despised, this figure is an unprepossessing character, carried with them along the road. This is how he appears in the Boturini screenfold, bundled up like a mascot and with a modest Humming-bird (huitzilin) disguise. When they attained power in Tenochtitlan, however, the Aztecs provided the world with a much grander image of the patron who had urged them on to glory. He was made into a solar god, his sanctuary next to Tlaloc's then being given to him. He was also said to have been miraculously conceived by Coatlicue (Snake Skirt), the earth-mother, who was impregnated by a ball of fluff or down when she was sweeping. Her family felt dishonoured by her unexplained fat belly and swore to kill her. As they closed in, Huitzilopochtli leaped out of Coatlicue's womb, fully armed like Tezcatlipoca, and slew them to a man. This feat has the solar analogy of sunrise 'killing' the stars and epitomises the power to strike instantly and definitely. In his annals of Tenochtitlan and the Valley of Mexico, the Nahua author Chimalpahin, writing about 1600, discussed this transformation of Huitzilopochtli from tribal mascot to sun-king. He showed how the Aztecs (like the imperialists of our own century) deliberately created and reshaped myths for political ends. In this respect, Huitzilopochtli is especially notable as one who was claimed to have been conceived miraculously. The moral and kinship problems caused by this special origin are resolved in his tremendous martial energy alone, this being provoked by doubts about legitimacy which are never explicitly denied.

Once acknowledged for what it is in the Priests' Speech, the Tenochtitlan triple paradigm of Aztec religion proves on inspection to be endemic to Mesoamerica as a whole, over a wide geographical area, at horizons long prior to that of the Aztecs, and in media that include sculpture and architecture as well as literature. A striking example comes from the city of Palenque which flourished in the Maya lowlands five hundred or so miles to the east, nearly a millennium before the Aztecs delivered their speech (see Figure 12.4). The text in question consists of three panels set in three temples atop pyramids that rise to the north, east and west of a plaza in the city (temples said to be of the 'Cross', the 'Foliated Cross' and the 'Sun' respectively); while the latter two match each other in height, the northern one rises far higher. Each of the panels has the same format: a central design flanked by columns of Maya hieroglyphic writing, the greater stand-

Figure 12.4: The Palenque Trilogy

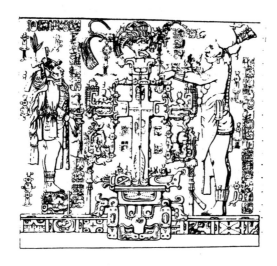

(a)

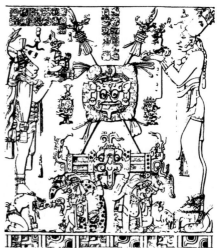

(b)   (c)

ing of the northern panel here being reflected in the fact that it has an extra column to left and right. Calendrically, all three follow a pattern whereby the left-hand columns record events early in the Maya and Mesoamerican Era that began in the year −3113 while the right-hand ones deal with history nearer to the probable date of composition 692 CE.

Using the Aztec Priests' speech as a guide to these three panels we are helped to interpret both their detail and their relationship to each other, and hence to appreciate the resilience of the priest-farmer-warrior paradigm in Mesoamerica and the holistic tendencies of its religion. About the priority of the first panel there can be little doubt, given its extra physical height, conventionally synonymous with a 'northern' placing in the Mesoamerican representation of space, and its extra columns of hieroglyphs. Moreover, it repeatedly invokes the name of the culture-hero Nine Wind who personifies *par excellence* the priestly Quetzalcoatl, the Feather-snake or Plumed-serpent after whom the Aztec priests named themselves, and whose Venusian aspect is pointed out in the accompanying glyph read as 'God 1' by Kelley and others. What is less sure is the identity of the central design customarily called the 'Cross' and of the small figure or manikin held in the arms of the officiating priest to the right. Comparisons with such texts as the Tepexic Annals (Vienna Codex obverse), which also repeatedly invokes Nine Wind over a span which likewise formally extends from the same era date as the Palenque text, would suggest a tree sooner than a cross and hence that the event is the 'tree-birth' of the priest-aristocracy of the city; such a birth theme is certainly present in other cradled figures at Palenque first reproduced by Stephens, could possibly be read from the 'Euripos' arrangement of signs for the inferior and superior planets to the left and right of the central tree stem, and appropriately echoes the fact that of all the male Mesoamerican gods Quetzalcoatl Nine Wind was the one most thoroughly identified with heritage and genealogy.

As for the other two panels facing each other east and west, they demand to be read as the stories of Palenque's farmers and warriors, complementary to each other as are their respective horizons beneath the 'northern' zenith. The farmers' 'Foliated Cross' is in fact not a cross at all but their consummate genetic achievement, the maize plant which began to transform Mesoamerica's economy not long after the −3113 Era date and whose sustenance is identified in the *Popul vuh* creation story with the flesh of this Era's people. The jade-skirt worn by the left-hand officiating figure, which has been cited as evidence of the local monarch Pacal's desire to own all qualities, male and female, finds a deeper echo within Mesoamerican culture in the skirted Tlaloc that guards the maize in the Fejervary screenfold. Diametrically opposite, to the west, stands the Sun panel which is architecturally designed so as to relate to a solstice sun motif also elaborated in the Temple of the Inscriptions and the shaft of Pacal's tomb below. At its most obvious, however, the actual centre-piece of the panel includes the shield and crossed spears of the warrior, below which crouch two captives, in the knightly uniforms of the jaguar and the eagle. The diagonal cross of the spears, moreover, schematically recalls the format of Mesoamerican tribute maps, like that of Tenochtitlan on the title-page of the Mendoza Codex. As for the recently detected Jupiter relevance of dates on this panel, it would also support rather than contradict this military reading.

Overall, the structural parallels between these two representations of religion, Aztec and Classic Maya, are the more striking given what otherwise amounts to major differences between those two cultures. The long-nosed Chac of the Maya farmer resembles Tlaloc only in part, while the chief weapon of his warrior gods, the blowpipe, is absent from the arsenals of Tezcatlipoca and Huitzilopochtli. Indeed, the roots of the triple paradigm must lie as deep in Mesoamerican cultures as the notion of Tula itself, the first named city, and take us back to the first Olmec settlements on the Gulf Coast, midway between Aztec and Maya, where the oldest surviving representations of Quetzalcoatl have been found.

The Good Shepherd of the Inca

To the south, in the course of their invasion of the New World, Europeans encountered in the Andean highlands a civilisation which for all its common native American traits, in curing, weaving and metallurgy for example, exhibited others quite distinctive to it. Indeed, the Inca empire Tahuantin-suyu penetrated by Pizarro remains to this day a source of theoretical enquiry, as a result of its highly organised religion and state system, which served to hold together many thousands of kilometres of territory, radiating out from the capital Cuzco, its means of communication being the *quipu*. Nowhere else in the Americas was such thorough control of population and economy achieved over such a vast geography; nor was there a religion even nearly so institutionalised and monotheistic.

At the same time, this region was the exclusive home of the four American camelids: the llama and the alpaca, the huanuco and the vicuña. Having in common with the Old World camels a remote and long vanished ancestor in the North American Ohio Valley, these animals differ somewhat in size and in quality and colour of wool, the first two having been domesticated and the other two not. While the larger llama, probably derived from the huanuco, has served largely as a pack-animal, the alpaca has been best known for its wool; the finest wool, however, belongs to the wild and rare vicuña. (The exact dates and places of domestication are still the subject of research, though bone evidence from Ayacucho points to as early as 4000 BCE.)

Given these two characteristically Andean phenomena, sociological and zoological, the question naturally arises whether they were connected, and if so, how. A prime aid towards any answer is the corpus of texts native to the region, which in many cases have only recently been published and edited. Written in Quechua and Spanish, and transcribed in part from *quipu* originals, these texts include the encyclopedic *Nueva coronica y buen gobierno* sent by Guaman Poma as a letter to Philip III of Spain and which structurally reflects, in its first part, Inca state organisation; the *Huarochiri Narrative* composed entirely in Quechua, which focuses chiefly on cosmogony and Christian attempts to incorporate native religion; other narratives like the *Relacion de antiguedades* of Santacruz Pachacuti, which includes a plan of the Inca temple Coricancha, as well as the Quechua originals of the Situa liturgy, in which the great god Viracocha is worshipped.

In the first instance, these native texts confirm the categorical change signified by domestication as such, that is, loss of wildness. Nowhere is this more fundamentally stated than in the general American cosmogony of world-ages, where the eclipse that ends the second age prompts a domestic revolt against masters who have lost their capacity to worship and respect the life-spirit. In Mesoamerica, this upheaval is led by mortars and kitchen utensils tired of unfeeling use, and not least by the Dog and Turkey, the two creatures whose long-standing alliance with American man is elsewhere celebrated in rituals that survive even today, for example in the south-west of the United States. That in Tahuantinsuyu this same contract was perceived to have extended to llamas is clear from the *Huarochiri Narrative*, where during the eclipse the revolt of the utensils is accompanied by one on the part of these creatures, who turn on their masters in herds. Later in the same *Narrative*, this motif recurs in the binary opposition established between the few wild vicuña who help the poor Huatyacuri and the teams of llamas enlisted by his rich antagonist (Chapters 4 and 5). For their part, Quechua poetry and drama nostalgically invoke the aesthetic attraction of the 'wild' llama, be it that of the beloved as a silky-haired, farouche vicuña, or that of the rebellious Ollantay who defies the Inca as a 'straying lamb'. Consistent with the terms of this domestic contract is the inclusion of the tamed creature as a ritual ally and even social companion. The actual process of inclusion is well-illustrated in Guaman Poma's report of the religious ceremonies proper to the month Uma Raima (October; see Figure 12.5), in which supplicants for rain included not just human children and dogs, whose tears and howls were elicited as sympathetic magic, as in Mexico for example, but a black llama as well. In Inca cosmogony it was the plaintive quality of the llama's faint cry or song that warned humans of the Flood that ended the first world-age (*Huarochiri Narrative*, Chapter 3), while socially this beast, this time coloured red, became the singing companion of the emperor himself in court performances of the Quechua *yaravi*. Indeed, for these capacities the llama, like our Ram, was elevated to the stars as a principal constellation and guide.

Besides these functions, however, for which parallels can be sought elsewhere in native America, the tame camelids of the Inca

Figure 12.5

had others, exclusive to them. For from all that has been recorded about the Inca state, it is clear that these creatures alternatively served just as units of value, mere items of exchange devoid of particular status or rights, and that as such they were transacted on the grand decimal scale of the *quipu*, whose first and most enduring use appears to have been to tally herds. In Umu Raimi, while one black llama sang for rain one hundred of his white brethren were simply slaughtered; and at the festival of Pariaca 'several thousand' were offered to his priests, such amounts being calculated and checked by means of the *quipu*, according to the *Huarochiri Narrative* (Chapter 9).

As a standardised arithmetical unit of value, especially for the purposes of Inca state religion, the llama in this respect can be well compared with other such units used both within Tahuantinsuyu and in urban economies beyond, like Mesoamerica. Hence, on the one hand it resembles Mesoamerican tribute units of precious feather, stone and metal in its durability; and on the other, in its immediate usefulness, it resembles rations of woven cotton and food, like the mantles and the bushels of maize and beans separately rendered as tribute to the Aztec emperor, for its wool could be variously spun according to quality, its flesh eaten fresh or as *charqui*, its dung spread as manure and so on. Besides uniquely combining these qualities the llama had two others. In the complete absence of any analogue except humans themselves, the llama served as transport, carrying about 45 kilos for up to 20 kilometres a day, chiefly crops from the estates of Empire and Religion back to the capital Cuzco, and thus provided labour as well as commodity value. Secondly, it increased and multiplied itself as sheer capital (whence 'cattle'). Inca attention to breeding, to the selection of prime males literally in 'races' and to penis size, is reported by the *Huarochiri Narrative* (Chapters 9 and 10).

Combined, these qualities of the domesticated Andean camelid, llama and alpaca, endowed it with a value that could not easily have been restricted to the type of domestic contract honoured throughout native American culture. How and where its particular qualities were exploited over time need still to be researched, but the process must have begun with domestication itself. For his part, Guaman Poma (pages 57–78) speaks of a sharp increase of llama and people in the age of the warlike Auca who succeeded the Purun, the first to measure out owned land distinguishing pasture from fields (*chacra*). Without doubt the process led to a new definition of land use and ownership, the edge between tutelary and wild territory being a powerful feature of Andean ideology still today. This meant another social definition of the agriculturalist, whose particular rivalry with the shepherd, rather than with the hunter-warrior, as elsewhere, is likewise evident in the modern ritual of the Collas in Bolivia. And it led to another formulation of religious control, of a flock obedient to its emperor-god, innocent of 'sin', and hence sheltered from the ravenous dangers beyond the frontier fence.

In the latter part of the story, a critical moment was certainly reached in the mid-fifteenth century, with the Inca Pachacuti's conquest of the Lake Titicaca region, the 'Collasuyu' renowned for its huge pastoral wealth and its own imperial past. For it was under this emperor and his son and heir Tupac Yupanqui that the Inca state was given its definitive shape, in dispositions which all point to the importance of pastoralism as an ideological as well as an economic force. Whereas the guarding of llamas could be relegated to boys and girls of twelve acting out of 'love' for the Inca, which is how Guaman Poma depicts it (pages 204 and 225), in incorporating the Collas the Inca emperors, in conjunction with the local chiefs, assigned the large herds they had appropriated to the care of professional shepherds. Though they worked full-time, these new appointees were privileged to retain their right to agricultural land, which was worked for them by their kin. Entrusted with the *quipu* accounts of Empire and Religion, these favoured few became pastoral retainers who among other rights could leave their post, patriarchally, to a son. At the same time the central administration set up by Pachacuti and Tupac Yupanqui made quite explicit the more general and significant equation between the llama flock and the human folk as complementary arithmetical components of the state, the latter being likewise counted on the *quipu* to the last unit and according to the ten categories and ages listed by Guaman Poma. This much is evident in the very term used for the police, *michic* or shepherd, responsible for surveillance of the population and for reporting absences from work and religious festivals once again by means of the *quipu* (*Huarochiri Narrative*, Chapter 31).

The same equation between flock and folk is made above all in the monotheistic worship of Viracocha exemplified in the following hymn from the Situa liturgy:

Oh dew of the world
Viracocha
inner dew
Viracocha
you who dispose by saying
'Let there be greater and lesser gods'
great Lord
dispose that here
men do multiply
fortunately.

Father Viracocha
you who say
'Let there be
the upper world
and the lower world'
you who fortify
the world below
hear me

attend to me:
Let me live in peace and in safety,
Father Viracocha,
with food and sustenance,
with maize and llamas,
with all manner
of skills.
Abandon me not.
Remove me
from my enemies,
from danger,
from all threat
of being cursed, ungrateful,
or repudiated.

In the Quechua cadences of this liturgy, the supreme god and paternalistic principle Viracocha is repeatedly asked to keep both men and llamas in peace and safety under the care of his representative on earth, the Inca emperor, and to favour their 'increase'; he is also asked to keep his flock from straying into disobedience and sin, again concepts otherwise foreign to native American liturgy. Actual confession was helped by the payment of llamas, and there are even reports of a black llama serving literally as a scapegoat during the Situa ritual, collective sin being heaped upon it. Disobedience towards Pachacuti the 'good shepherd', and its retribution, certainly provides the whole message of the play *Ollantay*.

The catalogue of pastoralist traits peculiar to Andean religion could easily be lengthened. Yet those noted already are enough to justify the connection in principle between fauna and society in that area and in so doing to raise larger theoretical issues like the standardisation of value, land appropriation, the concentration of power within what thereby becomes the 'state', the deep complicity between the -isms of capital and social, and the pastoral roots of monotheism itself. Indeed, set in as it were the laboratory conditions of the New World the Inca Tahuantinsuyu offers useful pointers to features of our own religion long saturated with pastoralist ideology, from the fable of Cain the agriculturalist and Abel the keeper of flocks, to the doctrine of Christ both shepherd and sacrificial lamb.

Further Reading

Brotherston, Gordon *Image of the New World. The American Continent Portrayed in Native Texts* (Thames & Hudson, London and New York, 1979)

Dewdney, Selwyn *Sacred Scrolls of the Southern Ojibway* (University of Toronto Press, Toronto, 1975)

Eliade, Mircea *Shamanism: Archaic Techniques of Ecstasy (Routledge & Kegan Paul, London, 1964)*

Krickeberg, Walter *Pre-Columbian Mexican Religions* (Weidenfeld & Nicolson, London, 1968)

New Religious Movements

13 | Introduction to New Religious Movements

Peter Clarke

There are no gospels which are immortal, but neither is there any reason for believing that humanity is incapable of inventing new ones.[1]

While some would undoubtedly question the first part of the above quotation from Durkheim's *The Elementary Forms of the Religious Life*, recent history has put the second part beyond all doubt. Over four hundred 'new' religions have emerged in Britain alone since 1945 and many of these and others are to be found in the rest of Western Europe. The figure is very much higher for North America,[2] and post-war Japan[3] has also witnessed, as have parts of sub-Saharan Africa[4] from the 1890s, what amounts to a thriving industry in new religions. Although we have no reliable statistics, the clientele of post-Second World War new religions must be estimated in millions rather than thousands. Although it can be argued that the religions covered in this section, or at least some of them, are not *new* in a 'cultural' and 'theological' sense,[5] as used in this introduction the term *new* is employed chronologically to refer to all those religions that have established themselves in Western Europe, North America and Japan since 1945, and in Africa over a somewhat longer time-span. It is worth pointing out here that the new religions that are known about and documented may constitute only the tip of the iceberg; below the surface there would appear to be a large mass of new religions which has neither been located nor measured with any precision. We can mention in this context the phenomenon of neo-pagan, esoteric and related movements. It is also worth mentioning that a number of new religions have burst upon the scene, flourished for a time and died, but in some cases not before having profoundly influenced the behaviour, thinking and general lifestyle of many thousands of people, and also the legal system in a number of societies, a notable and recent example being the Rajneesh movement discussed in Chapter 14, p. 163.[6]

New religions in the West and Japan derive from many different cultures and can vary enormously in terms of content, ritual, attitudes towards the older, albeit themselves once new religions, and towards one another and the wider society. They have also posed a great many questions for that wider society and the mainstream religions, in particular Christianity, obliging the former, for instance, to re-examine, and in certain instances to refine and develop among other things its legal concepts and definition of religion, and the latter to focus more of its attention on the mystical dimension of its tradition. Further, students of religion, including sociologists, psychologists, philosophers, theologians and historians, have also been pressed by the phenomenal growth in recent times of new religions to examine and improve their techniques of research, and reappraise some of their long held conceptual creations and notions about, for example, the meaning, nature and purpose of religion, the nature and method of interpretation of religious discourse, the mechanics of religious conversion, the question of religious freedom and tolerance, the process of secularisation and the character of modern society (both themes are treated by Bryan Wilson in his chapter on secularisation), the principle of and meaning of the term membership and the social location, nature and limits of charismatic authority. Numerous attempts have also been made to explain the rise and impact of new religions and the response of the wider society to this phenomenon and these are issues addressed by some of the contributors in this section of the volume and elsewhere.[7]

There is also the equally interesting question as to why some movements succeed while others fail, a question to which several of the contributions in this section attempt to provide an answer, pointing to, among other things, the process of rationalisation that is proceeding apace in modern society, leaving little room for that charismatic authority, precarious in itself, on which a number of the new religions are based. Of course, in this context success and failure are relative terms. However, if we limit the criterion here to no more than staying power or length of survival they would appear to have much to do not only with charismatic authority and the forces of rationalisation but also with the overall composition, size, structure and organisation of a particular movement, its methods of recruitment and evangelisation, the relevance of its message, its financial circumstances, the image it conveys of itself to the outside world, the response it meets with from the wider society, including the kind of media coverage it receives, the character and structure of that wider society, where and how the movement decides to insert itself and the extent to which it can in travelling to new areas assimilate to the local culture in which it finds itself without loss of purpose or identity.[8]

Rather than examining the foregoing questions in any detail here we can consider briefly some of the conceptions and stepping-stones to 'salvation' mapped out by some of the new religions and common in one form or another to many. There is first of all strong opposition to the rational, intellectual approach to religious truth. The mind, it is claimed, obstructs the quest for such truth and must, therefore, be controlled, some movements going so far as to encourage the complete abandonment of intellectual activity. In advocating this approach and at the same time criticising what they refer to as 'arid intellectualism' new religions would appear to be mistaken about the position of the student of religion and in particular the philosopher of religion who, far from maintaining that belief in God, however defined and understood, arises by irresistible logic either from a scientific investigation of the 'sources' or the world, holds almost as an axiom that such a belief can be achieved only by means of a much more complex process which takes note of experience and intuition as well as reason. For the new religionist, on the other hand, the only path to and authority for 'faith', which, as we shall see below, can dissolve into 'knowledge' even in this life, is experience; an approach which can sometimes lead to the suspension of all doubt and criticism in order to allow time for the old habits of mind and ways of thinking to be cast off.

A number of new religions are the creation of a charismatic leader and tend to be dominated by her/his personality and, despite at times disclaimers to the contrary, these leaders place great emphasis on the 'virtue' of surrender, a logical step considering their views on the limitations of the mind and/or intellect. Moreover, the relationship between master and disciple is considered to be of fundamental importance in the process of realising and perfecting the self, the primary goal of some of the more popular new religions, as the contribution to this section of the volume on the 'Self-Religions' makes clear. This relationship entails the absolute surrender of the disciple, for whom all other relationships, and especially those with family or friends, must become of secondary importance.

Realising and perfecting the self consists of being the *cause* of all one does, of determining events rather than being determined by them, of exchanging one's status of slave to events and circumstances for that of master of all that happens. It consists of becoming a creator. Unlike Christianity, many of the new religions are persuaded of the perfectibility of human nature in the here and now and much of the theorising which predicates this is grounded in the 'belief' that the individual is divine, is God. Once an individual realises that he/she is divine then all things are possible. What we see here, echoing Feuerbach, is a concern not with God as other but with a God who lives in and for the individual and whose real meaning lies in a conception of man.[9]

Given these related 'beliefs' in the perfectibility of human nature and the divinity of man, and their Buddhist and Hindu derived ideas and practices, it is not surprising to find that in many new religions the idea of faith as found in Christianity, whereby in the here and now we see only in part or 'through a glass darkly', is replaced by that of 'knowledge'.

New religions accept that there is a distinction between faith and knowledge but insist that this need not persist throughout this life for one can come to 'know' fully *now* the 'divine' or 'God', and thus faith becomes redundant.

An emphasis on the millennium is to be found in Soka Gakkai (Value Creation Society), almost all Japanese new religions, as another of the contributions to this section shows, and in many other new movements such as the Unification Church, more popularly known as the Moonies,[10] the Worldwide Church of God and the Rastafarian movement.[11] This is not unexpected in the light of what has just been said about human nature, the source of the divine, faith and knowledge. Moreover, millennialism can serve many purposes, operating in situations of rapid social change and upheaval as an appropriate and effective ideology.[12] Although there are differences in interpretation, for most new religions the millennium is close at hand and offers an escape from contemporary society and entry to a new, golden age, at times depicted as a highly spiritual realm but more often than not as a Utopia.

While others see them as attempts to grapple with the problems generated by the twin processes of rationalisation and secularisation, the new religions regard themselves, much in the same way as Christian and Islamic fundamentalists, as the instruments for the creation of a perfect order of society and as being in the forefront of the movement to regain the territory lost by religion over the past two hundred years and more since the Enlightenment. They may, however, prove to be something of a Trojan horse, quickening a process of internal secularisation rather than extending the frontiers of religion. Their more immediate aims can vary, but what is most striking is the attempt by many new movements, particularly those of Japanese origin, to enable people to cope with ordinary living, to provide solutions to ordinary everyday problems, to what Durkheim considered to be 'profane' matters.

Notes

1. E. Durkheim, *The Elementary Forms of the Religious Life: A Study in Religious Sociology*, trans. Joseph Ward Swain (Allen & Unwin, London; Macmillan, New York, 1915), p. 428.

2. J. Gordon Melton, *Encyclopedia of American Religions* (Gale Research Co., Detroit, 1986); D. Choquette, *New Religious Movements in the United States and Canada: A Critical Assessment and Annotated Bibliography* (Greenwood Press, Westport, Connecticut/London, 1985).

3. H. Byron Earhart, *The New Religions of Japan. A Bibliography of Western Language Materials* (University of Michigan Centre for Japanese Studies, Ann Arbor, 1983).

4. H.W. Turner, *Religious Innovation in Africa* (Boston, Mass., 1979); R.J. Hackett, 'Spiritual Sciences in Africa', *Religion Today. A Journal of Contemporary Religions*, vol. 13, no. 2 (May–Sept. 1986), pp. 8ff.

5. F. Hardy, 'How "Indian" are the new Indian Religions', *Religion Today. A Journal of Contemporary Religions*, vol. 1, nos. 2/3 (Oct.–Dec. 1984), pp. 15ff.

6. J. Thompson and P. Heelas, *The Way of the Heart: The Rajneesh Movement* (The Aquarian Press, Wellingborough, 1986).

7. R. Wallis, *The Elementary Forms of the New Religious Life* (Routledge & Kegan Paul, London, 1984); I.I. Zaretsky and M.P. Leone (eds.), *Religious Movements in Contemporary America* (Princeton University Press, Princeton, 1974); E. Barker (ed.), *New Religious Movements: A Perspective for Understanding Society. Studies in Religion and Society* (Edwin Mellen Press, New York, 1982), vol. 3; B.R. Wilson (ed.), *The Social Impact of the New Religious Movements*, Conference Series, no. 9 (The Unification Theological Seminary, Barrytown, New York, 1981).

8. J.A. Beckford, *Cult Controversies: The Social Response to the New Religious Movements* (Tavistock Publications, London, 1985); P.B. Clarke (ed.), *The New Evangelists* (Ethnographica Publishers Ltd, London, 1988).

9. L. Feuerbach, *The Essence of Christianity*, trans. by George Elliot (Harper & Row Publishers, London and New York, 1957), p. 281 and *passim.*

10. E. Barker, *Becoming a Moonie: Choice or Brainwashing?* (Basil Blackwell, Oxford, 1985).

11. E. Cashmore, *Rastaman: The Rastafarian Movement in England* (George Allen & Unwin, London, 1979); also P.B. Clarke, *Black Paradise: The Rastafarian Movement* (Aquarian Press, Wellingborough, 1986).

12. N. Cohn, *The Pursuit of the Millennium* (Paladin, London, 1970); J.A. Beckford (ed.), *New Religious Movements and Rapid Social Change* (Sage/Unesco, London/Paris, 1986).

The author would like to thank the British Academy for a research grant which made possible his research on new religions in Western Europe.

14 | North America

R. Wallis

Introduction

America possesses a free market economy *par excellence*. The mechanisms of the market extend not only to goods and services, but far into the sphere of culture, affecting even the realm of religion itself. Just as goods and services emerge and change in response to market forces, growing affluence, recession, the appearance of new consumer groups and new consumption desires, so too does the religious commodity. Existing suppliers seek to develop a new brand image, or continue to survive on the retained brand loyalty of old customers and sometimes their families, while forceful, even aggressive, marketing by new suppliers of salvation may lead to the capture of some section of the existing market, or the formation of new consumers from groups and strata hitherto ignored.

But the market is no longer a merely local phenomenon, even if the locality extends to the 50 states. The Western world and beyond have become enmeshed in the American market. Its products are promoted internationally through the multinational corporations. The Coca-Cola drinker keeps almost the whole world company. American cultural products too are enthusiastically exported, from films and television soap opera in Europe, to Pentecostalism in Latin America.

Not that the traffic is all one way, of course. Americans are willing to consume indigenous products of other economies and cultures, often, indeed, willing to believe that imported brands bear a certain superior cachet; although in time the product may become tailored and adapted the better to suit American palates and sensitivities.

The internationalisation of the market—at least in the non-Communist and affluent societies—both mirrors and extends an internationalisation of experience. Idiosyncracies of local production and culture are eroded by emulation and by the rationalisation of life in the pursuit of profit, efficiency, improved living standards and universal access to basic rights and privileges.

But although in one respect greater uniformity is the result—an airport hotel is much the same in London as in Los Angeles—in another, mass production encourages product diversification, to locate a niche in the consumer ecology unsatisfied by existing suppliers, servicing a particular clientele with distinctive consumer demands. Construing religion as a commodity thus leads to asking questions about factors operating to generate the consumer demands met by the new religions which have emerged or flourished on the American scene in the post-Second World War era.

Of course, the wave of new religions which emerged into prominence, even notoriety, in America after 1945 was by no means a unique phenomenon. There had been earlier waves. Immigration to a land of greater religious toleration had been a frequent recourse for embattled sects in earlier centuries. The Doukhobors, the Shakers, the Amish and a multitude of other religious groups found America to be an environment in which they might be left alone, if not accepted, and in which large tracts of available and cultivatable land permitted the formation of a comfortable agrarian style of life. The absence of an established church, jealous of its privileges and its flock, permitted the uninhibited development of indigenous religious innovations, and the American ethos of individualism and pragmatism ensured that there would always be an abundance of religious innovators, and of potential adherents for new beliefs and practices locally produced or imported.

Early in the nineteenth century Mormonism was to develop, recruiting in large numbers not only in America, but also in the British Isles. Alongside it, Millerism, a millennialist doctrine of the Second Coming developed in the eastern states, giving rise in turn to the Jehovah's Witness movement at the end of the nineteenth century. In the mid-nineteenth century, the Holiness movement was to spring from the Methodist tradition, giving birth in turn to Pentecostalism. Spiritualism too was a mid-century innovation, an American adaptation of European-originated Swedenborgianism. Christian Science and New Thought flourished in the late nineteenth century, and the World Parliament of Religions held in Chicago in 1893 gave a platform in America to Hindu thought in the form of Swami Vivekenanda and the Vedanta movement. Theosophy too, although in its early years centred in Britain and India, was founded in New York in 1875 and provided a further route for Eastern religious ideas to infiltrate American culture, spawning in turn a multitude of local heresies and adaptations. (An excellent source on all of these movements is B. Wilson's *Religious Sects*.)

The Variety of Modern New Religions

There is therefore, a considerable continuity between the new religions that emerged or flourished in post-Second World War America, and those that appeared in earlier generations. Indian thought found new vehicles in the Divine Light Mission of the Guru Maharaj-ji, Maharishi Mahesh Yogi and Transcendental Meditation, A.C. Bhaktivedanta Swami (also known as Srila Prabhupada) and the International Society for Krishna Consciousness (ISKCON), and later Bhagwan Shree Rajneesh and the Neo-Sannyas Movement (the 'Orange People' or Rajneeshism). Christian-originated movements were to arise from the radical conversionist tradition of American fundamentalism in the Jesus People and the more notorious Children of God (Family of Love). And Christian millennialist thought was to be reimported in the unusual form of a syncretic sect which combined Judeo-Christian adventism and Far Eastern Shamanic, Taoist and Buddhist thought in the form of the Unification Church of the Revd Sun Myung Moon (the 'Moonies').

From the 1950s, Zen Buddhism had found a small following among intellectuals and bohemians ('the beatniks' or 'beat generation'), and continued to thrive, if only among a rather small group of such people willing to suffer the rigours and austerity of Zen Buddhist discipline and practice and the rather arid intellectualism of its philosophy. The postwar occupation of Japan was to result in the return of GIs, often with Japanese wives, who had converted to the new religion of Nichiren Shoshu (Soka Gakkai), a Mahayana Buddhist heresy.

These movements were not, of course, all of a piece. Even among the Indian imports there were major differences. Transcendental Meditation provided only a meditational technique for the vast majority of its clientele. Customers would attend one or two preliminary orientation sessions, then a brief initiation at which they were given a *mantra*. Thereafter they were encouraged to meditate for twenty minutes twice a day. There was little expectation of any continuing involvement with the organisation or other adherents of the practice. The Divine Light Mission too offered a meditational technique, but also sought to encourage its followers, the *premies* or 'lovers' of Guru Maharaj-ji, to live communally, sharing a life of devotion to their guru, although often taking jobs outside the commune. Even more demanding as a way of life was that of devotees in the International Society for Krishna Consciousness, who adopted Indian dress, vegetarian food and a rigorous and ascetic mode of life in which sex, alcohol and tobacco were eschewed. Males were required to shave their heads but for a topknot by means of which Krishna would pull them up to heaven. Devotees rose before dawn in communal temples, for a demanding round of rituals before the temple deities, and *sankirtan*—chanting and witnessing in public—or street solicitation of funds in return for magazines, incense or records. While the Transcendental Meditation follower committed only the equivalent of one week's pay and forty minutes a day to the movement, the Krishna devotee committed himself twenty-four hours a day, subordinating his identity totally to its expectations.

The Jesus People and the Children of God involved a synthesis of lifestyle elements of the youth counter-culture—such as long hair, hippie dress and speech, rock music, and an emphasis on love and spontaneity—with American fundamentalism, a belief in the literal truth of the Bible, an expectation of imminent apocalypse and the Second Advent of Christ, a Jesucentric faith, and a commitment to the notion of the Holy Ghost still working in human lives as displayed through such signs as glossolalia, or 'speaking in tongues'. While the Jesus People (a disparate range of groups and movements which flourished in the late 1960s and early 1970s and was largely confined to North America) rose rapidly, peaked quickly and then virtually disappeared by the late 1970s, the Children of God were to survive, albeit in a rather different form. The Children of God emerged in the late 1960s in America as a more radical and zealous wing of the Jesus People. Its leader, Moses David Berg, a former itinerant preacher, was considerably older than most of his followers. Finding his message of cursing the apostate, materialistic worldly system and its compromising churches, and of the imminence of the Apocalypse and Christ's return eagerly accepted by many of the young people who came to hear him, Berg came to view himself as God's prophet for the End-time. He took a new young wife and began to introduce many new elements into the movement's system of belief and practice, including a belief in spirit guides, in Gadaffi as the probable Antichrist, in the likely return of Christ by 1993, and in the freedom of 'spiritual Israel', i.e. himself and his followers, to do 'all things' without sin, including engaging in increasingly indiscriminate sexual relationships.

Prominent among the new religions, however, was a range of groups and movements which—although hinted at in the structure and philosophy of Christian Science and the New Thought Movement—represented a relatively new departure. They diverged from traditional religions in being largely indifferent to the existence or will of any creator God. Rather, they construed the individual as a god in embryo or a spiritual being constrained by material or psychological bonds, and it was from ideas of psychological and psychosomatic therapy that such movements developed.

The Psychoanalytic Movement was the main progenitor of many of the psychological new religions. The more independently minded associates of Freud often departed from psychoanalytic orthodoxy by travelling in a more spiritual direction. Jung displayed a range of occult interests; Reich investigated forms of energy not located by conventional science, and the UFO phenomenon, as well as developing a form of therapy predicated on the assumption that psychological difficulties and traumas were absorbed into body musculature and would be released by physical as well as psychological techniques. Otto Rank shifted the locus of the major psychological trauma affecting adult behaviour back from the Oedipal conflict and other aspects of infant–parent interaction, to the trauma of birth itself. This development was crucial, because once the journey back had begun there was no intrinsically logical place to stop. Dianetics—the forerunner to Scientology—was to shift a stage further back from the birth trauma to traumatic experiences of intra-uterine life (the main one revealed by early Dianetics enthusiasts apparently being attempted abortion by the mother).

Dianetics was founded by L. Ron Hubbard, a pulp-fiction writer who had dabbled in hypnotherapy and the American occult underground. Employing regression and abreaction techniques adapted from medical hypnosis, Hubbard regressed his clients to earlier and earlier points in the life cycle, back to conception itself. Thereafter, although not initially encouraged by Hubbard, clients (known as 'pre-clears') began to produce 'memories' which they believed could not have come from this life at all. Thus a conception of reincarnation was combined with psychologically-oriented methods, and paved the way for a new religion, Scientology.

Scientology possessed a number of features in common with the other psychological religions and with related movements which offered a means of salvation from life's vicissitudes, even if they lacked overt spiritual reference. They shared a conception of man as perfectible. Human beings are believed to possess far greater potential ability, awareness, creativity, insight and capacity for emotional expression and experience than they currently display. Dianetics, for example, argued that the average human being used less than 10 per cent of his mental powers.

Through social conditioning and painful social interaction people lose their ability to manifest all their potential. They repress their emotional aspect, learn to act through the medium of constricting social roles and lose their spontaneity. However, they contain within themselves all that is necessary to be whole, to achieve their potential. Instead of *adding* anything, the individual may rather need to shed the constraints or impediments that have been acquired during the course of one or many lifetimes. By the practice of some technique, or series of techniques, often organised in a particular ritual format or training, the individual can break down conditioning and release the hidden powers beneath.

Just as had earlier been the case with Christian Science and the New Thought Movement, Scientology was to give rise to a myriad of smaller heretical movements and groups founded by individuals unwilling to subordinate themselves entirely to Ron Hubbard's authoritarian direction, and who believed that by synthesis or through their own insights or experiments, they too could develop such ideas and practices further. One of the most successful of such offspring was Erhard Seminars Training (or est) which synthesised ideas drawn from Scientology with practices from Gestalt therapy and a presentational technique drawn from Mind Dynamics, influenced in turn by Silva Mind Control, which reached back to New Thought and Couéism for inspiration. (Coué's most influential contribution to psychological development was probably the phrase—to be repeated several times every morning—'Every day, in every way, I get better and better'.) Est in turn gave rise to various other practices offering a slightly different package such as Lifespring, Actualizations and Insight.

These new psychological religions and related salvational systems adopted not only contemporary psychological ideas and practices, but also contemporary organisational structures and modern marketing methods. They promised not calendrically based collective worship, but rather individually-tailored, or consumer-convenient therapy, training, counselling or courses, available through weekend or evening sessions at a fixed fee and with cash discounts. The salvational commodity was purveyed through permanent outlets in major metropolitan locations, or by travelling teams which set up in large city centre hotels, offering their services to 150 or 200 clients at a time.

The major suppliers organised themselves as multinational corporations, often developing considerable expertise in international financial transfer and in corporate and public law. They marketed a particular range of brand-identified salvational services, striving to retain customer loyalty often by differentiating their product into a series of stages constituting a career which would take a considerable investment of time and money to complete. Some clients would be encouraged to make their hobby into a vocation by volunteering time to recruit or service clients, or by taking full-time employment with the corporation; or clients might be encouraged to pursue their course through the hierarchy of training with the expectation that they would be able to recoup their investment on completion, through professional practice.

Such large corporate suppliers inevitably attempted to maximise control over staff and committed clients, giving them a sometimes somewhat authoritarian character. Others required less exclusive commitment, and marketed their salvational commodity through facilities which provided a location for many different ideas and practices.

A major role in this respect was played by the Human Potential Movement which was a diffuse and eclectic congeries of ideas and practices drawn from the Psychoanalytic heretics; massage and other physical practices; humanistic psychology (Gestalt, Encounter, Transactional Analysis etc.); the corporate major suppliers such as Scientology, Primal Therapy, Arica etc.; and a variety of other sources. These ideas and practices were made available through centres which offered a rotating programme of therapy and training to a shifting clientele which might sample from among the advertised range of one centre and then another, without any necessary commitment to any one system, practitioner or purveyor. The most famous centre in the Human Potential Movement was undoubtedly the Esalen Institute at Big Sur in California, but more modest endeavours could be found during the late 1960s, and early 1970s throughout America, and in the major European metropolises.

One way, then, of considering the new religions of post-Second World War America is in terms of their origins, i.e. whether they are derived predominantly from indigenous religious traditions, from imported religious traditions, or from essential psychological sources.

Figure 14.1: Origins of New Religions in Post-War America

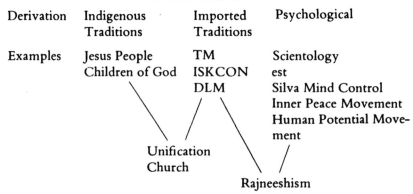

Derivation	Indigenous Traditions	Imported Traditions	Psychological
Examples	Jesus People Children of God	TM ISKCON DLM	Scientology est Silva Mind Control Inner Peace Movement Human Potential Movement

Unification Church

Rajneeshism

However, a classification in terms of origins can only take us a short way along the path to understanding such movements, their structure, functioning, development and sources of support. We can get somewhat further along if we conceive new religious movements as having three possible ways of orientating themselves to the world around them: they may reject that world, expecting or promoting its general transformation; they may embrace the world, accepting its goals and values, and promoting the means to cope with it more effectively; or they may merely accommodate to a world they view as potentially corrupting and dangerous, striving to cultivate their religious experience and heighten their religious sensibilities in an effort to provide a more effective example; in the world but not of it.

Figure 14.2: Orientations of New Religious Movements

World-rejecting	World-affirming	World-accommodating
ISKCON	est	Charismatic
Unification Church	Inner Peace Movement	Renewal
Children of God	Human Potential Movement	House Churches
		Subud
People's Temple	TM	

These three orientations produce different structures and patterns of behaviour and collective functioning. While there are clear examples of each in the new religions, many new religious movements may combine elements of two or more orientations, or shift between one and another over the course of time.

The world-rejecting movement typically adopts a communal way of life, recruiting the young or other radically disaffected groups on the social margins. Its hostility to the surrounding society may breed a lack of respect for social norms, a willingness to lie or break the law in what is seen as a good cause. Because of the sharp break involved in the transition from the conventional world to that of the movement, recruitment often involves intense, concentrated pressure to convert, with a high level of emotional display, and often an attempt to isolate the new recruit for a period from family or former friends until he is firm in the new faith. Rejecting the wider society will normally entail an unwillingness to engage in conventional occupations, and economic support will therefore be generated by street solicitation, street sales, unemployment and welfare payments, and other means which minimise the involvement of members in conventional social activities. The sharp break with the former life of members will often be marked by a new name and by handing over all possessions to the communal fund.

The world-affirming movement typically organises itself as a commercial operation, recruiting those who have a substantial investment in or commitment to the prevailing order, but who feel they are failing to attain some of the valued goals and attributes which their society makes available. Their full powers and potential can be unlocked by some practice or set of techniques which can be purchased in the same way as other luxury non-durables and services, from a convenient city centre outlet. The adherent becomes only gradually more deeply involved in the group as he invests progressively more time and money, acquires the language and conceptual scheme of the salvational group and begins to view the world in terms of it, and then finds that the only people who speak the same language and share the same interests as him are other members. Most followers must therefore inevitably remain deeply involved in the wider society. They not only see the movement as a recourse to improve their success in, and enjoyment of the world outside, but also have to earn sufficient funds in that world to pay for the therapy, counselling or training that the movement provides. There is no sharp break therefore on joining the group, and assimilation into its world-view and thought pattern, into complete commitment, may be a quite gradual process.

The world-accommodating movement likewise provides a recourse for people who generally continue to live and work in the world. However, they turn to such a movement not in order to become more successful or less guilt-ridden, but in order to heighten their experience of the supernatural, the transcendental, the divine. They are spiritually oriented people, often already committed Christians in the case of Charismatic Renewal and the House Church Movement, who have found the conventional religious institutions lacking in warmth and zeal, and unable to provide a clear *experience* of the spiritual world. Through 'speaking in tongues' and similar activities, neo-Pentecostals can feel themselves to have experienced the power of the Holy Spirit in their lives, reinvigorating their faith, recharging them to return to the materialistic world outside, and revivifying their commitment to moral and religious standards regularly challenged and affronted in that world. A number of small, non-Christian groups would also seem to follow this pattern: the Aetherius Society, Subud and various forms of Gurdjieffian and Ouspenskian study, for example. In addition, many groups tend to develop more in this direction over the course of time, from an originally world-rejecting stance. Some parts of the Jesus People shifted in this direction, and it is arguable that parts of the Unification Church and ISKCON are doing likewise.

Moreover, since these 'orientations to the world' and the syndrome of characteristics associated with each of them (see Wallis, *The Elementary Forms of the New Religious Life*) constitute 'ideal types', analytical constructs for the purposes of clarifying major features and central tendencies, we should expect to find that many actual new religions will contain—at least for a while—elements of two or more orientations. This may, indeed, have decided advantages at least during a movement's early years. The predominantly world-rejecting new religion risks completely alienating its social environment through the hostility it displays towards the wider society, and through its indifference to, or rejection of, normal social conventions. Such behaviour is likely to generate intolerable or at least very high levels of social control. This appears to have been what transpired in relation to the People's Temple, Synanon, and to a lesser extent the Children of God in various locations. Intense rejection of the world also jeopardises recruitment as potential converts come to find the distance between their world, and the world of the movement, too great to cross. Economic support is also jeopardised as a decline in new recruits may entail a drop in goods and income brought in with them, and sympathisers are likely to be alienated by the blanket condemnation and hostility toward a world which they still inhabit, thus rendering them less willing to donate, or to do business with such a group.

The predominantly world-affirming movement, with its very open boundaries, attracting in the public and requiring little initial commitment, risks the diffusion of its ideas and practices out through those boundaries, into the wider culture and other organisations beyond. Thus it risks the loss of any distinctive character for its salvational commodity as its ideas and practices are adopted by others and synthesised into quite different packages. Its clientele may therefore drop away as they find more or less the same commodity or service available elsewhere at lower cost.

The world-accommodating movement risks the classic problem of denominationalisation: the gradual attenuation of its distinctively enthusiastic character, and a loss of support as it becomes less clearly distinguishable from the established purveyors of salvation from which many of its followers originally came in dissatisfaction.

A new religion that can sustain elements of all three types may hope to attract three corresponding types of member. The now officially defunct Neo-Sannyas Movement of Bhagwan Shree Rajneesh, or Rajneeshism as it was called, may offer an example. Rajneeshism was founded in India in the late 1960s, but it was to attract a substantial American following, and in 1981 Rajneesh was to move to America, settling with a large number of his followers in central Oregon where he planned to found a large 'sannyasin' city.

Rajneesh preached a tantric-inspired philosophy which claimed that enlightenment came from acceptance and surrender to union with the cosmos. Achieving such a state involves 'dropping' the ego with its inheritance of social conditioning and patterns of learned belief, expectation and false needs. By total awareness of the present moment, by non-judgemental acceptance of oneself, one's feelings and circumstances, the individual will awaken from sleep, from mechanically responding to stimuli, and begin acting in harmony with the universe, spontaneously and in love.

Rajneesh initially attracted spiritual seekers and hippies on the guru circuit in the Indian sub-continent, but by the early 1970s, he was also attracting large numbers of Human Potential Movement therapists and group leaders, and through them in turn, many of their clients.

The faithful were gathered together around Rajneesh at an ashram in Poona in India, and later at Rajneeshpuran in Oregon. There they developed a programme of Human Potential activities which made those centres among the largest of all remaining providers of this salvational service. Smaller centres were also established throughout Europe, America and Australasia. The most intensely committed lived in the ashram or centre, and this inner elite constituted the most world-rejecting element of the movement. Not only did they carry out necessary administrative and fund-raising activities, but they also provided services and a role-model for less committed followers who continued to live in the world. Such people would remain in more or less conventional homes and jobs, but would visit the ashram or centre for a weekend or longer, to participate in activities there, revive their commitment, and return to the world with a strengthened vision of how life ought to be lived. Services were also provided through therapy, massage, group work and the like, for people with no great commitment to the Rajneeshee way of life, but who found in its facilities resources which equipped them better to cope with the conventional world.

Such a structure was particularly effective in that it provided a mechanism for supporting a world-rejecting elite from the gifts and fees of world-accommodating and world-affirming members and clients. It offered a graded, rather than entirely discontinuous pattern of entry from less committed client to totally committed and deployable member. It also provided a protective periphery of more conventional personnel to represent the movement and speak in its defence in the wider society (Wallis and Bruce, *Sociological Theory*, ch. 8).

Sources of Support

Where do the members of these new religions come from, and why are they attracted? The division of the field into the three analytical types facilitates the answering of this question. In the case of world-accommodating movements, we have almost answered it already. Such movements draw their support from the spiritually inclined who find that the established religious institutions offer little experiential confirmation of spiritual power in contemporary life. They are usually already committed to a religious faith or a spiritual quest, and find in the movement the concrete reassurance of the transcendent which they seek.

The world-rejecting movement draws its support from the social margins. The classic cases of such movements historically have found their support among the underprivileged and dispossessed, but in the modern world groups may feel themselves to be marginalised by their society, even though they may not objectively be poor or subjected to oppression. The world-rejecting new religions of the 1960s and 1970s largely found their following from among young people who had become part of the counter-culture, seeking to transform their society or their own situation through political radicalism, communal living, or drug use. The optimistic vision of change which informed the New Left, the student movement and anti-Vietnam war protests, the hippie and commune movements, had, by the late 1960s, become considerably tarnished. Student protests had led to violent deaths, communes had disintegrated, and the hippie playgrounds had become a focus of exploitation by drug dealers and freeloaders. Many young people active in, or sympathetic towards, these movements came to believe that human endeavour having failed, effective transformation could only come about through divine intervention. Post-war affluence had fostered optimism and a belief in the feasibility of progress and social justice. When secular means failed to produce it, some young people—often more spiritually inclined than before as a result of drug experiences—were prepared to believe that supernatural means might succeed where political endeavour and social innovation had failed. The world-rejecting new religions particularly appealed to the thwarted idealism of the young, their hostility to the corrupt, materialistic values of modern Western societies, and their commitment to a more intimate, caring community which would seek to promote a more mutually supportive, caring and principled world.

The world-affirming movement finds its clientele from among those who have been affected by the rationalisation of the Western world. The development of the economy and the advance of technology have created a situation in which the public sphere of life in the capitalist West has become dominated by the values of efficiency, predictability, rational planning and profitability. Success in the public sphere thus tends in most occupations to be incompatible with the fulfilment of a rich emotional life. Successful performance of public roles is often achieved at the cost of an impoverishment of private inner life. Emotion becomes harder to express, feelings are repressed. Spontaneity disappears as we become more deeply embedded in our public roles. The joy of discovery and experiment attenuate as our activities become more routinised, a habit rather than an adventure. Intimacy dissipates in the anonymity, impersonality, segmentalisation and privatisation of urban industrial society.

The world-affirming new religions provided, for those who were relatively successful in the modern world, resources for attaining the expressive release and intimacy denied them in their everyday lives. Through cathartic exercises, encounter, massage and the like, the adherent could escape the guilt and trauma of the past, the inhibition of the present, and attain some temporary community and the opportunity to indulge emotions and secrets normally repressed.

For those who were less successful, the world-affirming movements offered resources for releasing hidden abilities and powers, holding out the promise of achieving the valued goals of the conventional world, greater success in their jobs, increased intelligence, improved interpersonal relations and the like. Those who entered Scientology and est were often likely to be aspirants to corporate success. Those who went to Esalen or the Rajneesh ashram in Poona or Oregon were more likely to be drawn from social and educational backgrounds which gave a certain amount of choice as to the future, and sought to direct their lives into creative and imaginative occupations or those providing a service to other people, particularly in respect of human development. They were often teachers, social workers, therapists, performing artists and the like. But of course the attractions of liberation from social conditioning and constricting social roles was far more widely attractive at a time of affluence and economic expansion. Many people were willing to expend surplus income in a possible salvational programme in economically buoyant times. Come the recession, however, they were more likely to save on such expenditure, or to direct it to means of holding onto their jobs in more competitive times.

As for the world-rejecting movements, they too were affected by the changing economic climate, albeit indirectly. Recession meant that fewer young people took time out to follow some personal quest for fulfilment in the expectation that worthwhile opportunities would still be available should they decide to return to the conventional world later.

Recession meant that leaving the normal career path almost inevitably entailed unemployment. The counter-culture receded as a significant social phenomenon and fewer young people were on the streets or otherwise unattached, available to be recruited by a new religious movement which offered a vehicle for their idealism.

Conclusion

The evaporation of the counter-culture has meant that the recruitment base for the world-rejecting new religions has largely disappeared, and in consequence many of them have declined, while others have had to change their style, accommodating more to the wider society to secure new bases of support. The Unification Church has begun a parochial mission; ISKCON has begun to locate a new source of support among East Indians living in the West who wish to avail themselves of the devotional facilities of the movement, without becoming themselves totally committed to it.

A deepening of the religious life, a magical recipe for securing more of what this world has to offer, or a millenarian programme for the transformation of a world conceived to be altogether unsatisfactory, these are three responses to life's vicissitudes which recur constantly, in many societies and historical epochs. The new religions which emerged or flourished in America in the post-Second World War era reiterated these recurrent themes, but they did so in ways which sharply reflected and refracted the particular circumstances of the world in which they appeared or flourished.

Bibliography

Wallis, Roy *The Elementary Forms of the New Religious Life* (Routledge & Kegan Paul, London, 1984)
—— and Bruce, Steve *Sociological Theory, Religion and Collective Action* (The Queen's University, Belfast, 1985)
Wilson, Bryan *Religious Sects* (Weidenfeld & Nicolson, London, 1970)

15 | Western Europe: Self-Religions

P. Heelas

Self-religions offer participants the experience of god. What they experience is themselves, the god within. The self itself is divine. Many will be perplexed by such claims. However, there is little that is new about this form of monism. The self-religions point to parallels, in both Western and Eastern traditions. Thus one of the first self-religions (Psychosynthesis, the Italian psychoanalyst-cum-mystic Assagioli founding the Instituto di Psicosintesi in 1926) cites the Renaissance Neoplatonist Paracelsus: 'In every human being there is a special heaven, whole and unbroken.' And the founder of est (the highly influential seminar training established by Erhard in 1971) observes that, 'Of all the disciplines that I studied, and learned, Zen was the *essential* one.' In fact Eastern traditions, whether the teachings of Patanjali, Sufism, or various forms of Buddhism (in particular Vajrayana), lie at the very heart of the self-religions. They are basically Eastern in nature.

But this is not to say that there is nothing new about them. They are Eastern manifestations in a particular Western context. They are new in that they fuse two domains which we have become accustomed to see as antagonistic—the religious and the psychological. The fusion has occurred by virtue of two innovations. On the one hand the self-religions have moved beyond the parameters of religion as established in the West. Participants do not worship and surrender to an externally envisaged theistic being. Instead, they live 'as' gods. On the other hand the self-religions have moved beyond the parameters of mainstream psychoanalysis and psychotherapy. Participants do not simply engage in psychological activities for reasons of therapy, growth, self-improvement or even to fulfil their human potential. Instead, they use psychological techniques to reveal the god within. That these movements are self-orientated qualifies what is normally understood by 'religion'; that they are religiously-orientated qualifies what is normally understood as 'self'.

These movements can easily be distinguished from new religions of a theistic nature. Hare Krishna, Transcendental Meditation and Meher Baba's movement, for example, are not self-religions in that god is attributed an external locus of agency. As new religious movements the self-religions can also be distinguished from those Eastern imports which might be monistic but which have not fused with Western psychological traditions and institutions. Yogananda's Self-Realization Fellowship, the paths of Sai Baba and Sri Chinmoy, and countless yoga and Buddhist schools are not new in the fashion of the movements under discussion.

The great majority of the self-religions active in Europe owe their immediate ancestry to developments in the United States. Going back a step, however, these developments in turn largely derive from events in Europe. One event, above all others, stands out: Gurdjieff's establishment, in 1922, of the Institute for the Harmonious Development of Man. Housed in a château on the outskirts of Fontainebleau, Gurdjieff's Institute paved the way for what was to follow. Gurdjieff taught that we are all capable of obtaining what he called 'objective consciousness', namely, the 'enlightened state'. But we do not know it. We are 'prisoners'. Gurdjieff introduced a model of human nature, a model which both explains why this is so and what can be done about it. Part of the model (reminiscent of behavioural psychology) is, as he puts it, that, 'Man is a machine. All his deeds, actions, words, thoughts, feelings, convictions, opinions and habits are the result of external influences, external impressions. Man does not love, hate, desire—all this happens.' We are trapped by the mechanics of our socialised selves. We are driven by how we have learnt we should present ourselves to win approval, and so on.

The remainder of the model has to do with the techniques which must be used to gain liberation, to awaken spirituality, to reach the 'real and unchanging "I"', to come to act, not to react. To use a Sufi term, Gurdjieff was perhaps the first to function as a 'context-setter' in the West. He provided the (often) group contexts, complete with rules and techniques, to effect transformation. All the basic ingredients of the self-religions are thus in evidence. And as well as provoking what was to come, Gurdjieff's 'The Work' is still alive and well. Although it is impossible to estimate how many are currently engaged in 'The Work' in Europe, if England is anything to go by the numbers are not inconsiderable. Between five and ten thousand attend centres (including the Gurdjieff Ouspensky School), and then there are those attached to such neo-Gurdjieffian movements as Arica, the Emin Foundation (700) and the School of Economic Science (5,000).

Other European figures have also contributed to the development of the self-religions. All belong to the psychoanalytical tradition. All have made contributions to that spiritualising of psychology which is such an important aspect of that fusion discussed earlier. Mention of the self-religion which I know best, namely London-based Exegesis, serves to introduce one such contributor. D'Aubigny, the leader, has had an office devoid of books, except the collected works of Jung. If for no other reason this is because Jung wrote of 'individuation', 'the psychological process that makes of a human being an "individual"—a unique, indivisible unit or "whole man"'. Bearing in mind that individuation involves integrating the 'ego-consciousness' and the 'unconscious', and that the 'unconscious' takes a decidedly mystical form, it is not surprising that Jung, like his contemporary Groddeck, should be on the reading list of contemporary context-setters.

It is also worthy of note that the fusion of psychological techniques and Eastern spirituality, the hallmark of all self-religions, was long ago formulated by Gurdjieff in a way which incorporates psychoanalysis:

> Man has become an uprooted creature unable to adapt himself to life and alien to all the circumstances of his present existence. This is what the psychological system of M. Gurdjieff asserts by means of psycho-analysis, showing by experiment that the world-picture of a modern man and its own effect on life are not the personal and voluntary expression of his entire being, but that on the contrary are only the accidental and automatic manifestations of several parts of him.

Developments within the psychological tradition have provided many of the ingredients of the self-religions (see Wallis in this volume for further details). The tendency to spiritualise psychology (as well as to psychologise spirituality) has made specific impact in that the psychotherapeutic tradition itself has generated a considerable number of self-religions. Clare and Thompson, for example, have gone so far as to write of 'the inexorable thrust which propels every new therapy into a creed of salvation'. As they continue, 'Reichian massage, Moreno's psychodrama, Rogerian psychotherapy—they each began as a relatively circumscribed approach to helping the mentally distressed and ill and ended up as a programme for living, a philosophical statement and a religious message.' Along similar lines Vitz has written a book with the revealing title *Psychology as Religion. The Cult of Self Worship.*

Heavily psychologised forms of self-religions are today well in evidence in Western Europe. As well as those already mentioned, one can think of forms of Transactional Analysis, Primal Therapy and Co-Counselling; of Rebirthing (a movement which is becoming increasingly popular); of various Esalen-like growth movements which have sprung up during the last twenty or so years, such as London's the Open Centre, the Human Integration Centre and the Constructive Teaching Centre of the Alexandra Technique (there is also, for example, the Skyros Centre in Greece); one can even think of certain drug addiction units, employing the

Minnesota model and engendering monistic sentiments. Then there is the International Society of Analytical Triology, with roots in the Freudian tradition but which, in common with all the self-religions, works with a much more optimistic, Pelagian, model of man. And there are the various centres of Transpersonal Psychology, Mind Dynamics and so on.

Together with Eastern traditions, Western therapeutic thought has also influenced one of the best known self-religions, Scientology. The movement appears to be enormous, 300,000 in Great Britain, 80,000 in West Germany, 30,000 in Sweden, 10,000 in Switzerland and 8,000 in Holland. These figures can be put in perspective by the admission, reported in *The Sunday Times* of 28 October 1984, that membership in Britain is actually 1,000. But it is clear that it is one of the larger self-religions. And it is also clear that it is one of the most radical.

A Scientological Operating Thetan, living as a *Homo Novus*, believes that he has moved beyond the illusory albeit real restrictions imposed by the everyday world. He has become a 'spiritual agent of infinite creative potential that acts in, but is not part of, the physical universe'. This allows Operating Thetans to communicate telepathically, perform psychokinesis and mentally materialise things. For reasons which will become apparent, such radical claims are not characteristic of the great majority of self-religions, including those which owe much to Scientology.

These are the est-like movements. Erhard of est and D'Aubigny of Exegesis both acknowledge their debt. So too, I imagine, would the leaders of those other est-like movements which are operative in Europe—the Church for the Movement of Inner Spiritual Awareness/ Insight, Self Transformation, the Life Training/the Kairos Foundation, Relationships and the like. Movements of this variety are seminar based. With reference to est, what is offered is 'a sixty-hour educational experience which creates an opportunity for people to realize their potential to transform their lives'. Drawing on a whole range of techniques or 'processes', including many drawn from the 'therapies' mentioned earlier, seminars also include lengthy talks and interchange sessions. The aim is to allow each participant to see who he really is; the overall process is one of de-identification. As Erhard puts it, 'The person de-identifies with his mind, de-identifies with his body; he de-identifies with his emotions, he de-identifies with his problems, he de-identifies with his maya, he begins to see that he is not the Play.' Since Enlightenment is knowing what one really is, and since this is a 'machine', est trainers say, 'An asshole is a machine that thinks he's not a machine; an enlightened man is an asshole that knows he is a machine.'

Unlike Scientology, where there is a clear dualism between the mechanical self and the indwelling spiritual agency, monistic identification of the mechanical and the spiritual means that there is no *sui generis* god within to exercise 'magical' powers. As a trainer says, 'You're the source and creator of all you experience, you're a God, but what you, the individual entity bouncing around inside the big universe you've created, what you do is totally out of your control.' A far cry perhaps from the powers of the Operating Thetan. However, this is not to say that knowledge of mechanicalness is held to be without efficacy. The purpose of the seminar is to 'transform your ability to experience living so that the situations you have been trying to change or have been putting up with clear up just in the process of life itself'. The machine can come to be experienced as perfect (cf. Relationships and their cry, 'You are perfect just the way you are').

Those graduating from est and other est-like seminars typically report improvements ranging from physical well-being to such factors as a new sense of responsibility, greater self-esteem and confidence, greater communicative skills, being in control and 'the experience of personal power'. These results go some way in explaining the popularity of the movements. They are almost certainly the fastest growing form of self-religion in Europe. Some 70,000 have been involved with est in West Germany (5,000 are are full time), est is popular in Israel (est-Kibbutzim), and 8,000 have taken the seminar in Britain. These figures are higher if one includes graduates who have become involved in courses since the 'closure' of est in December 1984. Another, more direct indication of the growth rate of these movements is provided by the fact that Self Transformation Seminars has only been active in Britain since 1982, yet already realistically claims in excess of 7,000 graduates.

Like other self-religions, only perhaps more so, the est-like movements are not simply in the business of transformation. They are equally concerned with the transformation of business. In the United States this is well developed. The *Network Review*, reporting Erhard's organisation, for example, writes of the fact that 'Two independent enterprises, "Action Technologies" and "Transformational Technologies", join "Hermenet" in offering a wide range of new programs that make the technology of transformation widely available within the business and corporate communities.' In Europe it does not appear that things are yet so well organised. However, a number of companies employ est graduates (including Saatchi and Saatchi and Gold Greenlees Trott, reported in *Marketing*, 14 July 1983), a number of Exegesis graduates have decided to work together and so have formed or joined various businesses, and a number of movements put on courses or training for secular companies (Findhorn, whose philosophy is not so very different from that of est, has close ties with the Business Network and The New Initiative Ltd). Many concrete illustrations of how the self-religions as a whole attempt to transform mainstream institutions and life could be given. And these are not limited to business: est/the Network has the World Hunger Project; self-religions are moving into the fields of schooling, social work and so on.

Although the self-religions, especially those of an est-like variety, are expanding, they are not expanding as fast as they are in the United States. No European city comes anywhere near the 'one out of 34 adults have taken est' figure provided by this organisation for Boston. It is likely that Europeans are put off by what they perceive as a brash form of American positive thinking and idealism. On the other hand, and this helps explain why these movements are growing, the self-religions are by no means alien to the European sensibility. Gurdjieff, Jung and Frankl, to name but three, worked in this part of the world. To the extent that Erhard, for example, is a latter-day Gurdjieffian (it is surely not a coincidence that he devotes himself to what he calls 'The Work'), he can appeal to a similar clientele as those attracted to the Institute for the Harmonious Development of Man. Add to this the ever-increasing 'therapeutic awareness' of Europeans and the progress of self-religions hardly stands in need of further explanation. Therapy offers salvation through 'knowing oneself'; monistic spiritual paths offer a far from dissimilar route to salvation. The paths enhance one another. The desire to fulfil human potential is taken further by the addition of the god within. We have a transformed humanism. Feuerbach's and Durkheim's prediction, of religion and god becoming internalised, has in measure been validated. God, one might say, has been put to work by the psychological-therapeutic culture; has been put to use in perfecting a conception of man.

To close here is a list of some of those self-religions which have not already been mentioned: Silva Mind Control, Science of Mind, DMA, CAER (a human potential centre), Self-Formation, Playworld, the I am Institute of Applied Metaphysics, the Taking Risks workshop, the Emissaries of the Divine Light, the Centre for Psychological Astrology and much of the work of the Wrekin Trust. Many other movements have much in common with the self-religions but contain additional ingredients. Rajneeshism, especially active in Germany, and with offshoots such as Focus of Life, is one such instance. It is a self-religion in that there is talk of 'the psychology of the Buddhas', of the fact that we are all 'Gods and Goddesses in exile'. But there is also worship, and Rajneesh is more than a context-setter. Much the same goes for the Laughing Man Institute(s). Lifewave ('Man is the only God'), Eckankar, the 'I am' movement (Christian monism) and Inner Light Consciousness also have much in common with the self-religions but, so to speak, go well beyond the human self. Yet more movements are discussed by C.W. Henderson in his excellent survey, *Awakening. Ways to Psycho-Spiritual Growth*. Mysticism is certainly showing signs of being active in the modern world.

Further Reading

Clare, A. with Thompson, S. *Let's Talk About Me. A Critical Examination of the New Psychotherapies* (British Broadcasting Corporation, London, 1981), p. 142
Groddeck, G. *The Book of the It* (Vision Press, London, 1979), original 1923
Henderson, C.W. *Awakening. Ways to Psycho-Spiritual Growth* (Prentice-Hall, New Jersey, 1975)

Rhinehart, L. *The Book of est* (Holt, Rinehart and Winston, New York, 1976)

Vitz, P. *Psychology as Religion. The Cult of Self Worship* (Lion, Hertfordshire, 1977)

Wallis, R. *The Road to Total Freedom: A Sociological Analysis of Scientology* (Heinemann, London, 1976)

Webb, J. *The Harmonious Circle. The Lives and Work of G.I. Gurdjieff, P.D. Ouspensky, and their Followers* (Thames & Hudson, London, 1980)

16 | Japan

A. Lande and Peter Clarke

Introduction: Common Features

An estimated two hundred 'new' religious movements, known as *Shinko-shukyo*, 'newly arisen religions' or the preferred title of the groups themselves, *Shinshukyo*, 'new religions', are to be found in present-day Japan. Very many of these are indigenous in that their beliefs and practices are for the most part derived from traditional Japanese religions, among which we include Buddhism and Confucianism although they both originated outside Japan. They have, however, a long history in that country and have been influenced, shaped and moulded by Japanese society over a relatively long period of time.

The non-indigenous new movements tend to have a more pronounced Christian or Hindu doctrinal dimension and include the Unification Church, more commonly known as the Moonies, which has an estimated two hundred thousand followers in Japan, and the International Society for Krishna Consciousness (ISKCON), also called Hare Krishna, with a very much smaller following.

From the perspective of the Japanese the indigenous new religions are neither unfamiliar nor exotic and if considered in a Western context they would seem to parallel more closely Christian revivalist movements rather than for example the new religions of India or the self-religions (see pp. 154–66 and pp. 167–73). In almost every instance these new religions are built around the personality of a charismatic founder, usually seen as an *ikigami*, that is as one possessed by a deity. Among the founders of new religions possessed by a Shinto deity are Miki Nakayama of *Tenrikyo*, the Teaching of Heavenly Truth, and Kawate Bunjiro of *Konkokyo*, the Teaching of the Golden Light.

The differences that are to be found in these new religions can often be attributed to the differences in the personality of the

174

founders or leaders in question. Moreover, while each of these religions has its own spiritual and socio-cultural centre point or 'Mecca' they all tend to be highly syncretistic, holding to a mixture of beliefs and practices. Some of these derive from traditional Japanese religion, for example the belief in the continuing presence and power of the spirits of the dead, in the efficacy of various forms of magic, and in practices such as exorcism as a means of healing, and in purification through ancestor worship. There is also in many new religions a close link between Shamanism (see pp. 67–77 *re* Shamanism) and ancestor worship. Shamans are believed to enter into contact with the *kami*, spirits of the ancestors, receive and transmit messages from them and acquire from them powers of healing and prediction. Not only the new religions but Buddhism and Confucianism have given a central place to ancestor worship in order to appeal to the Japanese.

New religions such as *Risshokoseikai*, Establishment of Righteousness and Friendly Intercourse, began with the teaching that the family was the centre of human life and this was based in large measure on the belief in the continuing presence and influence of the ancestors. There are those, moreover, who believe that the worship of the ancestors is of great benefit to the nation. Further, the new religions lay great emphasis on the psychological, emotional and in general medical and social benefits to be derived from membership; virtually all of them are millenarian, stressing that the Kingdom of God on earth is near at hand and that great rewards both of a material and spiritual kind will be bestowed on the faithful. These religions are also characterised by a spirit of optimism and, with some exceptions, most notably Soka Gakkai, they teach the relativity of all religions.

We can now move on to consider in more detail examples of some of the better known of these new movements, beginning with those that have been strongly but not exclusively influenced by Shintoism, before turning to those that display a pronounced Japanese Buddhist character.

Nineteenth-Century Japanese New Religions

From the mid-nineteenth century until the end of the Second World War many of the Japanese new religions derived much of their mythology and many of their deities and rituals from Shinto sources while at the same time drawing heavily on other local religious traditions. Prior to 1945 these new religions had a somewhat ambiguous relationship with State Shintoism. On the one hand, since they worshipped Shinto deities and professed belief in Shinto myths they could be regarded, officially, as legitimate religions—in 1868 the Japanese recognised thirteen Shinto religions and Buddhism and Christianity—while on the other hand they could be and indeed were seen as alternatives to State Shintoism and as a consequence were at times persecuted and suppressed.

Three new religions which emerged during the period of religious revival in the mid-nineteenth century deserve particular attention. These are *Tenrikyo*, Heavenly Wisdom (the suffix kyo means religion or teaching), *Konkokyo*, Golden Light, and *Omotokyo*, the Great Origin. The first of these three, Tenrikyo, was founded by Miki Nakayama (1798–1887), the daughter of a farmer who received her first revelation in 1837. She taught that the Heavenly Kingdom was drawing near bringing a world of sickness and poverty to an end, and appealed in the main to farming communities who had lost their property and status during the Meiji land reforms. Tenrikyo has an estimated 153,000 teachers and 2,500,000 members for whom the object of worship is God the Parent, the creator and sustainer of all life, who is assisted by a number of lesser gods. Miki Nakayama, it is believed, is both the shrine of God the Parent and the mediatrix between this god and humanity. The movement also has a holy shrine or centre at Jiba in Tenri City.

Despite the fact that the Tenrikyo creation account placed Japan at the centre of the universe and presented the Japanese as the original and supreme race, ideas compatible with those held by the new centralising administration, the movement was, none the less, persecuted by Meiji officials. This, however, did little to curtail its growth and in 1909 it received official recognition.

Konkokyo was founded in 1859 by Bunjiro Kawate (1814–83) whose father was also a farmer and who likewise was the recipient of numerous revelations. It was in one of these many revelations that he was told that the prosperity of mankind was the ultimate purpose of the 'Parent-God of the Universe' and that without the realisation of that purpose God himself would be morally imperfect. While this movement retains many Shinto rituals and services it is, nevertheless, 'new' in that it has discarded other Shinto beliefs and practices such as exorcism and divination. But what distinguishes it most clearly from Shintoism, and the same can be said of Tenrikyo, is its belief in a mediator between God and man. This movement's 'holy centre' is at Asaguchi City and the principal object of its worship is the Parent God of the Universe who is believed to be the Spirit of the Founder. It has an estimated membership of just under half a million.

Omotokyo was founded in 1899 by Nao Deguchi (1836–1918), at one time a member of Konkokyo. Not surprisingly, therefore, she preached a message of world reformation which was similar in many respects to that preached by Miki Nakayama. Deguchi proclaimed that 'The Greater World shall be changed into the Kingdom of Heaven where peace will reign through all ages to come.' However, it was her adopted son Onisaburo Deguchi (1871–1948) who was largely responsible for the development and spread of Omotokyo. Onisaburo also propounded the 'Three Great Rules of Learning' which provided many Omoto offshoots with much of their doctrinal content.

The first of the three rules lays down the principle that the body of God is Nature, the second that the energy of God is the source of the Universe's movement and the third that every living creature possesses the soul of the true God. Therefore, everything is divine. Onisaburo also preached the imminent arrival of the Kingdom of God and became seriously involved in political issues criticising among other things Japan's annexation of Korea, Manchuria and Taiwan. Further, he presented himself as the only leader capable of ruling Japan, and by way of giving symbolic expression to this belief in his own unique ability to rule, he began to imitate the lifestyle of the Emperor.

The government responded in 1921 by arresting and imprisoning Onisaburo and by destroying the movement's temples. After his release Onisaburo became a firm supporter of the Emperor and membership of the movement grew rapidly, reaching a total of almost three million by the mid-1930s. But once again in 1935 Onisaburo was arrested and charged with lese-majesty and the movement was dissolved and its temples and other property destroyed. Omotokyo began to experience something of a revival after Onisaburo Deguchi's release in 1942, but it soon began to stagnate with the latter's death in 1948. Today Omotokyo has an estimated 7,000 teachers, some 150,000 members and two sacred temples or centres, Kameoka and Ayabe, in Kyoto Prefecture. It has also developed strong links with other religious traditions, including Christianity, both in Japan and in Western Europe and the United States. Moreover, although numerically quite small when compared with a number of the other Japanese new movements, Omotokyo continues to exercise a considerable influence on Japanese society. One of its main concerns has been world peace. It maintains that religion is the basis of society and that the pursuit of peace should begin with religion. Omotokyo also emphasises the close link between religion and art. According to Onisaburo, 'Art is the mother of religion', and the movement has organised a number of art exhibitions in the West for the purpose of demonstrating this relationship and for the promotion of world peace. These and other ideas, many of which are contained in the eighty-one-volume encyclopedia produced by Onisaburo Deguchi, have served as a source of inspiration for other Japanese new religions, among them *Sekaikyuseikyo*, Church of World Messianity, *Seicho no Ie*, House of Growth, and Perfect Liberty Kyodan. Indeed it makes sense to speak of these three movements as Omoto-derived new religions.

Twentieth-Century Examples

Sekaikyuseikyo, founded in 1934 by Mokichi Okada, at one time a member of Omotokyo, has for its main object of worship the True God of the Marvellous Light, and concentrates on healing. The principal healing rite is *jorei*, spirit purification, which consists essentially in raising the palm of a hand of a member wearing an amulet called *ohihari* towards a recipient, who may or may not believe in the movement's teachings. Critical of the Western medical approach to the treatment of illness as found in Japanese hospitals and in private medical practice, Okada developed a theory of healing which related sickness to spiritual clouds and also prescribed, among other things, the use of herbal medicines for the removal of such clouds. Further, believing like Omotokyo that religion is the source of peace, both inner and collective, this movement has constructed models of paradise at Atami and Hakone, situated between Tokyo and Kyoto, and these are not only meant to serve as prototypes of a world where peace reigns supreme but also to promote a consciousness of a new age of peace and harmony. Sekaikyuseikyo has over 800,000 members in Japan and has also established itself in the West, Latin America and Thailand.

Sekai Mahikari Bumei Kyodan, World True Light Civilisation, established in 1959 by Okada Kotama (1901–74), also lays great stress on the importance of healing through radiation transmitted via the hand. However, whereas Sekaikyuseikyo attributes evil and sickness to spiritual clouds, this religion believes that the cause of evil is to be found in unpacified spirits. It is chiefly known for its *o-kiyome*, purification, which is used to eradicate the misfortune and disease caused by the angry spirits of the ancestors and of the rest of the dead. Once these spirits have been placated then wholeness, harmony and peace can return to the troubled individual or society.

Mahikari like Omotokyo and Sekaikyuseikyo has its cosmic vision and grand theory of history. As for the present, this is a time of crisis described using both Buddhist and Christian imagery and myth—the Old Testament story of the Flood being one of the illustrations used to depict the contemporary situation—and people are warned that now is the time to enter the ark of salvation provided by Mahikari. So far an estimated 50,000 people have joined this movement which now has centres in a number of Western countries and which specialises not only in healing but also in clairvoyance, ecstasy and prophesy. There is also a splinter group *Sukyo Mahikari*, Religion of True Light, which broke away from the main body in 1978 and is at present building a temple or sacred centre for the 'Civilisation of Light' in the mountains north of Tokyo. In some Japanese traditions mountains are regarded as holy places and have been treated by shamanistic diviners and exorcists, among others, as *shintai*, that is *kami* objects charged with the power of the spirits. Traces of this mountain worship are to be found in some of the new religions and the climbing of a sacred mountain such as Mount Fuji, an act of worship in itself, is seen by members as a means of purification, of acquiring spiritual strength and of contributing to the well-being of the nation.

Seicho no Ie, House of Growth, also derives many of its beliefs from Omotokyo. Its founder Masaharu Taniguchi (b. 1893) was formerly a member of Omotokyo and in fact a scribe in the employment of Onizaburo Daguchi. In 1930 Taniguchi started a publishing house and since then this movement has stressed the 'word' in its spoken or written form as the principle of the cosmos. This is a clear example of Omotokyo influence. The words of the founder are believed to be the divine media *par excellence* and to have the power to heal, and it is for this reason that his books are read aloud. Taniguchi has paid great attention to the concept of the *word* or *logos* as found in St John's Gospel and has even written a commentary on this theme.

Seicho no Ie, then, is primarily about healing. It regards sickness as in essence an illusion or 'deceit of the mind' to be conquered by spiritual means and in particular through the healing power of the word. Like a number of other Japanese new religions this movement has altered its political views and its views of Japan on more than one occasion. Prior to 1945 it was an ultra-nationalist movement which proclaimed that Japan was the centre of the universe and its Emperor its overlord. Since 1945 these beliefs have been modified and although today members are among the strongest supporters of emperor-worship they now see the Emperor as the centre of the Japanese nation only.

Seicho no Ie has a large following in Japan, estimated at over three million members, and many branches in North and South America and several others in Europe and Africa. Its main temples or sacred centres are in the Nagasaki Prefecture and at Uji in Kyoto, while the principal object of worship is the Great God of the House of Growth.

Perfect Liberty Kyodan was first established in 1924 as *Hitonomichi*, the Way of Man, but was dissolved by the government in 1937 on the grounds that, like Omotokyo, it was a threat to the position of the Emperor. Reorganised in 1946 by Miki Tokuchika (b. 1900) under the name Perfect Liberty, it emphasised the importance of art as a religious pursuit. Its use of computers and other forms of modern technology for providing members and other interested parties with information, of English in contrast to Omoto's use of Esperanto, and of fashionably-dressed female attendants known as 'angels', all give to this movement the appearance of a modern, international organisation. This religion is also well known for its golf courses and other sporting activities and for its highly colourful display of fireworks put on to celebrate the founder's birthday, a display which is regarded as remarkable even by Japanese standards.

The members believe that God has revealed a number of precepts, one of which is that the individual is a manifestation of the divine and another that individuals suffer if they do not 'show forth' or express their 'divine' nature. Furthermore, they see artistic and religious pursuits as means to happiness which is the ultimate goal of Perfect Liberty Kyodan. Believers regularly assess by questionnaires the progress they have made towards this goal. The movement promotes itself at home and abroad under the slogan 'a joyful religion' and compares and contrasts itself with the 'gloomy' religion of Christianity which, it believes, places too much emphasis on sin and suffering. Perfect Liberty Kyodan which, according to some estimates, has over one million followers, has its main centre of worship at Osaka.

Nicheren Buddhism and the New Religions

It was suggested above that some of the Japanese new religions have been greatly influenced by Buddhism and particularly by the Nicheren tradition. Nicheren (1222–82), a Japanese monk of the Tendai sect, founded a distinctly Japanese tradition of Buddhism based on the Sutra of the Lotus of the Good Law, in Japanese *Hokkekyo*. This scripture was regarded by Nicheren as the final and supreme embodiment of Buddhist truth. Moreover, he not only initiated the worship of the Lotus Sutra, having himself devoted a strong faith in its supernatural powers, but also believed himself to be the Bodhisattva prophesied for the last days. The formula of worship, known as the 'sacred name' or *Daimoku* invocation, consists in the chanting of 'Nam-myoho-renge-kyo' (I take refuge in the glorious Lotus Sutra). This invocation, believed to have been inscribed by Nicheren on the sacred mandala or scroll known as the *Gohonzon* and housed in the main temple of the Soka Gakkai movement at Taiseki-ji, near Mount Fuji, is held to be the law of life and for all living beings the principal means of attaining enlightenment. Nicheren Buddhism, defined as the Buddhism of *True Cause*, is seen as transcending the Buddhism of Gautama Buddha, the Buddhism of *True Effect*, and the Lotus Sutra. Among the important elements of the Lotus Sutra stressed by Nicheren were a this-worldly concept of salvation, the religious equality of all social classes, the possibility for all to achieve the state of Buddhahood and the duty to evangelise and convert others to the Buddhist Way.

Nicheren was also concerned with the welfare of society as a whole and believed that true religion and proper worship were necessary conditions for its peace and happiness. He held that since the state did not honour true Buddhism, national disasters would befall Japan by way of divine judgement, and his prophecy was believed to have been fulfilled with the Mongol invasion of Japan in 1274 and again in 1281. Nicheren's prophetic powers and the veneration and respect he showed for the ancestors greatly enhanced his authority and led many to believe that he alone could save Japan from religious *malaise* and political domination. His teachings, which he spread with determination and even aggression for over thirty years, were characterised by a tendency to identify religion with national life, an intolerance of other people's beliefs and an apocalyptic mysticism based on Mahayana Buddhism. After the death of Nicheren a split occurred among his disciples and this resulted in the emergence of different Nicheren traditions roughly divided into *Nicheren-Shoshu* (Shoshu means true religion) and *Nicheren-Shu* (Shu means religion).

The Nicheren Shoshu Tradition and Soka Gakkai (Value Creation Society)

One of Nicheren's disciples, Nikko, acquired a considerable following and what he taught was later given shape and coherence by Nikkan (1665–1726). According to these teachings Nicheren is the eternal Buddha and Gautama Buddha is assigned the significance and role of a precursor. While the latter's teachings are said to be incomplete, the substance of what he taught is contained, it is maintained, in the Lotus Sutra, and in the invocation or *Daimoku*.

Soka Gakkai is the largest of the new religions belonging to the Nicheren Shoshu tradition and of the new movements in Japan as a whole. The movement was started in the 1930s by Tsuneburo Makiguchi (1871–1934), a teacher from Hokkaido in north Japan, who developed a theory of education based on Nicheren's teachings that emphasised that what was of value and profitable was paramount. Makiguchi, who was imprisoned during the war along with his assistant Josei Toda (1900–58), died in gaol. The latter after his release began the rebuilding of the movement, previously called *Soka Kyoiku Gakkai* and now known simply as *Soka Gakkai*.

The methods used by Toda to recruit more members, in particular the 'break and subdue', or *shakubuku* approach to 'false believers' proposed by Nicheren, brought strong criticism of the movement. Toda and his assistants literally pressed their beliefs upon people and the movement grew from several hundred at most in 1945 to around three-quarters of a million families in 1958. The majority of these recruits came from the working and lower middle classes and under Toda's successor Daiseku Ikeda (b. 1928) the movement increased its influence in Japanese politics under the umbrella of the *Komeito*, Clean Government Party, the third largest political party in Japan today. At the same time the *shakubuku* approach to evangelisation was moderated and this gave the movement a better image.

Soka Gakkai is a lay organisation. However, it has links with the priests of Nicheren Shoshu who since they are the guardians of the original *Gohonzon* are in a position to provide the movement with its spiritual legitimacy. Members of the movement are committed to chanting twice daily before a shrine which contains a replica of the *Gohonzon*, the invocation, *Daimoku*, and two chapters of the Lotus Sutra. Chanting, or *Gongyo*, it is believed, can alter karma, the law of cause and effect, and also, as many members testify, bring great benefits of an emotional, psychological and material kind for individuals in the present. There are also discussion groups, *zadakandai*, which usually take place in members' homes and it is on these occasions that followers recount the benefits they have received from chanting and the difficulties of an emotional, spiritual, psychological or material kind that they may be experiencing. Soka Gakkai seeks to bring religion down on to the factory floor or kitchen table, so to speak, and is very much a world-affirming religion. Members also undertake missionary work. This is the message they preach: religion and daily life are inseparable in the sense that the former, if true and practised regularly and correctly, unfailingly improves and enhances the latter. Moreover, those who can afford it make the 'pilgrimage' to Taiseki-ji, the *Kaidan* or place of dedication and instruction and the sacred place of Nicheren Buddhism.

All the positions of responsibility and leadership are filled by lay people. Lay leaders not only play a very important administrative role but also provide direction and counselling on personal matters. In terms of its organisation the movement is divided vertically into local, district, regional, national and international sections, and horizontally into a number of different groupings; for example, there is a section for young men, another for young women and another for children. But this horizontal grouping is not always maintained, especially in those areas where the membership is small.

Soka Gakkai, like other Japanese new religions, places great emphasis on art, music, dance, gymnastics, festivals, parades and education. It has its own university, a number of other educational institutions and an art museum. Furthermore, one of its major preoccupations, especially in recent times, has been with world peace, stressing that the safety and survival of the planet depends on the dissemination and application to daily life of true beliefs and practices.

The present estimated size of membership of this movement is ten million families and although the vast majority of these are in Japan it has been making steady progress in North and South America and Europe.

The Nicheren-Shu Tradition

Among the new religions that may be said to belong broadly to the Nicheren-Shu tradition are *Reiyukai*, the Association of Friends of the Spirit, founded in 1925 by Kubota Kakutaro (1892–1944) and Kimi Kotani (1901–71), and *Risshokoseikai*, the Establishment of Righteousness and Friendly Intercourse, begun in 1938 by two former members of Reiyukai, Naganuma Myoko (1889–1957) and Niwano Nikiyo (b. 1906).

Many of the Reiyukai teachings, being based as they are on the Lotus Sutra, are almost identical to those of Nicheren Buddhism discussed above. Initially, however, it placed even greater emphasis on ancestor worship which, as we have seen, it regarded as central to its belief in the family as the centre of human life. Moreover, like Mahikari it believes that suffering and evil are the result of neglect of the ancestors to whom, along with all other Buddhas and spirits of the universe, we are indissolubly connected.

182

Further, it believes that spiritual power is contained in the *mandalas*, those scrolls produced by its own founder and by Nicheren and which provide graphic illustrations of teachings. Through reading these scrolls believers can obtain direct access to the Buddhas and Bodhisattvas, that is those enlightened ones who delay entry to Nirvana in order to help suffering humanity. Moreover, it is believed that by reading the Lotus Sutra members can acquire merit for the ancestors. It was this movement that introduced the *Hoza* system, a method of group counselling which provided adherents with the opportunity to discuss in open forum, so to speak, their personal difficulties and problems. This system was adopted, as we shall see, by Risshokoseikai. It is also deeply committed to social and welfare programmes, including work for the physically handicapped and the Red Cross. The membership of Reiyukai is estimated at over two and a half million, some three thousand of whom are teachers. The Shaka temple in Tokyo is its holy centre and, as we have seen, its special object of worship and source of inspiration is the Lotus Sutra.

Risshokoseikai, it has already been pointed out, split off from Reiyukai in 1938 and made its own the *Hoza* group system which the latter had initiated. While in Reiyukai the believer acquires merit principally by chanting the *Daimoku* formula given above, in Risshokoseikai the stress is placed on personal development which must begin with the self. It is through self-transformation that the world will be transformed, also a central tenet of the self-religions discussed elsewhere in this volume (see pp. 925–31).

The concept of the Bodhisattva, defined above, is also central to Risshokoseikai teaching and practice, as is ancestor worship. The principal aim of group counselling and other practices is the fostering of the bodhisattva spirit which enables individuals to triumph over the law of karma and break through the cycle of *samsara* or rebirth. However, following Nicheren, and similar to the other Japanese new movements influenced by his teaching on the intimate relationship between religion and society, Risshokoseikai believes in an indissoluble link between the religious and social and political spheres. Religious development is not seen as a purely private and personal affair with no bearing on the wider society, for, as we have already indicated, religion is believed to have important social and political consequences and to be the foundation of individual and collective peace, stability and prosperity. This explains the movement's involvement in world peace, among other things, through its agency the World Conference of Religion and Peace. Also central to its belief and practice is the Nicheren mandala and the Lotus Sutra.

This movement's sacred centre or headquarters is the Great Hall in Tokyo and since its reorganisation after the Second World War it has made steady progress. According to a recent estimate there are as many as five million members, making it one of the largest of the new religions in Japan.

Conclusions: Some Problems of Classification

In the foregoing the focus has been on indigenous Japanese new movements and it has been implicit throughout that any attempt to classify these religions will encounter immense problems. It is extremely difficult, for example, to construct a typology of Japanese new religions on the basis of their content since many of them have drawn on a variety of religious beliefs and practices, and this in turn creates problems for those who might attempt a classification by relating them directly to either of the two major Japanese religious traditions, Shintoism and Buddhism. For example, *Tenshokotaijingukyo*, the Teaching of the Almighty God of the Universe, founded by Kitamura Sayo (1900–67), not only has a Shinto name and uses many Shinto terms and expressions but has also adopted a number of Buddhist and Christian beliefs and practices.

Moreover, the historian will want to ask whether it makes any sense at all to apply the term 'new' to many of the religions that have been discussed here. These religions have been referred to as 'Children of the Emperor system' and classified according to the Meiji (1868–1912), Taisho (1912–26) and Showa (from 1926) periods, with an additional historical period, the post-Second World War era, incorporated into this chronological framework. The post-Second World War period has witnessed what amounts to a veritable growth industry in new religions, many of which have a distinctively different character and orientation from the older, pre-Second World War and nineteenth-century movements, and fulfil somewhat different functions.

It is important, none the less, not to lose sight of the fact that although much has changed in the 'new religions' field during the past century and more many of the new movements form part of an ongoing historical process. In other words, we should not expect to find outbreaks of entirely 'new' new religions that are peculiar to and only intelligible in the context of one or other of these historical periods. If this is borne in mind then the emergence of Japanese new religions can be linked with political and economic developments during the Meiji, Taisho and Showa eras, that is from 1868 onwards. They were also, in part, a reaction to the rigid formalism and increasing irrelevance particularly during the nineteenth century and the first quarter of this century of the two mainstream Japanese religions, Shintoism and Buddhism, and a response to rapid post-Second World War industrial development, urbanisation and modernisation. And working within this historical framework the social historian of religion may well discover that what is 'new' is not to be found in the content of these movements but in the fact of their emergence as socio-religious organisations whose primary function has been the reworking and revitalisation of traditional religious beliefs and rituals in order to make them directly relevant to daily life in a society in transition.

Given the difficulties of classification on the basis of content, derivation, structure and historical context, perhaps the most satisfactory approach to the problem is that devised by the sociologist Bryan Wilson, who has constructed a typology of new religions based on their response to the world. According to Wilson, Japanese new religions, while they manifest a pronounced thaumaturgical dimension, especially in their early years, as they develop come to approximate more to the 'manipulationist' type of sect than to the 'thaumaturgical' type. By this Wilson means that their main concern becomes the provision of a modern, relevant faith for a society whose traditional belief systems are not easily accommodated to the new conditions created by the rapid process of industrialisation and urbanisation.

However, the fact that there is nothing necessarily fixed or determined about the doctrines, rituals, symbols and orientation of some of these new religions must in itself mean that even the most useful of typologies is in need of frequent refinement if it is to be of wide and general application. Sekaikyuseikyo, the Church of World Messianity, founded by Mokichi Okada (1882–1955) is but one of a number of examples of a Japanese new religion whose teachings, ritual and public official image has changed significantly since its emergence in 1935. This movement which began as a healing cult, and healing is still one of its central concerns, has called itself by several different names, indicating a shift at this public level from a Buddhist to Christian orientation, while at the same time making far greater use than was previously the case of Shinto ritual and of art as the medium for transmitting its message. Evidently such twists and turns and changes of emphases and orientation can greatly reduce the life-span and impose strict limits on the usefulness of any typology.

However, when considered within the chronological framework outlined above it would seem to be the case that most if not all of the modern Japanese new religions display the principal characteristic of revitalisation or renewal movements: they rework and reshape traditional beliefs, rituals and symbols in such a way as to make them relevant to the cultural, social and spiritual needs and aspirations of the present.

Further Reading

Blacker, C. *The Catalpa Bow. A Study of Shamanistic Practices in Japan* (George Allen & Unwin, London, 1975)

Byron Earhart, H. *The New Religions of Japan. A Bibliography of Western Language Materials,* 2nd edn (University of Michigan Center for Japanese Studies, Ann Arbor, 1983)

Kitagawa, J.M. *Religion in Japanese History* (Columbia University Press, New York, 1966)

Thomsen, H. *The New Religions of Japan* (Charles E. Tuttle Company, Vermont, 1963). (For a critique of this book and Western approaches to new religions in general see R.J. Zwi Werblowsky's review article in the *Journal for the Scientific Study of Religion* (JSSR), V, no. 2 (Spring 1966))

Wilson, B.R. *Religious Sects. A Sociological Study* (Weidenfeld & Nicolson, London, 1970)

17 | *Africa*

H. W. Turner

In earlier centuries first Christianity and later Islam came as new religions in Africa, took root and expanded until today they are the dominant faiths of the continent. Their predominance was long confined to Africa north of the Sahara and east of the Nile but in recent centuries their expansion into sub-Saharan or 'black' Africa has led to a fresh and increasing interaction with the indigenous African religions. One massive result, more extensive in the Christian context than in the Islamic, has been the emergence of a wide range of new religious movements which draw on the local traditions and one or other of the introduced faiths to produce new syntheses. These are usually referred to as new religious movements and they should be distinguished from the missions, churches or communities associated with these two faiths, from other religious bodies that have more recently taken root in parts of Africa, such as Baha'i, the Mormons and Jehovah's Witnesses, as well as from the original primal religions of the African peoples. They represent a creative attempt to meet African needs in African ways by a reworking of all available religious and cultural resources.

Different Kinds of Movement

The thousands of movements across hundreds of African peoples naturally exhibit many varieties. Among these, five different groups may be distinguished according to their religious content and intention, and the various degrees of syncretism between the African and the Christian or Islamic contributions.

Neo-Primal Movements

These stand closest to the indigenous tradition but have adopted some

187

important new features from one of the other faiths, such as a single universal divinity, God or Allah, the rejection of magic or the adoption of new elements such as preaching or parts of the Mosaic decalogue. Islamic-related examples have taken the form of new voluntary possession cults adding Muslim powers to local spirits, and in east Nigeria a sophisticated religion known as Godianism rejects Christianity and much of local tradition in favour of a new single God of Africa who is derived from ancient Egyptian sources.

Synthetist Movements

These consciously attempt a combination of elements from each tradition to form a new religion for Africans. Although there are few clear examples from the Islamic milieu there are many with a Christian component, such as the extensive Déïma religion in the Ivory Coast or those sections of the Bwiti cults in Gabon which are increasingly adopting Christian forms and ideas.

Deviationist Movements

These endeavour to depart from indigenous traditions by the adoption of an Islamic or a Christian content, but in fact so deviate from some of the basic elements of these faiths as to be unacceptable to them. In the Islamic context this may mean neglecting the Qur'an, as with the movement of Yakouba Sylla from the 1930s in the Ivory Coast. He claimed a new revelation from Fatima, the daughter of Muhammad, depreciated prayer and made fasting optional. In Nigeria since 1934 the God's Kingdom Society has claimed to be a Christian movement but has replaced Christmas with a Feast of Tabernacles and would be closer to the classic religion of Israel.

Africanised Movements

These intend to be either Islamic or Christian but are more concerned with practical relevance in Africa than with Christian or Islamic orthodoxies. In West Africa the reforming and missionary Islamic brotherhood founded by Hamallah in 1925 regarded its own holy city, Nioro, as more important than Mecca, developed a more exuberant form of worship and dealt with social problems by supporting greater freedom for slaves, the lower classes and women. Christian examples of this form are commonly called 'aladura' churches in Nigeria, 'spiritual' churches in West Africa, Botswana and other areas, and 'Zionists' in southern and central Africa. A general term for these would be 'prophet-healing' churches.

Orthodox Movements

Such movements aim to be fully Islamic or Christian and even to reform or renew their African communities, but do so by adapting to African situations and needs under African leadership and independently of outside influences. In Islam this concern usually leads to mahdist movements which are rather different from those dealt with here; by the nature of Islam strictly independent orthodox movements are rare. Christian examples, however, are numerous since about the 1880s. The largest and best known is the Kimbanguist Church in Zaire and central Africa, dating from 1921; in 1970 it became the first such body to be admitted to the World Council of Churches, after the question of its doctrinal orthodoxy had been dealt with.

It must, however, be remembered that these movements usually lack established traditions and strong institutions and so are free to respond to the rapidly changing African situation. They are also often still in the process of working out their new religious syntheses or forms. There is therefore considerable mobility in beliefs and practice so that a movement seemingly belonging to one of the above groups may within a few years be better understood in terms of a different group.

What are the Causes of these Movements?

If there is any general common factor it lies in the great social and cultural upheaval consequent upon increasing interaction with the world outside Africa. While this includes the Arab world, the main influence has come from the West and from its Christian religion, first in the exploration and colonial periods, and now in the era of independence, modernisation and development. These movements have sometimes been seen as essentially political protests against colonialism. This is only part of the truth for there has been a substantial increase in religious independency in the post-colonial period and many movements are not protesting against anything but are seeking positive spiritual goals.

Among the many factors that can be identified there are the stress and rootlessness arising from the great cultural, social and political disturbances, bringing new values and lifestyles, and from particular issues such as employment, marriage, alcohol and, above all, sickness. There is more ill health today in Africa than ever before in its history and the majority of the new religious movements offer some form of spiritual healing. Western medicine is too limited in extent and seems unable to reach the real cause of much African sickness; the Christian churches which first brought Western methods have relied on these and seldom offered spiritual healing. This is now prominent in the independent movements and makes a real contribution to some dimensions of African ill health.

This should be seen as part of the overall search for a spiritual power greater than that of the traditional faiths, and more freely available in relevant forms than through the older Christian churches. There is a further search for independent revelation from God direct to African founders and prophets, and often through visions and dreams. This means that African relations with the divine are no longer tied to Arab or Western channels and forms but have their own identity and status in the sight of God and man.

Some of their Common Features

Despite the diversity of the different groups surveyed above there tend to be certain features characteristic of these movements, which may be summarised as follows:

1. They begin with a founder who has a mystical experience of a new revelation from the spirit world, often described as dying, visiting heaven, being given a new way and then being sent back to earth to start the new religion. The latter is therefore no man-made invention but has divine authority.

2. The divinity is now seen as a single personal supreme being who has ultimate power and will help people if they obey him.

3. The founder is accepted as an authentic African prophet called by God, occasionally as a new Messiah; contrary to traditional locations of authority the founder is often young and is sometimes a woman.

4. There is a selective rejection and retention of different elements of local culture. Magic, divination and dealings with the occult are usually discouraged, but revelatory dreams and visions, polygamous marriage, drumming and dancing, food taboos and colour and other symbolisms are retained and perhaps reshaped.

5. Considerable creativity is shown in the development of new forms of worship. There are new hymns, vestments, styles of architecture, and new major festivals, often at a new holy mountain or community centre with a biblical name such as 'New Jerusalem'.

6. The new blessings or salvation offered include healing, guidance from God, protection from evil powers and membership in a new and disciplined community as a 'place to belong'.

7. Receipt of these blessings depends on following the new rites and the new ethic, which commonly stresses love, discipline and industry, bans luxury and alcohol and tobacco, and sometimes transcends tribe and nation.

8. Expansion by deliberate missionary activity is a major innovation as compared with primal religions. It is based on the new universal deity, on the revelation from this source, and on being a new open and voluntary society in distinction from traditional age-grade, vocational or secret societies. Thus

the Kimbanguist Church is established in a number of central African nations and some Nigerian independent churches have spread around West Africa and into Europe.

9. The contribution to modernisation and development may be quite substantial but is seldom recognised. A change of world-view has begun when magical control of power is replaced by rational and scientific methods; when their own past story and future hopes introduce the dimension of history into an outlook dominated by myth; when the traditional closed, sacral, tightly integrated society is replaced by the new open, desacralised, pluralist forms implied by these movements; and when evil begins to be internalised so that one takes responsibility for one's own misfortunes rather than always blaming them on external evil powers. Psychologically and culturally there is a break with the past and an openness to an innovative future. This is sometimes expressed in new low-technology economic activities and better farming, coupled with a new work ethic. The Mourides Islamic movement in Senegal, with its groundnut farming and other activities, is a notable example of new forms of organisation and discipline playing a major role in the national economy.

The Size and Distribution of the Movements

Not all areas of Black Africa have produced these new religious movements to the same extent. Islamic movements seem concentrated in West Africa and especially in Senegal. Christian-related movements are a second-stage response rather than a preliminary substitute and so have first appeared and have proliferated where this faith has been longest established, in Ghana and Nigeria, in South Africa and in Zaire. Certain tribes, such as the Lovedu in South Africa, and some areas, such as Cameroon and Tanzania, have produced few movements of this kind; the explanation is to be sought in terms of the particular cultural features and mission history of each area.

It was once widely believed that such movements arose only in Protestant mission areas and that Catholic areas were immune, partly because they did not provide the model of many denominations and did not freely translate and distribute the Scriptures. Earlier there was some truth in this but since the 1940s there have been notable movements arising within a Catholic milieu as well as many Catholic individuals who have joined these movements. The Eastern Orthodox tradition has been interacting with Black African peoples from about 1924, first indirectly through Marcus Garvey's African Orthodox Church in North America, and, when its authenticity was questioned, through the Alexandrian Patriarchate of the Greek Orthodox Church. The complex of Orthodox-related independency has developed mainly in East Africa and since the 1970s has been extended through the presence of a missionary bishop of the Coptic Orthodox Church in Nairobi.

Estimates of the total number of distinct movements reach as high as 20,000; in Ghana alone some five hundred were known in the 1970s. Some, however, are very small, with perhaps no more than twenty members. Others are large, with several million members—for example the Kimbanguist Church, and the Zion Christian Church in Southern Africa which was reported to have over three million assemble at its annual Easter festival at Zion City Moriah in the northern Transvaal in 1985. A fairly firm figure for South Africa, based on the 1980 census, indicates that about thirty per cent of all Blacks, about 5.9 million members, belong to these movements in that one country. While specific statistics in this field should be treated with caution it is clear that taken together these movements represent a massive new religious development in Africa.

Islam's Relations with Africa's New Religions

Compared with the colonial setting of much of the relation of Christianity to the peoples of Black Africa Islam has enjoyed considerable freedom in its dealing with African peoples. At certain points it has stood over against African traditions, especially where divinities were represented by images, where ancestor cults challenged the prerogatives of Allah, or secret societies stood for independent authorities in face of Islam's emphasis on the unitary community. At other points Islam has been able to accommodate readily to a wide range of African practices. Polygamy has been accepted and regulated, and the traditional male dominance in most African societies has been confirmed. Much divinatory practice has been retained, together with reliance on dreams as revelatory and the use of various forms of magic.

Traditional spirit-possession cults where the spirit power was present in human embodiment rather than in cultic image or object could develop in new ways by adding Islamic spirits, as found in the Qur'an. Many of the Islamic-related movements have been of this form and have exhibited the further novelty of being voluntary societies of adherents and initiates rather than public cults of the whole community, and of appealing especially to women. Among these cults we may mention the Zar cults of Ethiopia and the Nilotic Sudan, the various Bori cults among the Hausa of Nigeria in the nineteenth and twentieth centuries, and the spirit-possession movement among the Lebu women of Senegal, which operates alongside the more orthodox mosque religion of the men.

The Lebu people have also provided a more distinctive new religion founded by an illiterate fisherman, Seydina Limamu. In 1883 he experienced a call from God to fulfil the mission of Muhammad by reviving and expanding orthodox Islam through new fraternities of God-fearers (hence their name *layens*, from the Lebu word for God). As a charismatic saint, miracle worker and preacher, he imposed a strict ethic upon his followers and he himself was accepted by the orthodox and learned Muslims.

192

Opposition, however, arose from his more Africanising teaching, which rejected the obligation of pilgrimage to Mecca, the limitation of wives to four and the rigours of the Ramadan fast. The dominance of Arabic gave way to the religious use of the Lebu vernacular, Wolof, with a repertoire of songs and poems still widely used. He suffered much persecution from the French authorities. Since his death in 1909 the leadership has been held by two sons and then a grandson. The Laye movement survives as a small but religiously intense community being reintegrated into Islam. Limamu remains perhaps the most notable example of an African prophet inspired by Islam but equally concerned with the Africanisation of the faith.

The Positions of Islam and Christianity

While new Islamic-related movements still appear, as in the heretical movement of the prophet Maitatsine that has clashed violently with the government of Nigeria since the late 1970s, their paucity as compared with those related to Christianity requires some explanation. Since Islam lacks the distinction between Church and state, or religion and politics, there was more control of religious developments in Muslim areas. At the same time individuals had more freedom to achieve religious status or leadership than within the tighter organisation of Christian missions and churches with demanding requirements for ordination, and strong moral discipline. It is also possible to become a Muslim through easier stages than with Christian conversion and baptism.

On the other hand, independent forms of African Christianity have been encouraged by the extensive translation of the Christian Scriptures into hundreds of vernaculars and by the deliberate mission policy of developing non-Western indigenous forms. There has been no equivalent in Islam, with scriptures untranslatable in principle and a certain in-built disdain for 'primitive' African tribal cultures.

Nevertheless, there are many similarities between the movements these two faiths have engendered. Both have notable examples of new holy cities, often with the tomb of the founder, and serving as places of major festivals and of pilgrimage. Both have contributed to tribal revival and renewal: the Mourides for the Wolof, Limamu for the Lebu and Shembe's Nazarite Church among the Zulu. There is a tendency in both towards regarding the founder as a Messiah or Mahdi, but this usually fades with time, as it did with Limamu and with Shembe and Kimbangu. The passing of leadership by lineage descent is common in both, likewise disputes over the leadership and over property and money. In ritual and ethical matters there is much in common: the removal of footwear for worship, the emphasis upon prayer, the use of water for purification, the importance of dreams and visions, discipline through fasting and food and other taboos and the acceptance of polygamy. The presence of most of these features in classic

Islam also helps to explain why there has been less need of independent developments in that milieu.

Characteristic differences can also be identified. Movements in a Christian context have been more fissiparous, more hostile to Western forms and concerned to develop a religion adapted to Africa. They have also produced a number of young women founders, as seen in Alice Lenshina in Zambia, Victoria Akinsowon of the Cherubim and Seraphim in Nigeria, Gaudencia Aoko of the Maria Legio in Kenya and Marie Lalou of the Déïma religion in the Ivory Coast. Equally remarkable is the centrality of healing in the Christian context and the lack of a similar emphasis in the other group. In the latter the Qur'an tends to be a mystic sacred object, recited but not avidly studied; the Bible serves as a creative stimulus, within which African peoples find their own story and a normative reference point. It also serves as a means of contact for the increasing relationships between the church sector of the movements and Western mission agencies which offer help in Bible study and leadership training, and also with Christian councils, both national and international, which have admitted some bodies from this sector into their membership.

These new religious movements are still increasing and have come to represent a distinctive part of the religious scene in Black Africa, a major new phenomenon that neither African nor other nations can readily ignore.

Further Reading

Baëta, C.G. *Prophetism in Ghana: A Study of Some 'Spiritual' Churches* (SCM, London, 1962)

Barrett, D.B. *Schism and Renewal: An Analysis of Six Thousand Contemporary Religious Movements* (Oxford University Press, London, 1968)

Peel, J.D.Y. *Aladura: a Religious Movement among the Yoruba* (Oxford University Press for The International African Institute, London, 1968)

Sundkler, B.G.M. *Bantu Prophets in South Africa*, 2nd edn (Oxford University Press, London, 1961)

Turner, H.W. *African Independent Church: Church of the Lord (Aladura)*, 2 vols. (Clarendon Press, Oxford, 1967)

18 | 'Secularisation': Religion in the Modern World

Bryan Wilson

From the perspective of religion, the single most important feature of the modern world is its secularity. Sociologists of contemporary affairs regularly refer to 'this secular age'; 'secular society' and 'the process of secularisation', and the Christian clergy and Jewish rabbinate (as the religious professionals of the dominant religious traditions of advanced Western countries) frequently acknowledge the prevailing secularity which has depleted their congregations and diminished their social influence. The term 'secularisation' is, however, unspecific, and the very width of its application has given rise to controversy and uncertainty. It may allude to religious practice (which, in such matters as congregational attendance, is perhaps the most easily available and apparently objective indicator). It may refer to religious institutions and the changes that have occurred in the internal character of their ideology, ritual and organisation. It may allude to the place of religion within the social system taken as a whole. There are other possible applications. The evidence with respect to the relative vigour of religion is various and not necessarily all one way, and whilst most commentators allude to secularisation as a readily assumed matter of fact of contemporary Western society, some apparently contrary indicators can be invoked and need to be taken into account.

One source of confusion arises from the confusion of secularisation with secularism. Secularisation is a sociological concept which refers to an aspect of processes of structural change in society. By way of illustration, we may take the structural change that occurs as work techniques develop. More extensive division of labour and increase in productivity follow. In turn, these developments historically facilitated urban growth. One consequence was the decline of the influence of the local community and the growth of a more impersonal society (the replacement of the *Gemeinschaft* by the *Gesellschaft*). In such a society, the role player (rather than the total person) became the effective operational unit of the social system. This radical process brought consequential changes in other social institutions and in their value-orientations. Thus, to pursue the example further, education in Western countries once accepted religious dogmas as its basis, and was extensively employed to sustain the moral order and to assist the transmission of moral values. Today education has changed its character. The context of education has become—and increasingly becomes—scientific. Detached observation, empirical investigation, rational deduction and pragmatic application have come to characterise all academic disciplines, even including the humanities. These orientations have displaced erstwhile premisses of a supernaturalist, revelatory, or transmundane character, and have even modified where they have not entirely superseded more general humanistic and aesthetic dispositions.

Once secularisation is understood as a process occurring within the social system, as an objective fact denoted by an ethically-neutral term, it can be distinguished from a concept with which, especially in the minds of theologians, it is readily confused: namely secularism. Secularism is an ideology: that is to say, it denotes a negative evaluative attitude towards religion, and might even be appropriately seen as a particular 'religious' position, in the sense that secularism adopts certain premisses *a priori* and canvasses a normative (albeit negative) position about supernaturalism. Secularism may, in certain limited respects, have promoted secularisation, but it is more convincing to regard the secularity of modern society as a consequence of structural change (as posited by the secularisation thesis) rather than as a result of the advocacy of secularism. Even in the self-proclaimed secularist Soviet Union, sociologists attribute secularity much more emphatically to processes of structural change than to the state-sponsored advocacy of secularism.

Whilst the concept of secularisation originally referred to the sequestration of church properties by the political authorities, the concept has expanded to take into account the many diverse ways in which religious power and control has passed into non-religious hands. Secularisation may be defined as that process by which religious thinking, practice and institutions lose social significance, and become marginal to the operation of the social system. In advanced societies, religion has now lost that presidency over social activities which once it exercised, as various institutional orders of social life (the economy, the polity, juridical institutions, education, health, recreation) have ceased to be under religious control, or even to be matters of religious concern. Even in the most intimate areas of social relationship—in marriage, and in family matters—religion has no longer the influence that once it had. The process in which specialised institutions develop—functional differentiation, as it is termed by sociologists—has been a process in which religious ideas and practice have lost their social significance. The evidences are of many kinds, ranging from the dominant values expressed in society to the most personal concerns of everyday life. Thus, whereas the dominant ideal values of society were once formulated as the fulfilment of the will of God, today the transcendent and overarching social values are more likely to canvass the welfare of the people. Whereas once, to turn to personal intimacies, children were welcomed as God's gifts, and fertility was a primary focus of religious concern, today families are carefully planned, conception prevented, or foetuses aborted in the interests of rational family organisation.

As the social order has itself come to conform to rational precepts of action, so religious intimations respecting values and behaviour have given place to conscious calculation in economic terms of the utilisation of resources and the demand for material evidence of cost-efficiency, profit and expediency in their use. The growth of instrumental values, and the diminished potency of supernaturalist or transcendent ideals, affects religious institutions and religious professionals. A simple comparison of the stipends paid to professional groups indicates the relative weakness of the clergy and the diminished evaluation (even in money terms) of their social worth. A comparison of stipends over, say, the past two hundred years, would reveal the steady erosion of the value of clerical incomes in contrast to the experience of other professionals. The proportion of a society's gross national produce devoted to supernaturalist concerns (support of churches or other religious properties) would reveal the same emphatic trend.

It is clearly much less easy to document changes in the thought-processes of the general public, yet, if a liberal interpretation is made of what constitutes a religious mode of thought (and, in this sense, one may say patterns of thought which invoke superempirical concepts or processes) one may well conclude that modern man has become progressively less disposed to believe that supernatural influences operate in his day-to-day life. Whether the instances are those of pure superstition (which must count as part of the religious dimension when contrasted with rational pragmatic attitudes) or recourse to prayer, supplication, belief in revelation or mystical experience, there has been a dramatic change in the course of the last century. We may note, to consider a more fully institutionalised aspect of official (Christian) religion, that less regard is paid to rites of passage. Baptisms have shown considerable decline in recent decades; confirmations become less usual; marriages have become increasingly secularised: burial alone remains an activity firmly within the control of the churches, but this may be at least in part sustained by superstition and also by the fact that the churches operate a very considerable continuing control over the public facilities for burial in cemeteries and crematoria.

These elements of religious practice tell a broadly similar story to patterns of church attendance, although these patterns vary considerably as between Western societies. The steady decline in attendances in Europe during this century is not matched by the evidence from the United States, where church-going continues to be a popular activity, with something approaching half the population attending church on any given Sunday. However, this particular indicator of religiosity must itself be interpreted in the light of other evidence: church-going does not carry the same cultural meaning in all societies. Clearly, there are many motives for this very conspicuous form of religious activity, and sociologists have suggested that some of these are operative in a vigorous way in the United States which, by other evidences, some have regarded (with Japan) as perhaps the most totally secularised nation. Some of those additional motives are held to be the search for community in a society which has received successive waves of immigration and in which there is a very high incidence of geographic and social mobility. Others have maintained that, in a society without very long traditions and without a mystical and mythic sense of its own origins, church-going is a way of establishing national identity, so much so that it little matters to which church people go—all are equally potent as expressions of Americanness. Clearly, this hypothesis is one which is difficult to test, although here is abundant evidence that Europeans, from the time of de Tocqueville, have found religion in America to lack spiritual content of the kind with which they were familiar in Europe.

This last consideration relates to the internal secularisation of religious institutions. It has been contended that processes of secularisation are not merely patterns of diminishing religious influence over other areas of the social system, but are also evident in the changing quality of religious performances and beliefs. It is clear that in the case of Christianity there has been a steady erosion of many elements that were once considered central to the thought and practice of the Church. Some of this process of change has been gradual, such as is exemplified in the diminution of votive offerings to the effigies of saints, which has been recorded in, say, Catholicism in France, or in the gradual abandonment of anthropomorphic conceptions of deity which appears to have occurred very generally in Protestantism. Other changes have come as forthright and vigorous challenges to previous ideas and practices. Such have been the rejection by some modern bishops of central Christian truths including the virgin birth, the resurrection and even the Trinity, and by the dramatic liturgical changes introduced in the Catholic Church after the Second Vatican Council. Verbal formulas sometimes continue after their content has ceased to express the convictions of those who use them: thus, one may doubt how actively Christians, who weekly affirm belief in the Second Coming of Christ, actually believe this proposition.

All of these diverse evidences may be seen as facets of a secularisation process in advanced societies: they are, however, to be regarded as attendant phenomena rather than as the core manifestations of the process. The loss of religious influence over the major social institutions is the fundamental issue. Thus, the Christian Church once closely regulated economic matters in Western society, specifying dates for agricultural pursuits; regulating the practice of trade, by forbidding such devices as forestalling and ingrating; controlling the operation of craftsmen and stipulating the rules by which they worked. Today, the church has no influence in matters of this kind, nor in the more important and centralised functions of industrial and financial operations. Once, politics was an arena in which major churchmen played a vigorous role and even local clergy were often active: the affairs of the Church continued to occupy the minds of Prime Ministers in Britain up until the time of the First World War. Today, in contrast, church affairs are generally a very quiet bywater of the political mainstream. Less than a century ago, the presence of the Church in education was predominant, and Church Schools were still a majority of all schools, whilst university dons were mainly clergymen. That has all been swept away, as the structural differentiation of the social system has produced specialised agencies for different social functions. These phenomena, and the less formalised but equally apparent diminution of religious and/or church influence in health, recreation and family and moral affairs, represent the core of the secularisation process in advanced nations.

The structural differentiation of the social system is accompanied by the increasing dependence of society on the articulation of distinct roles, particularly in the economic sphere. Role relationships characterise advanced society in which interaction is governed by impersonal criteria: individuals who 'man' these social roles set aside their personal attributes and dispositions and confine their role performances to the relevant skills. It is this impersonality of role-articulated social systems which makes them uncongenial to religion. Religion has its natural locale in the small community, and functions best, as Max Weber long ago noticed, in circumstances where people interact as total persons in face-to-face contexts. In such situations, the moral precepts of Christianity have their fullest purchase: these moral injunctions are much less easily applied to the impersonal context and role-performances of the *Gesellschaft*. As modern society has been reorganised, with increasing tendencies for vital functions to be centralised (and 'societalised'), so religious influence, always greatest at the level of the local community, wanes, and so occurs the attendant phenomenon of diminished recourse to religious thought and practice. Modern man learns, of necessity, to function in a rational environment, in social situations which are increasingly 'man-made'. As men, in their role-performances, contribute rationally to the upbuilding of the social context, so the paradox occurs that the man-made environment is itself more rational (more the product of well-co-ordinated role performances) than are the individuals (as sensate human beings) who have created it. Thus, we have the spectacle of irrational man in rational society. The society is the product of role players, but each role player has another dimension to his life—the vibrant, sentient, emotional dispositions of his total humanity. Thus, although the major thrust of contemporary social organisation is to elicit from individuals rational responses to their situation (in the role, as profit-seekers, as negotiators of traffic system, electronic devices, the bureaucracy and the whole apparatus of the modern social system) of necessity, there remains still, in each individual, a fund of personal dispositions which are not satisfied by rational solutions. It is to these that modern expressions of religiosity, to which some have pointed as counter-evidence to the process of secularisation, frequently appeal.

Before turning to these creative religious responses to the current situation it may be instructive to examine one response by which some sought to resist and contain the process of secularisation in some European countries. The religious divisions which have been activated in the last century (between Protestants and Catholics in Holland, for example, and between Catholics and Free-thinkers in Belgium) led to the attempt by the churches to insulate themselves from secularising influences. The churches sought to create for their own following alternative agencies and institutions which fulfilled a variety of institutional functions. This process, known as 'pillarisation', saw the development of distinctively Catholic (or less significantly, Protestant) organisations, such as schools, universities, hospitals, insurance companies, trade unions, recreational organisations and even travel agencies. The attempt was to provide something like a state within a state, or at least to provide religious believers with a safe enclave within which the major requirements of modern life could be satisfied. The Catholic child, in Belgium, for example, would be born in a Catholic hospital, go to a Catholic school, on to a Catholic university, join a Catholic union or professional association, take out Catholic insurance and so on. These 'pillars', replicated for those of other persuasions, jointly made up the state. The Catholic pillar was a manifest attempt to prevent the influence of secularisation which elsewhere appeared as an autonomatic consequence of structural differentiation in society. But the pillarisation experiment may be said to have largely failed in the face of the impress of rational techniques and organisation. It may, first of all, be less cost-efficient than state systems because of duplication and loss of economies of scale. Beyond this, and more important, is the fact that the skills and competences of each profession (university teachers, doctors, bureaucrats) are increasingly dictated by essentially secular criteria. Studies of 'Catholic' hospitals and universities have found that they differ very little from their secular counterparts—professional ethics and advanced techniques dictate the style of these institutions and the personnel who operate within them, and these have been shown to be of greater saliency in determining institutional character than the confessional basis of their foundation and their work-force.

The concept of secularisation does not in any sense imply that the process by which religion loses influence is a regular, uninterrupted decline. Religious phenomena are themselves so diverse, and religion's influence over society has, in times past, been so pervasive at many levels, that any idea of a unilinear development must be at once rejected. Counter-currents occur, and there are clear reactions to contemporary secularity which, if they fall short of full-scale religious revival, indicate the persistence of a will to sustain religion on the part of some sections of the public even in the most secular societies. A review of the diverse contemporary manifestations of religiosity in the world might, indeed, at least superficially, lead to the conclusion that the present day was an age of unprecedented religious vigour. In the face of the overwhelming evidence of the diminution of influence discussed above such a view is untenable, but contemporary expressions of religion cannot be dismissed as merely incidental. Religion responds to certain deep-laid, perhaps atavistic, human needs, and, as such, something which passes for religion, no matter how different it may be from established, traditional and well-institutionalised forms, may well be a permanent phenomenon of human society, even if it prevails only at the margins and in the interstices of an increasingly rational structure.

The most conspicuous evidences of the vibrancy of religion come from societies in which social conflict is expressed in religious terms, in which men are, apparently, prepared to lay down their lives for the sake of religious convictions. The conspicuous cases are the civil strife in Lebanon and Ireland; the religious revolution in Iran; and the passive resistance to the Communist state in Poland. In each case, special factors are at work. In both Lebanon and Ireland it might not be too much to say that religion here functions as a legitimation of what are tantamount to tribal allegiances of populations which live on the periphery of the religious confessions to which they claim adherence. In such cases, marginal groups frequently over-identify with the values of the tradition to which they belong: Irish Catholics are notoriously 'backward' compared to Catholics in Europe, in the sense that they have retained the ultramontane and triumphalist stance of nineteenth-century Catholicism long after its abandonment in most other Catholic countries. Similarly, the Ulster Protestants represent an extreme fringe at the margin of Britain, more Protestant than the British, and capable of using this Protestant heritage to assert that they are, indeed, more British than the British. Over-identification is a well-known ethnic, nationalist and/or religious phenomenon, particularly among culturally deprived or retarded constituencies. All this being said, it must be recognised that the violent terrorism on both sides, but more pronouncedly on the supposedly Catholic side, owes nothing to the religious traditions in the name of which it acts. The marginality of Lebanon's mixed population of seventeen divisions of Muslim and Christian conviction might yield to similar analysis: religion becomes the symbol in terms of which embattled groups take cognisance of themselves.

The Iranian case is manifestly a case of resurgent religiosity, but religion proclaimed in an underdeveloped country in which religion is a rallying-ground against modernisation, or, perhaps more accurately, against the inequalities, corruption and social divisiveness which modernisation produced. Iran, as a less developed country, scarcely exemplifies a reversal of secularisation, although there is no doubt that secularisation—diffused from more advanced countries—might be retarded in contexts where external influences can be resisted, as for instance in pre-war Tibet. How long such self-imposed isolation can persist is a matter for speculation. The Polish case turns on different considerations. The Catholic Church has long been the repository of national identity for a much-conquered and long-occupied people, regularly deprived of their national leaders. Religion is here a surrogate for political expression in a context where such expression is prohibited. Religion regularly takes this role in contexts in which there is, apart from religion, no possibility of freedom of speech or action. The symbolic significance of the Catholic Church for Polish nationalism, and the recurrent recourse of Poles to the Church in search of national leadership (as has occurred also in Ireland and in Greece in times past) is a large part of the explanation of the revitalisation of religion in this instance.

In nations more advanced than any of these, there are also instances of religious revivalism. In these, quite different, circumstances, we may suppose that personal discontents with the increasingly impersonal, large-scale, societally-organised social system, induce a response in which religion—with its emphasis on personal relationships and transcendent values—is a ready-made focus for the expression of contemporary alienation. (This point might, of course, be made in strictly religious terms, expressed as man in search of spiritual values, mystical experience, or ultimate reality.) These examples of renewed religious vigour take many diverse forms, both within and without the existing church structures. Many of them are grassroots movements which emerge to express some generalised consensus of protest against existing social or political arrangements, or to experiment with new forms of religious expression.

The so-called 'new American Right' appears as a loosely formed and diffuse agglomeration of people who appear to be principally concerned with the erosion of American moral values which they see as being embodied in fundamentalist religious positions. The influence of television religion ('the electronic church') and the impact of television revivalists has been significant in the emergence of this movement, the supporters of which accept the label of 'the moral majority'. This inchoate movement is, however, one of the least well-defined and most unorganised of modern religious constituencies claiming a large following among people who are not formally drawn into separately organised congregations. The influence which this form of religion exercises is difficult to assess, and claims of direct political weight are disputable. Its attempts to resist, for instance, the teaching of evolution in schools, or to demand equal time for creationist theories, have not produced convincing evidence of the movement's strength.

A more specifically religious reaction to modern society, and perhaps also to the rigidity of church structures, has been the movement known as Charismatic Renewal, which began in California in 1958. Charismatics believe, as has been believed since the beginning of this century by those sects which took the designation 'Pentecostal', that the gifts of the Spirit, as described in 1 Corinthians, are still in operation today. Most attention is paid to the gift of speaking to the congregation in 'unknown tongues'. All the major Christian denominations, including the Roman Catholic Church, have been affected by this movement, and many inter-denominational prayer meetings have encouraged individuals to seek the experience of 'Spirit baptism' and the (usually subsequent) experience of exercising the gifts of the Spirit. The major churches have generally not resisted this spontaneous manifestation of religious enthusiasm, and some prominent church leaders (including Roman Catholic archbishops) have endorsed charismatic practice: on the other hand, the churches have not come forward to endorse as thoroughly orthodox this style of religious worship. Most of those who have accepted charismatic worship have remained in their church fellowships, and some congregations of main-line denominations have become well known for their manifestations of this enthusiastic phenomenon. The diffuse nature of the movement makes it impossible to say how many people have been drawn into charismatic practice, or how long they remain committed to this form of religion.

Charismatic renewal is perhaps significant for its incidental comment on both contemporary religion and church structures. The spontaneity, immediacy, emotionalism and, at times, anti-intel-lectualism, of this form of worship stand in sharp contrast to the formalised, hierarchically organised, solemn and ritualised order of the churches as they had developed into the present century. This movement represented an assertion of democracy, but it also implied a distrust of the mediated relation-ship to deity. If, as in the exercise of charismatic power, the individual believer can directly receive inspiration from a member of the Godhead, then the need for the church establishment and the ministration of priests may seem to be put in question. In this sense, charismatic renewal represented, whether its votaries were conscious of this or not, a latent and implied assault on the received structures of the churches. In practice, it may be recognised that despite this tacit criticism of religious leadership and the implicit democ-racy of this enthusiastic form of religion, many charismatic fellowships actually evolved new patterns of (sometimes very authoritarian) leadership: thus, a measure of control was exercised over what might otherwise have been highly volatile and disruptive religious activities.

Although the majority of Charismatics appear to have remained within their original church fellowships, this movement has also spawned new forms of religious organisation of a minimalist kind. Rejecting the formalism of church services, groups have come into being which emphasise the informality of worship by holding their meetings in houses, hence the collective name of 'house churches'. Some of these groups have tended to become at least loosely affiliated and there is evidence of an incipient process of denominationalism, even with the development of the purchase of new properties for religious meetings, so leading away from the idea of the house church. Some of those who have sought this style of religion have left their former churches altogether. In some cases, strong leadership has emerged, and different groups are identified by reference to the particular preacher whose teachings they accept. This movement owes something to earlier Nonconformist organisation and style, particularly that of Baptists and (Plymouth) Brethren.

The general decline in church practice in Europe, and the erosion of denominational differences (particularly in the United States) has seen the development of increased interest in amalgamations. Ecumenicalism has been part of the advocacy of many churchmen for several decades, but the process of amalgamation has not been especially swift. Some conspicuous examples have occurred, particularly the Church of South India. Generally amalgamations have been more easily effected in mission countries, since in those contexts denominational differences which were (at one time) of real social significance in the homeland more easily lost their particular *raison d'être*. Time and distance diminish these distinctions, and several amalgamations have taken place (in Scotland, the United States, Canada and Australia). In America, denominational labels had, by the mid-twentieth century, come often to represent little more than different organisations, the distinctive tenets of which had fallen into desuetude. In Britain, there have been some successful amalgamations among smaller bodies, and the United Reformed Church, composed of Congregationalists and Presbyterians, is the best known among these. Contrary to the expectations of some of those urging such mergers, however, these amalgamated bodies have not grown as a consequence of their new structure, but rather have experienced continuing decline.

Innovation within church communities, or at their fringes, is merely one form of contemporary religious activity, however. The sectarian tradition, in Protestantism, has persisted, albeit leading to the growth of a few sects rather than to a further proliferation of smaller groups. Some nineteenth-century sects and smaller denominations— Christadelphians, Unitarians and Quakers, have shown no capacity for growth in England; Irvingites have virtually died out; and the Exclusive Brethren have suffered a process of serious attrition. On the other hand, Jehovah's Witnesses, thanks in large part to the vigour of their doorstep evangelism, have continued to grow in England, and in most countries (particularly so in predominantly Catholic countries such as Italy, Portugal and Chile). Although it is well established that this movement has a considerable turnover of membership, perhaps associated with its particular preoccupation with the Second Coming of Christ and the periodic disappointments which the failure of prophecy occasions, none the less, the overall rate of recruitment is such that losses are, in most countries, more than compensated by continued gains.

Pentecostal sects, of which there are a great many, have also experienced considerable growth in recent decades, and particularly so in Third World countries. The Assemblies of God in particular has been successful, and this movement is now a vigorous presence in many parts of the world. It appears that the strength of traditional Pentecostalism has not been in any way vitiated by the development of Charismatic Renewal within the main-line churches, but it also appears that the Pentecostal sects do appeal to a different constituency, mainly of less well-to-do and less well-educated people and to people in less developed countries.

Two other major sects have shown great growth in recent decades, albeit in somewhat different countries. The Seventh-day Adventist Church, with several million members world-wide, succeeds in recruiting principally in Third World countries, the membership in which now considerably exceeds the membership in North America, Australia and Europe, where the movement has not experienced such dramatic patterns of growth. The Church, which maintains a vigorous programme of education and a health system of its own, finds its resources stretched by its recruitment of increasing numbers of people in poor countries. The Church in Britain has not escaped problems of racial tension because of its mixed composition of indigenous white and immigrant West Indian members.

The Mormons have also enjoyed a period of pheno-menal growth with a membership of nearly six million, with continuing success in North America and in Europe, as well as in parts of the Third World. The Church, which organises its membership for social, welfare and recreational purposes as well as for religious practice, has been particularly successful in recruiting young families in European countries. Mormon temples, in which special rites are performed (including baptism for the dead by living proxies), have been built in many parts of the world for a member-ship which is no longer dependent on Salt Lake City for its facilities, although the church remains powerfully centralised and effectively organised from its American heartland.

A large number of new religious movements have sprung up in Western countries, particularly since the 1960s, but many of these remain relatively small even if well publicised, and it is a common characteristic that they encourage their members to accept work overseas and to engage in proselytising activity there. A number of these movements have drawn on oriental traditions which they have introduced to the West (Krishna Consciousness movement; Bhagwan Rajneesh; the Divine Light Mission; Transcendental Meditation, for example). Some, conspicuously the Children of God (later called Family of Love), grew up in the Christian tradition, although departing considerably from Christian morality in some respects. The Unification Church is conspicuously Christian but incorporates ideas which accommodate the assumptions of its Korean votaries. A different stream of contemporary religiosity flows from ideas that had some early expression in Christian Science and the New Thought movements which, in themselves, have shown little capacity for sustaining their numbers in the modern world: the modern variants of this tradition are represented by Scientology and some other 'human potential' movements, which emphasise the opportunity for individuals to increase their health, intellect and success in the world. Unlike the earlier representatives of this so-called gnostic tradition, which mainly recruited middle-aged votaries, most of whom were women, these movements tend to appeal to people in their twenties and early thirties.

Religious innovation is by no means confined to modern Western countries. New movements emerge regularly in other traditions, even if forms of worship and beliefs show less radical departures from the received tradition. The Sai Baba movement and the Swami Narayan movement are indications of the vibrancy of contemporary Hinduism and, unlike earlier variants of that tradition, these movements now seek to proselytise beyond the confines of India, initially among migrants but, in the case of Sai Baba, also among Westerners. Sometimes, too, the secular currents from other countries affect these new movements, as appears to be the case with the Brahma Kumaris in which women have acquired the conspicuous leadership positions in contrast to normal Hindu practice. Since feminism has not yet been significantly represented as a specifically religious intimation, we may suppose that this development owes more to secular ideas than to specifically religious ideas.

Japan is often regarded as one of the world's most secularised countries, yet it is in that country that some of the most successful and vigorous new religions have developed in the decades since the Second World War. These movements, Buddhist and Shintoist in inspiration, sometimes retain elements of traditional Japanese shamanism, particularly in the experiences claimed by their founders (several of whom were women). Many of these movements have a specific concern with healing practices. Some, such as Reiyukai and Rissho Kosei Kai, strongly counsel members to give all due attention to ancestral spirits and ancestor worship: others, chief among which is Soka Gakkai, entirely reject this aspect of traditional religious practice. Sociologically, the arresting fact about the new Buddhist movements is that, although they have attached themselves to one or another of the monastic sects of Japanese Buddhism, they are themselves entirely lay movements, with lay leadership and control. This process of lay revitalisation of otherwise increasingly ineffective and, at times, almost moribund ecclesiastical systems, is itself an eloquent commentary on one aspect of processes of secularisation.

New religious movements, whether in the Christian, Buddhist, or any other tradition, are not in the strict sense revivals of a tradition: they are more accurately regarded as adaptations of religion to new social circumstances. None of them is capable, given the radical nature of social change, of recreating the dying religions of the past. In their style and in their specific appeal they represent an accommodation to new conditions, and they incorporate many of the assumptions and facilities encouraged in the increasingly rationalised secular sphere. Thus it is that many new movements are themselves testimonies to secularisation: they often utilise highly secular methods in evangelism, financing, publicity and mobilisation of adherents. Very commonly, the traditional symbolism, liturgy and aesthetic concern of traditional religion are abandoned for much more pragmatic attitudes and for systems of control, accountancy, propaganda and even doctrinal content which are closer to the styles of secular enterprise than to traditional religious concerns. The new religions do evidently indicate a continuing interest in, perhaps a need for, spiritual solace and reassurance on the part of many individuals, but, in the West at least, they are also very much the creations of a secularised society.

An examination of the contemporary religious situation reveals that, at least in advanced countries, religion has necessarily abandoned many of its former functions. It no longer provides the overarching symbolic structure—the sacred canopy—in terms of which total societies take cognisance of themselves and affirm their supernatural origin. In considerable measure, religion has become a very private affair. In most societies there is a wide variety of religions and no religion is able to claim societal monopoly, nor even to represent the social system. Religion becomes—in a way which was not possible within the orthodoxies of the past—a matter of choice or preference. In consequence of this measure of privatisation, religion in the West ceases to claim a very significant societal position or to fulfil social functions. Religious movements might, of course, mobilise opinion. As voluntary bodies they are still perhaps the largest agencies for the expression of unconstrained opinion (in a way which is not true of trade unions—in which commitment is lower and which, in many countries, can scarcely be considered as truly voluntary organisations). Religious movements may serve primarily as mediating institutions between the individual and the increasingly powerful state, enclaves in which some vestige of communal association may be sustained. This is particularly evident in Japan, where, in this respect, their functions are of great importance. Religion may still have this significant function in societies which are increasingly impersonalised by formal, rational, bureaucratic structures and technological work operations.

In the face of persisting secularisation of the social order, we might expect religious movements, and particularly new forms of religion, to arise, perhaps as recurrent phenomena. Alienation is one source of religious demand, which, more in its associational features than in its doctrinal teachings, religion may serve to counteract. Alternatively, as long as society emphasises competitive success and the struggle for achievement, religions offering short cuts to social mobility, or enhanced personal power (whether intellectual, sexual, social or physical) may be expected to recruit a clientele. We may expect, with the speed of social change, religious expression to become diversified for different constituencies, as specified by age, education, social class and perhaps gender or sexual preferences. Religious diversity is quite consistent with secularised society, testifying in its own way to the limitations of what religion can actually do.

Further Reading

Bellah, R.N. *Beyond Belief: Essays on Religion in a Post-Traditional World* (Harper & Row, New York, 1970)

Hammond, P.E. (ed.) *The Sacred in a Secular Age* (University of California Press, Berkeley and Los Angeles, 1985)

Wilson, B.R. *Religion in Sociological Perspective* (Oxford University Press, Oxford, 1982)

Index

Index

resurrection, doctrine of
  influence of in Melanesian
    religions 93
  rejection of 198
revelation and new religions 190
revivalism and secularisation 202–4, 207
Rios Codex of Tenochtitlan 136, 137
Risshokoseikai (Establishment of
  Righteousness and Friendly Intercourse)
  175, 182, 183, 206
ritual, in traditional religions 80–4, 85–90,
  116, 118–22, 132–3
Robertson Smith, William 6, 8
Russell, Bertrand 41, 46, 54
Russia, Orthodox Church in 47

sacred, the, and the mundane 25–6
sacrifice, in traditional religions 80, 90, 91–2,
  121, 135, 137
Sai Baba movement 168, 206
salvation
  in Buddhism 180
  in new religions 158–9, 16, 162–3, 165,
    172, 178, 190
  see also liberation
Santeria, Cuban cult 74
Sasaki, K. 75
Schill, E. 42
Schmidt, Wilhelm 64
science of religion 14–15, 20, 22
Scientology 158, 165, 170, 206
secularisation
  and modern religion 195–208
  reaction to 200, 201–8
  of religious institutions 197–201
  of society 195–7, 207
secularism 195, 196
Seicho no Ie (House of Growth) 178–9
Seikai Mahikari Bumei Kyodan (World True
  Light Civilisation) 178, 182
Sekaikyuseikyo 177–8, 185
Self Transformation Seminars 171
'Self-Religions' 151, 167–72, 183
Seventh-day Adventist Church 205
sexuality
  in new religions 156–7
  and shamanism 73, 76–7
  in traditional religions 89
Shaker communities 155
shamanism 67–77
  definitions of 67–8
  and ecstasy 68–71, 73, 74–5, 76

in North America 75, 118–19, 121–2, 125
  in South America 126–34
  and women 73, 74, 75, 206
Shamanistic religions 74–5, 175
Shembe, Isaiah 193
shepherd, significance in Inca religion 144–6
Shintō 75, 206
  and new religions 174–6, 184
Shirokogoroff, S.M. 67–8, 72, 75
sin, in Inca religion 146
slave trade, in Africa 112
society, cohesion of 79, 81, 83–4, 85, 88, 90,
  107–8
Soderblom, Nathan 57
Soka Gakkai ('Value-Creating Study Group')
  152, 156, 175, 180–2, 206
soul, concept of, in traditional religions 101–2,
  122, 131
South Africa, Christianity in 46
South America
  Christianity in 127, 128, 132, 134
  traditional religions in 125–46
    monotheism 141–6
    social organisation 134–41
    trance journey 125, 126–34
Spencer, B. and Gillen, F.J. 78–9
spirits
  in African religions 109–12
  in shamanism 67, 68–71, 74, 76
  in traditional religions 80–1, 86–9, 113,
    118–21
Stanner, W.E.H. 81
suffering, in Buddhism 182–3
Supreme Being, in traditional religions 80,
  110–11, 113, 117, 118, 190
syncretism and new religions 175, 187, 188

taboos 88–9, 119
Tarantism 72
Tawney, R.H. 37, 39
Tenrikyo (Heavenly Wisdom) 174, 176
Tepanec religion 137
theology of world religions 13–14, 15–16
Theosophical movement 155
Tlaloc, Mesoamerican rain-god 136–8, 140–1
tohunga, Maori expert 96–8, 100
Toltec religion 137
tradition, oral 64, 108–9
trance
  in shamanism 67, 70, 71, 75, 119, 126–34,
    136–7
  in traditional religions 125

213